Due Respect

DUE RESPECT

Essays on English and English-Related Creoles in the Caribbean in Honour of Professor Robert Le Page

Edited by Pauline Christie

UNIVERSITY OF THE WEST INDIES PRESS
Barbados ● *Jamaica* ● *Trinidad and Tobago*

University of the West Indies Press
1A Aqueduct Flats   Mona
Kingston 7   Jamaica

© 2001 by The University of the West Indies Press
All rights reserved. Published 2001.

05 04 03 02 01   5 4 3 2 1

CATALOGUING IN PUBLICATION DATA

Due respect : essays on English and English-related creoles in the
Caribbean in honour of Professor Robert Le Page / edited by Pauline
Christie.
p. cm.
Includes bibliographical references.
ISBN: 976-640-105-5
1. Creole dialects – Caribbean, English-speaking. 2. English language
– Study and teaching – Caribbean, English-speaking. 3. Conversation
analysis – Caribbean, English-speaking. 4. Le Page, R.B. (Robert
Brock), 1920–. I. Christie, Pauline. II. Le Page, R.B. (Robert Brock),
1920–.

PM7834.C37D84 2001   417'.22'09727–dc20

Book and cover design by ProDesign Ltd, Red Gal Ring, Kingston, Jamaica.

Printed by Stephenson's Litho Press, Jamaica

Contents

Dedication	*vii*
R.B. Le Page: Selected Publications	*x*
Acknowledgements	*xiii*
List of Symbols and Abbreviations	*xiv*

General Introduction

Forty Years On — 1
Pauline Christie

Section One

Creole and English: In the Society and in the School — 22

1. The Status of Creole in the Caribbean — 24
   Lawrence Carrington

2. Competence, Proficiency and Language Acquisition in Caribbean Contexts — 37
   Hazel Simmons-McDonald

3. Language Education Revisited in the Commonwealth Caribbean — 61
   Dennis R. Craig

4. Defining the Role of Linguistic Markers in Manufacturing Classroom Consent — 79
   Beverley Bryan

5. "A Singular Subject Takes a Singular Verb" and Hypercorrection in Jamaican Speech and Writing — 97
   Velma Pollard

Contents

6 English in the English-Speaking Caribbean: Questions in the Academy   *108*
   Monica Taylor

Section Two

Aspects of Structure   *122*

7 The Mysterious Case of Diminutive *yala-yala*   *124*
   Silvia Kouwenberg and Darlene La Charité

8 The Use of *Se* in Jamaican   *135*
   Dhanis Jaganauth

9 A Comparison of Tense/Aspect Systems in Caribbean English Creoles   *155*
   Donald Winford

10 On the Sierra Leone-Caribbean Connection: Hot on the Trail of "Tone-Shifted" Items in Anglo-West African   *184*
    Hubert Devonish

Section Three

Analysis of Conversational Interaction   *206*

11 Contrapuntal Conversations and the Performance Floor   *208*
    Kathryn Shields-Brodber

12 Working out Conversational Roles through Questioning Strategies   *219*
    Valerie Youssef

Glossary   *247*

Appendix 1
   Cassidy–Le Page Writing System: An Illustration   *253*

Appendix 2
   Caribbean Students who Gained Higher Degrees in Linguistics at the University of York, 1967–1988   *254*

Contributors   *255*

Dedication

To anyone observing the population of the South London borough of Eltham today, the Caribbean connection is obvious. But its complexion was very different in the 1920s when young Robert Le Page was growing up there. Nothing about his early upbringing suggested that he would ever have much contact with Caribbean speakers, let alone devote most of his career to their language. He received his secondary education at Christ's Hospital, a private school in Horsham, Sussex, to which he had won one of the very few open scholarships available, and, on leaving school, was apprenticed to a firm of chartered accountants. However, his budding career there was cut short after four years by the outbreak of World War II. Young Le Page joined the Fleet Air Arm of the Royal Navy and served in it for the duration of the war.

In 1945, after his discharge from the Navy, he took the first steps in the direction which was to bring him eventually to Jamaica. He registered for a BA degree in English Language and Literature at Keble College, Oxford University and, after graduating in 1948, became a teaching assistant at the University of Birmingham and a tutor at Oxford, while working on a PhD thesis on Early English prosody.

September 1950 saw Le Page taking up a position as an assistant lecturer in the Department of English at the new University College of the West Indies, Mona, Jamaica. His interest in Early English verse soon paled before a growing fascination with the Jamaican vernacular. During his second year in Jamaica, Manfred Sandmann, Professor of Modern Languages, aware of this development, introduced him to Frederic Cassidy, a visiting Fulbright scholar from the University of Wisconsin. Cassidy, who was soon to become Le

Dedication

Page's collaborator and close friend, had been born in Jamaica and had spent his early years here. What is more, he had a deep interest in dialectology. Not long after that meeting, Philip Sherlock, then Deputy Vice-Chancellor at Mona and Head of the Extra-Mural Department, passed on to Le Page the entries in a competition which had been organized by the *Gleaner* newspaper in 1944 for the "best list of dialect words and phrases". These further stimulated his interest. Together with Cassidy, he started collecting "dialect" words and later Old Witch and Anansi stories among the Maroons of Accompong.

In 1953, Bob Le Page launched a relatively informal linguistic survey of the British Caribbean with financial assistance from the Commonwealth Fund of the Carnegie Foundation. Soon afterwards began the collaboration with Fred Cassidy which was to result eventually in the *Dictionary of Jamaican English*, published by Cambridge University Press in 1967 (second edition 1980). To better equip himself for his new ventures, he took courses in linguistics at the University of Michigan, United States. He also benefited from the assistance of other scholars who shared his broad interest, chief among them David DeCamp, a Fulbright scholar in Jamaica in 1957, Beryl Loftman Bailey, a Jamaican working towards a PhD on Jamaican Creole at Columbia University, New York, who had come home for a short while to do fieldwork, and Jack Berry, a British-born Africanist. Help was forthcoming, too, from Louise McCloskey, who had had training in dialect survey work at the University of Edinburgh. She worked as his research assistant for a year. The survey took him all over the region collecting data and at the same time familiarizing himself with West Indian life and also with a cross-section of those who were normally part of it. The experience was to serve him well in later years.

In 1959, Le Page convened the first ever international conference on Creole language studies at Mona. He was then also putting together an account of Jamaica's settlement history. It was published in 1960 in a volume entitled *Creole Language Studies I: Jamaican Creole*, which also included transcriptions and analyses by DeCamp of recorded stories told by a Maroon, Emmanuel Rowe. This is the first attested use of the label, "Jamaican Creole". It was patterned on the term "Haitian Creole", which had been used by Professor Robert Hall for his description of that variety, published in 1953. In 1961, a second volume appeared, *Creole Language Studies II*. This contained proceedings of the Mona conference, edited by Le Page.

Dedication

After ten years, Bob Le Page left Jamaica to become professor of English at the University of Malaya. Four years later, he returned to England to head the Department of Language at the new University of York. This department was to a large extent his own creation. Among other things, students specializing in linguistics were exposed to Creole. There came a succession of graduate students from the Caribbean, most of them assisted by scholarships arranged through Professor Le Page's efforts. (The list appears in Appendix 2.) Before long, York had become known throughout the country – and internationally – as a centre for Creole studies.

Le Page's direct involvement with the Caribbean did not end with his resignation from the University College, Mona. He was partly responsible for the second international conference on Creole language studies at Mona in 1968, out of which came the seminal volume, *Pidginization and Creolization of Languages*, edited by Dell Hymes. He was also one of those instrumental in the establishment in 1972 of the Society for Caribbean Linguistics, of which he was elected president four years later. In the early 1970s he directed a survey of multilingual communities concentrating on Cayo District, British Honduras (now Belize) and St Lucia. The research was to form the basis for *Acts of Identity*, which appeared in 1985, produced jointly with Andrée Tabouret-Keller of the University of Strasbourg, France. He encouraged the introduction of courses in linguistics at the University of the West Indies, which had become, in 1962, a degree-granting institution in its own right, and was, for some years, the external examiner for the courses taught. York graduates in linguistics have been among the members of the teaching staff on all three campuses over the past three decades.

Professor Le Page retired in 1988, but remained active until recently as Professor Emeritus at York. On his retirement, he generously donated copies of the tapes and other documentation from his surveys of multilingual communities to the Department of Language and Linguistics at Mona.

Forty years after the first international conference on Creole languages in 1959, we pay special tribute to Robert Brock Le Page, a pioneer. *Rispek juu!* "Respect is due."

R.B. Le Page: *Selected Publications*

1952a. The English language. *Caribbean Quarterly* 2, no. 2: 4–11.

1952b. A survey of dialects in the British Caribbean. *Caribbean Quarterly* 2, no. 3: 49–50.

1955. The language problem in the British Caribbean. *Caribbean Quarterly* 4, no. 1: 40–49.

1957–1958. General outlines of Creole English dialects in the British Caribbean. *Orbis* 6: 373–91; 7: 54–64.

1960a. Editor, *Creole Language Studies I*. London: Macmillan.

1960b. Jamaican Creole: An historical introduction. Le Page, ed., 3–124.

1961a. Editor, *Creole Language Studies II (Proceedings of the Conference on Creole Language Studies, Mona, 1959)*. London: Macmillan.

1961b. (with F.G. Cassidy). Lexicographical problems of the *Dictionary of Jamaican English*, edited by Le Page, 17–36.

1964. *The National Language Question*. Oxford: Oxford University Press.

1967. (with F.G. Cassidy). *Dictionary of Jamaican English*. Cambridge: Cambridge University Press. Second ed. 1980.

1968a. Problems to be faced in the use of English as the medium of instruction in four West Indian territories. In *Language Problems of Developing Nations*, edited by J. Fishman, C. Ferguson and J. Das Gupta, 431–41. New York: Wiley.

1968b. Problems of description in multilingual communities. In *Transactions of the Philological Society*, 189–212. Oxford: Blackwell.

1968c. (with P.C.C. Evans). *The Education of West Indian Immigrant Children*. London: National Council for Commonwealth Immigrants.

1969. Dialect in West Indian literature. *Journal of Commonwealth Literature* 7: 1–7.

1972. Preliminary report on the sociolinguistic survey of Cayo District, British Honduras. *Language in Society* 1, no. 1: 155–72.

1973a. (with Andrée Tabouret-Keller). L'enquête sociolinguistique a grande

R.B. Le Page: *Selected Publications*

échelle. Un exemple. / Sociolinguistic survey of multilingual communities, Part 1: British Honduras survey. *La Linguistique* 6, no. 2: 103–18.

1973b. The concept of competence in a Creole/contact situation. *York Papers in Linguistics* 3: 31–50.

1974. (with P. Christie et al.). Further report on the sociolinguistic survey of multilingual communities. *Language in Society* 3: 1–32.

1975. Polarizing factors: Political, social, economic, operating in the individual's choice of identity through language use in British Honduras. In *Les États Multilingues/Multilingual Political Systems*, edited by J.G. Savard and R. Vigneault, 537–51. Quebec: Presse Université Laval.

1977a. (with Andrée Tabouret-Keller et al.). Report to the DGRST, Paris, on the Sociolinguistic Survey of Multilingual Communities, Stage II: St Lucia. Department of Language, University of York. Mimeo.

1977b. Processes of pidginization and creolization. In *Pidgin and Creole Linguistics*, edited by Albert Valdman, 222–55. Bloomington: Indiana University Press.

1977c. Decreolization and recreolization: A preliminary report on the Sociolinguistic Survey of Multilingual Communities, Stage II: St Lucia. *York Papers in Linguistics* 7: 107–28.

1978a. Projection, focusing, diffusion, or steps towards a sociolinguistic theory of language, illustrated from the Sociolinguistic Survey of Multilingual Communities, Stages I: Cayo District, Belize (formerly British Honduras) and II: St Lucia. SCL Occasional Paper 9 (reproduced in *York Papers in Linguistics* 9: 7–32).

1980. Theoretical aspects of sociolinguistic studies in pidgin and Creole languages. In *Theoretical Orientations in Creole Studies*, edited by A. Valdman and A. Highfield, 331–51. New York: Academic Press.

1981. *Caribbean Connections in the Classroom*. London: Mary Glasgow Language Trust.

1985. (with Andrée Tabouret-Keller). *Acts of Identity*. Cambridge: Cambridge University Press.

1987. The need for a multidimensional model. In *Pidgin and Creole Languages: Essays in Memory of John E. Reinecke*, edited by Glenn C. Gilbert, 113–29. Honolulu: University of Hawaii Press.

1988. Some premises concerning the standardization of languages, with special reference to Caribbean Creole English. *International Journal of the Sociology of Languages* 71: 25–36.

1989. What is a language? *York Papers in Linguistics* 13: 9–24.

1992. "You never can tell where a word comes from": Language contacts in a diffuse setting. In *Language Contact, Theoretical and Empirical Studies*, edited by E.H. Jahr, 71–101. Berlin and New York: Mouton de Gruyter.

1994. The notion of linguistic "system" revisited. *International Journal of the Sociology of Language* 109: 109–20.

1997. Co-editor (with Andrée Tabouret-Keller et al.). *Vernacular Literacy. A Reevaluation.* Oxford: Oxford University Press.

Acknowledgements

The editor wishes to acknowledge the role of the Institute of Caribbean Studies, University of the West Indies, Mona, in conceiving the idea for this book and also in granting her the honour and privilege of putting it together. Thanks are also due to Dr Kathryn Brodber, who set the process in motion by soliciting essays, and to the contributors who responded.

Appreciation is expressed, too, to the readers who commented on the original manuscript, for their invaluable suggestions, and finally to the staff of the University of the West Indies Press for undertaking the task of publication and all that it entails.

Symbols and Abbreviations

Symbols

[ ] usually encloses phonetic notation, that is, transcription of pronunciation. In a few instances square brackets are used otherwise in this text, but in such cases the interpretation is specifically indicated.
/ / encloses phonemic transcription, that is, representation of the significant sound units of the language being discussed.
[indicates the start of overlap between utterances (in the transcription of conversation).
marks word boundary.
* indicates that an item is ungrammatical.
?? precedes a sentence about the grammaticality of which one is uncertain.
`_ indicates Low tone.
´_ indicates High tone in phonetic transcription, High Low in phonemic transcription.
'_ indicates primary stress on the following syllable.
^_ indicates Falling tone over a single vowel.
(.) indicates a pause of five seconds or less.
= indicates lack of a discernible gap between utterances.
< derives from
> changes from

Symbols and Abbreviations

Abbreviations

AAVE	African American Vernacular English
ASP	Aspect
AUX	Auxiliary
BelC	Belize Creole
BICS	Basic interpersonal communication skills
Br. Eng.	British English
BJC	British Jamaican Creole
BJE	British Jamaican English
C	Consonant
CALP	Cognitive academic language proficiency
CARICOM	Caribbean Community
CBU	Caribbean Broadcasting Union
CEC	Caribbean English Creole
CLT	Communicative Language Teaching
CXC	Caribbean Examinations Council
D1	The first dialect learned
D2	A dialect learned after the first
DCEU	*Dictionary of Caribbean English Usage*
DEM	Demonstrative
ESD	English as a second dialect
ESL	English as a second language
GC	Guyanese Creole
H	High tone
IGSVL	International Group for the Standardization and Vernacularization of Literacy
IPA	International Phonetic Alphabet
IRE	Initiation/Response/Evaluation
IS	Information-seeking (question)
JC	Jamaican Creole
L	Low tone
L1	First language
L2	A language learned after first
LJ	London Jamaican

Symbols and Abbreviations

LOC	Locative
NAm. Eng.	North American English
NEG	Negative
NPE	Nigerian Pidgin English
PIC	Providence Island Creole
SCL	Society for Caribbean Linguistics
SE	Standard British English (unless otherwise indicated)
SN	Sranan
SPCL	Society for Pidgin and Creole Linguistics
TL	Target language
TMA	Tense/Mood/Aspect
TRP	Transition relevance place
UG	Universal grammar
UWI	University of the West Indies
V	Vowel
VP	Verb Phrase

General Introduction

Forty Years On

Pauline Christie

The Le Pagean View of Language

This volume appropriately reflects the slogan which was adopted by the University of the West Indies for its fiftieth anniversary celebrations in 1998: "Celebrating the Past, Charting the Future". For a few of the contributors, Professor Le Page is a figure of whom they have only vaguely heard, one whose name they may associate mainly with the *Dictionary of Jamaican English* (Cassidy and Le Page [1967] 1980). Others are his former students. Still others have, in various ways, been closely associated with him and his work over many years. Despite these differences, in paying tribute to him as a pioneer in this collection of essays, they are all revisiting or opening up for the first time one or more routes along which future research on Caribbean language might proceed. The past and the future are never altogether separate. Forty years on the work continues, building on foundations which others, outstanding among them Robert Le Page, have laid.

Le Page's exposure to language in the Caribbean and Malaysia radically changed his thinking on the subject. His *National Language Question* (1964) raised the topical issue of language choices facing newly independent nations, including those of the Caribbean. It was followed in 1968 by "Problems to Be Faced in the Use of English as the Medium of Instruction in Four West Indian Territories" and "Problems of Description in Multilingual Communities", titles which speak for themselves. Discussion of language in the

Caribbean, approximately forty years after the 1959 Creole conference at Mona, would be incomplete without special consideration of the development of his ideas during the interval.

Problems of description in the early days forced him to admit that to portray the linguistic situation in the Caribbean in terms of two discrete entities, Creole and English, was to misrepresent the facts, since no clear boundaries were discernible. For him, the individual is the starting point in matters concerning language. He sees language as primarily a manifestation of human behaviour in which it is individuals who create the "rules" as they seek to identify themselves with (or distance themselves from) particular groups, subject to certain social and psychological constraints. Some communities are highly "focused"; that is, their members are fairly similar to each other in their linguistic behaviour. On the other hand, in cases such as those characteristic of the Caribbean, the situation is quite diffuse; individuals readily identify with very different groups on different occasions and this results in marked variations in their everyday language. Professor Le Page sees the reification of language varieties as particularly inappropriate in such communities. In fact, he has consistently argued against seeing any language simply as a closed and finite rule system (see, for example, Le Page 1989: 9).

Acts of Identity

The Le Pagean view of language has received its fullest expression in *Acts of Identity* (Le Page and Tabouret-Keller 1985), the theme of which he defined as the concept of "linguistic behaviour as a series of acts of identity in which people reveal both their personal identity and their search for social roles" (p. 14). The data he used to test his hypothesis were drawn mainly from Belize and St Lucia, each of which is more clearly multilingual than most of the other "Anglophone" Caribbean territories. In Belize, Spanish, English, lexically English Creole, Maya, Kekchi and Garifuna are recognized. In St Lucia, lexically French Creole is in contact with English. In each of these territories, too, the search for new individual and social identities, at the time of Le Page's survey in the early 1970s, was affected by the approach of political independence.

Having recognized the impossibility of devising formal statistical methods that would be suitable for testing his hypothesis, he established groups or "clusters" of informants based on correlations between the use of specific linguistic variables and differing formal and informal contexts. This provided documentation of the variability which had given rise to his investigation, since each group so identified represents a different cluster in a series of overlapping clusters.

Le Page rejects the concept of a linear continuum for describing the Caribbean language situation, as he does not think that every utterance can be arranged on a scale from more English to less English, or from more Creole to less Creole. Similarly, he does not agree that all linguistic features can be assigned to some named system such as basilect, acrolect, mesolect, or, for that matter, English or Creole. What is necessary for an appropriate description of Caribbean language behaviour, he claims, is a multidimensional model which can account for the very complex mixing that takes place in individual and group performance. While admitting to problems with the design and execution of his own research (Le Page and Tabouret-Keller 1985: 153), he has expressed disappointment (Le Page 1989: 20) that only a few creolists seem to have recognized the need, first highlighted in his foreword to Beryl Bailey's *Jamaican Creole Syntax* (Bailey 1966: vii), for descriptive techniques analogous to quantum mechanics to handle such situations.

Perhaps the real problem resides in the enormity of the task. Rickford so concluded in his statement that "the multidimensional approach may be too all-encompassing or unnecessarily complex, and it is theoretically useful for us to attempt to constrain it as far as possible" (Rickford 1987: 28–29). For Rickford, the unidimensional model, even if it cannot represent the full picture, does not really distort the facts and should be retained as an ideal. From an apparently similar viewpoint, Devonish (1989b) described cases where co-occurrence restrictions could be identified, in Guyana and Jamaica at least. The challenge of a multidimensional model remains, however, as does the need for data collection in other less obviously multilingual communities on a scale similar to Le Page's for Belize and St Lucia.

Due Respect

The Stereotypes

Discussion of stereotypes surrounding language is especially relevant in a volume concerned, as this one is, with the Caribbean. Linguists and nonlinguists alike in this region conceive of Creole as an entity distinct from another entity labelled, for example, English, notwithstanding the linguistic complexity which is the reality. The bias is, of course, largely a consequence of the stereotyping which has traditionally been fostered, on the one hand, by our education system and social structure and, on the other, more recently by the search for a postcolonial identity. Le Page understands this, despite being very conscious of how much the stereotypes distort the true picture. Referring to language generally, he has written:

> If one takes the view about the centrality of the individual to any scientific study of language, then one has to build outwards from that to accommodate the indisputable fact that cultures tend to throw up various stereotypes about the autonomy of their languages and that these . . . sometimes exert a powerful influence on the community so that people defend their implications . . . (Le Page 1992: 76)

The Creole stereotype is alive and well in the Caribbean, whether it is called Patwa (as are Jamaican and the lexically French Creoles of Dominica and St Lucia), Creole (as in Belize), Creolese (as in Guyana), or Bajan (as in Barbados). The Jamaican situation is detailed here, taken as generally representative of situations throughout the region. What is usually referred to in Jamaica as Patwa (and more recently as Creole in some circles) is speech perceived as being furthest removed from Standard English. Judgements about this are regularly made by Jamaicans, although the criteria on which they are based are often as much social as linguistic. Much depends on what is known about speakers. Thus, if we know Speaker X to be educated and/or economically well off, for example, we tend to associate him or her with Standard English speech, ignoring what may in fact embrace a wide range of linguistic features. Similarly, more English features used by Speaker Y, whose appearance and social background make us associate him or her with the other end of the linguistic scale, may be overlooked.

As for the English stereotype, few educated Jamaicans are aware of the extent to which their own usage differs from the traditionally accepted model of Standard British English. The concept of English is, moreover, a highly normative and conservative one which contrasts more and more with actual usage. It is also noticeable that many persons who deplore what they see as the decline of English are often guilty of the very practices against which they inveigh. Such departures are usually diagnosed as resulting from increasing Creole interference, despite the fact that many of them reflect informal usage long established throughout the society, and have as their source more than a century's imperfect learning of English in the classroom as much as direct transfer from Creole (see Pollard, this volume).

Attitudes to Creole and Their Relationship to Actual Behaviour

Where acceptance of Creole as something other than "bad English" is concerned, it sometimes appears that little progress has been made over the last forty years. The motives of those who express different views about Creole are still often misinterpreted and their credentials ignored, not least by authority figures. The stereotype is still generally associated with ignorance and a lack of discipline, even by many of those whose parents and friends, and often themselves, speak something which closely reflects it, more often than not, as they quietly go about their daily lives. On the face of it, the situation seems not to have changed at all since the 1950s when a Jamaican journalist, the late Vere Johns, roundly attacked Robert Le Page in his newspaper column for daring to suggest that "bad talk" could be worthy of scholarly attention. Similar negative comments still come from journalists and important public figures whose own written and spoken "English" more and more reflects local features which they fail to recognize as such. Even the admission that the first language of the majority of the Jamaican people is not English is still treated by many as akin to heresy and/or is automatically interpreted as a call for Creole to replace English. This not only illustrates the usual tendency to perceive language situations in terms of dichotomies, but it is also a consequence of the fact that most of the population cannot even conceive of Creole as a real language. This does not simply reflect a desire on the part of the elite to maintain the linguistic status quo as some outside observers have suggested.

Due Respect

From the point of view of the so-called elite, and for many others in the society as well, Creole cannot replace English, whatever the claims of a few "misguided" intellectuals, any more than for our ancestors, putting a man on the moon was possible. More significantly, their reaction illustrates the strength of entrenched ideas about language in general, according to which, among other things, a language must at least have an established written form and grammatical categories that parallel those traditionally identified for English.

However, there are some indications pointing in another direction, which should not be ignored. Back in the 1950s, Patwa was not something one talked about. Some people enjoyed the poems of Louise Bennett or the feature, "Law and Laughter in Court", for example, which appeared regularly in the weekly Jamaica Times newspaper, but humour was all they saw in them. They took it for granted that some people spoke "dialect", not themselves, of course, and that such speakers were often funny. Nowadays, many people think seriously about it and talk about it, even if only to condemn it. In 1959, there were few if any articles or letters in the press on the subject. Nowadays, what is portrayed by journalists, usually inaccurately, as the English versus Creole debate, occupies a place in the media at regular intervals.

Creole has come to be taken for granted in Jamaica in other areas of the public domain where once only English would have been expected (see Carrington, this volume, for references to other parts of the Caribbean). For example, callers to the growing number of talk shows do not hesitate to express themselves using clearly non-English forms and structures and, more and more, moderators of these programmes, all of whom are perfectly capable of producing what would normally be regarded as English, adjust their speech to that of their callers. At least one such host deliberately does so on principle. For a large part of his programme, his language indicates that he identifies with the group he associates with the Creole end of the spectrum and many of this group in turn identify with him, judging from the popularity of his programme. In contrast, his frequent abrupt switches to English during a single conversation on this programme, and the Englishness of the language he used consistently in a series of interviews with public figures on television, indicate membership of a very different group, one considered more compatible with his position as a tutor at the University of the West Indies. The only thing unusual about his case is the drastic nature of the switching in the former context and the obvious general difference in his behaviour, depending on the type of occasion.

Creole has almost superseded English as the language of the theatre, as nearly all plays nowadays are written by Jamaicans who choose to write primarily for other Jamaicans. This includes Jamaica's responses to popular North American soap operas on television. The settings are Jamaican and the language reflects a wide cross-section of local usage. Even the few plays of foreign origin which are still performed are usually adapted for the same purpose. Last but not least, reggae songs, the lyrics of which are inevitably in Creole, have represented the most widely listened to form of music for some time now and are frequently learned from early childhood. The increasing use of Creole in writing is another significant development (for a discussion of this, see Devonish 1996). Newspaper columns in Creole are more frequent than they were even a decade or two ago, and Creole is more and more deliberately used in advertisements in the press and in posters on public display. As well, over the last two decades alone, there have been at least half-a-dozen popular booklets produced by amateurs, mostly glossaries, the primary aim of which has been to introduce Jamaican speech to visitors to the island. In addition, writers of letters to the newspapers increasingly switch from English to Creole to show their Jamaicanness. A recent letter to the *Gleaner* newspaper in which the joint signatories described their trip to the World Cup matches in France in 1998 illustrates this. It was written for the most part in Standard English, as the following opening sentence illustrates: "It was the experience of a lifetime. It had always been a dream, a secret wish, to watch a World Cup match." The penultimate paragraph read, however: "Finally, in true Jamaican style it did nice nuh. Nuff nuff merriment fi real. We caan tap chat bout it an we tell yuh true true seh wi did luv it bad bad" [Finally, in true Jamaican style, it was nice, it really was. Much merriment indeed. We can't stop talking about it and we tell you truly that we loved it very very much] (*Gleaner*, 3 July 1998). These writers, too, are deliberately using Creole to express solidarity with other Jamaicans while, at the same time, by using Standard English in parts of the letter, declaring their membership of the educated group.

The foregoing example supports Le Page's hypothesis about language behaviour, although his focus is mainly on unconscious and relatively unfocused acts of identity. The psychological and social constraints he identifies apply, that is, adaptation of our language behaviour to resemble the behaviour of groups with which we wish to identify can only take place to the extent that

- We can identify the groups.
- We have both adequate access to the groups and the ability to analyse their behavioural patterns.
- The motivation to join the groups is sufficiently powerful and is either reinforced or reversed by feedback from the groups.
- We have the ability to learn, that is, to change, our habits where necessary. (Le Page and Tabouret-Keller 1985: 182)

The Development of Caribbean Language Studies

On the academic level, the seeds planted four decades ago and more by Professor Le Page and others fell on fertile ground. Creole studies have prospered and now represent an internationally recognized developing area of linguistics. Work on Caribbean language, not only in the "Anglophone" territories but also significantly in Haiti and Suriname, prepared the way for this and still makes the most comprehensive contribution to the field. In the early days, the work was carried out mainly by foreign-born and/or foreign-based scholars, among them Robert Hall, Jr, Frederic Cassidy, Jan Voorhoeve, Douglas Taylor, Albert Valdman, Derek Bickerton, Beryl Bailey, David DeCamp and David Lawton, in addition to Bob Le Page. For some time now, however, Caribbean-born scholars, working mainly at home, have been taking the lead. Some of these, notably Richard Allsopp, Mervyn Alleyne, Christian Eersel, Dennis Craig, Lawrence Carrington, John Rickford and Jean Bernabé, must be considered pioneers in their own right. Researchers on Caribbean language are now to be found in significant numbers in the Caribbean, North America and Europe. The Society for Caribbean Linguistics (SCL), founded in 1972, is still going strong, as evidenced by the popularity of its biennial conferences held in different parts of the Caribbean. Its more broadly based North American counterpart, the Society for Pidgin and Creole Linguistics (SPCL), has a strong Caribbean component. The Societies have held joint conferences in Guyana (1994) and New York (1997).

Linguistics (Including Creole Studies) at the University of the West Indies

Linguistics has been taught at the University of the West Indies since the 1960s. For some time the courses were organized under the auspices of the Senate Subcommittee on Linguistics which spanned the three campuses – Mona in Jamaica, St Augustine in Trinidad and Cave Hill in Barbados. Departments responsible for teaching the subject replaced the subcommittee in 1975. Since then, the course offerings have gradually expanded at both undergraduate and graduate levels and currently cover general linguistics, sociolinguistics, historical linguistics, language planning, language acquisition, gender studies, discourse analysis and, of course, Creole studies.

Issues within Caribbean Linguistics

Up to the late 1960s, the main concern of scholars dealing with Caribbean language was to show the structural autonomy of Creoles, in an attempt to break away from the tradition which saw them as unsystematic mixed varieties inevitably linked to their European lexifiers (see, for example, Bailey 1966). This approach indubitably served a useful purpose but, as Le Page and others discovered, what was described was very much an abstraction which masked the significant variations characteristic of most situations.

The 1970s were marked by attempts to describe what was now conceived by many to be a linear continuum, the extremes of which were represented by English and Creole. David DeCamp (1971) introduced the idea of using implicational scales to account for the co-occurrence of selected linguistic variables from the Jamaican spectrum. A few years later, based on his experience in Guyana, Derek Bickerton (1975) proposed a polylectal grammar of that community to which the grammars of individuals could be related both synchronically and diachronically. He identified three abstract levels available to Guyanese speakers: the basilectal level furthest removed from Standard English, the acrolect closest to Standard English, and the mesolect or intermediate level. As was indicated earlier, Le Page favours a multidimensional approach to the continuum, which is in contrast with the linear approach taken by both these scholars. His own survey of multilingual communities, which was to provide much of the data for *Acts of Identity* (Le Page and Tabouret-Keller 1985), had been launched in Belize in 1970.

The concept of a linear continuum nevertheless continued to be generally utilized (see, for example, Escure 1980; Rickford 1987). However, it has not been uncritically accepted. For example, Carrington (1992: 96), while noting that its survival probably provides evidence of its closeness to what it was designed to illustrate, expresses his own doubts as to "whether it has not shaped the space it seeks to describe, designing its own aptness, rather than mimicking the reality of the nature of the space". Illustrations of the continuum tend to focus on a few linguistic features such as tense/mood/aspect markers, pronouns and the distribution of the copula, while ignoring the fact that there are many other features for which no gradation is observable and also features whose formal resemblance to Standard English mask functional parallels with Creole. Some controversy has been sparked off by the notion that the continuum resulted from decreolization, a consequence of continued contact with the lexifier. Observable change is not always as unilateral as this implies and, as has been pointed out by Alleyne (1971), among others, some variation must always have existed on Caribbean plantations, since the slaves were not all equally exposed to the language of their masters. We cannot, of course, be certain that there is a direct relationship between the variation which is evident today and that which existed in an earlier era.

Correlation between linguistic variation and social variables has been a feature of much of the research involving the continuum concept. For example, although in illustrating his implicational scales David DeCamp (1971) relied on linguistic criteria alone, he followed this up by considering the sociolinguistic implications of the variation. Similarly, in Le Page and Tabouret-Keller (1985), cluster membership was correlated with socioeconomic and demographic factors. From the more general perspective of the sociology of language, the significance of sociocultural factors in the development of Caribbean language was first illustrated by Alleyne (1971), while Pollard's work on Dread Talk, the language of the Rastafari (for example, Pollard 1983, 1994), illustrates the relationship between language choice and social identity. These, along with, among others, Young's (1973) study of Belizean, Edwards's (1975) investigation of Guyanese, Muhleisen's (1993) discussion of language attitudes in Trinidad, Peter Patrick's (1999) sociolinguistic examination of linguistic variation in Kingston, Jamaica, and Carrington's call (this volume) for a proper survey of the use of Creole languages in the light of social changes during the past few decades, point to continuing recognition of the importance of not treating language in isolation from the environment in which it is spoken.

Research into the genesis and development of Creoles as a group and their social history also requires sociolinguistic information. Over the last two decades in particular, significant progress has been made in these areas. The debate on Creole genesis was the first to occupy the stage. In the beginning, the arguments had been between the proponents of various monogenetic and polygenetic theories (for example, Taylor 1961; Hall 1966), but Bickerton's Language Bioprogram Hypothesis, which claimed that children on the slave plantations invented Creole using their innate linguistic capacity (Bickerton 1981), provoked a new round. This time the contrast showed up between the universalists, like Bickerton, and substratists, including Alleyne (1980), who stressed the importance of the role of African languages in Creole formation. It is generally agreed, however, that universalist and Afrogenetic viewpoints are not incompatible (see, for example, Mufwene 1986; Carrington 1993).

In testing the validity of any theory of Creole genesis, one must take into account the demographic and ethnographic contexts in which creolization occurred. Until recently, few relevant details were available. However, demographic studies by Arends (1995) on Suriname, Singler (1995) on Haiti and Martinique, Jennings (1995a) on Cayenne and St Christopher/St Kitts, Cooper (1998), Jennings (1995b) and Parkvall (1995) on St Kitts, and Mazama (1998) on Guadeloupe, are helping to fill the gap.

General descriptions of groups of Creoles or of individual Creoles which appeared during the last forty years are to be found in, for example, Bailey (1966), Alleyne (1980), Carrington (1983) and Roberts (1988). Some of these provide more structural information than others. Since 1958, at least two previously unrecognized Creoles have been brought to light. The first of these, Palenquero, a Spanish-based variety spoken just south of Cartagena in Northern Columbia, has been the subject of descriptions by Bickerton and Escalante (1970), Lewis (1970) and Schwegler (1992). Berbice Dutch was first unearthed in Guyana and described by Ian Robertson in his doctoral thesis

(Robertson 1979). A book-length description of it, based on her own thesis, has been published by Kouwenberg (1994).

However, the most striking feature of descriptions of Creole structure published over the past two decades has been a focus on specific syntactic topics, mainly predication, including tense/mood/aspect (for example, Gibson 1982, Singler 1990; Winford 1993), complementation (for example, Byrne 1987; Winford 1993), serial verbs (for example, Jansen et al. 1978; Sebba 1987). Some of these studies illustrate application of recent grammatical theory to Creole language structure. Phonological investigation has lagged behind the investigation of syntax, but in this area Devonish's work on tone (for example, Devonish 1989a) must be singled out.

A few creolists have also recognized the potential contribution of dictionaries towards improving the status of Caribbean language varieties in addition to their value as reference works. Cassidy and Le Page's *Dictionary of Jamaican English* led the way in 1967, to be followed after a fairly long interval by the *Dictionary of Bahamian English* (Holm and Shilling 1982). The French-lexicon Creoles of Dominica and St Lucia are represented by Fontaine's *Dominica's Diksyonnè*, a Creole-English and English-Creole dictionary, the text edited by Peter Roberts, which appeared in 1991, and Mondesir's *Dictionary of St Lucian Creole* (1992), the text edited by Lawrence Carrington. Most recently, Richard Allsopp's comprehensive *Dictionary of Caribbean English Usage* was published in 1996 after more than two decades of meticulous preparation, during which the author investigated a wide range of oral and written sources from all over the region and status-labelled the items where appropriate.

Language acquisition in the context of Trinidad and Tobago has received special attention from Valerie Youssef. She has proposed that children growing up in the twin-island state and in other Caribbean environments, where what she identifies as "codemixing" is the norm, acquire an underlying "varilingual" competence (Youssef 1996). Le Page would deny that separate codes are easily identifiable in the multidimensional space that characterizes such unfocused situations, but he would certainly agree that the Chomskyan model of individual competence as the knowledge of an ideal speaker–hearer in a homogeneous speech community is particularly inappropriate for Caribbean speakers.

Discussion of the place of Creole in Caribbean educational policy is another area to which much attention has been paid over the past forty years. In this regard, special mention must be made of the work of Craig, Carrington, Robertson and, most recently, Simmons-McDonald. As indicated by Craig's article in this volume, however, the decision makers have paid little heed to recommendations made by linguists.

Le Page played a pioneering role in opening up discussion of practically all the issues mentioned here. As well as his work in lexicography, mentioned earlier, his outline of Caribbean Creole structure (1957–1958) and his socio-historical introduction to *Jamaican Creole* (1960) were firsts for the "Anglophone" Caribbean. He has repeatedly called for cooperation with trained Africanists in the effort to assess the African contribution to Creole genesis (see, for example, Bailey 1966: viii). His was also one of the voices which very early called for a new approach to education in Jamaica that recognized that English was not the first language of the majority of learners. Discussing the obvious disadvantage of Jamaican children from poorer homes with regard to selection for secondary education, he asked: "What tests are there in which language plays no part? How can the selectors take the language differential into account unless adequate descriptions of the Creole exist? How can the teachers themselves be trained to get the best out of the children unless the problems of communication and expression are fully understood?" (Bailey 1966: v). These questions have still not been fully addressed by those in charge of educational policy (see Craig, this volume) and the repercussions of the situation which prompted them are now being felt even at the tertiary level.

Back home in the United Kingdom in the 1960s and 1970s, Le Page devoted much of his attention to the problems that arose in teaching children of Caribbean origin in the classrooms of that country. Students at York who specialized in English language were encouraged to spend a year in a school in an immigrant community or in a Creole-speaking environment abroad, as well as being formally introduced to Creole in one of their University courses. More recently, Le Page turned his attention to the question of literacy, a matter of extreme relevance for contemporary Jamaica at least, where one of the most frequent complaints in the 1990s has been about the large number of graduates from secondary schools who are considered functionally illiterate.

Due Respect

The activities of his informal International Group for the Study of Language Standardization and the Vernacularization of Literacy (IGLSVL), convened biennially between 1986 and 1992, includes case studies from both non-Creole-speaking and Creole-speaking situations in various parts of the world and examination of the conditions favourable to the development of vernacular literacy. The term *vernacular* in this context is not confined to the contrast between the low prestige everyday spoken language of a community and the coexisting high prestige standard or official variety. It also includes the contrast between actual usage and the conventional stereotype of discrete and homogeneous varieties normally promoted in teaching literacy. For example, in the Caribbean it could refer to local varieties of English as well as to Creole. The deliberations of the group are reflected in *Vernacular Literacy: A Re-evaluation* (Tabouret-Keller 1997).

Conclusion

The focus on Anglophone Creoles in this introduction reflects not only the title of the volume, but also the geographical focus of Le Page's work on the Caribbean. Nevertheless, it should be evident that the issues which have been presented here are by no means restricted to the areas where these particular Creoles are spoken, but are of equal relevance to other Caribbean varieties and, indeed, to the entire Creolophone world. They have been included without detailed discussion or evaluation. Such details are considered to be beyond the scope of an introductory chapter, the main objective of which has been to outline the main developments in Creole Studies since the 1959 international conference on Creole languages and to highlight Professor Le Page's contribution to Caribbean language studies.

A partial list of events involving Creole languages in the "Anglophone" Caribbean and the authors and titles of the occasional papers published to date by the Society for Caribbean Linguistics (1973–1998) both suggest the range and significance of Le Page's work.

1959   First international conference on Creole languages, University of the West Indies (UWI), Mona, Jamaica.

1968	Second international conference on Creole languages, UWI, Mona, Jamaica.
1972	UNESCO conference on Language and Educational Development, St Augustine, Trinidad. Formation of the SCL.
1973	First occasional paper published by the SCL.
1975	Establishment of departments responsible for teaching linguistics at UWI.
1976	First biennial conference, SCL on New Directions in Creole Studies, University of Guyana.
1978	Second biennial conference, SCL on Semantics, Lexicography and Creole Studies, UWI, Cave Hill, Barbados.
1979	Symposium on Theoretical Orientations in Creole Studies, St Thomas, US Virgin Islands.
1980	Third biennial conference, SCL on Redefining Creole Studies; The Social History of Creole Languages; Non-Creole Languages; Extending the Use of Vernacular Languages in the Caribbean, Aruba, Netherlands Antilles.
1982	Fourth biennial conference, SCL, Paramaribo, Suriname.
1984	Fifth biennial conference, SCL, UWI, Mona, Jamaica.
1986	Sixth biennial conference, SCL (joint with American Dialect Society), UWI, St Augustine, Trinidad.
1988	Seventh biennial conference, SCL, Nassau, Bahamas.
1990	Eighth biennial conference, SCL, University College, Belize.
1992	Ninth biennial conference, SCL, on Creole Language Studies at the Crossroads, UWI, Cave Hill, Barbados.
1994	Tenth biennial conference, SCL (joint with Society for Pidgin and Creole Linguistics), University of Guyana, Guyana.
1996	Eleventh biennial conference, SCL on Creole Languages: Theory and Social Practice, St Maarten, Netherlands Antilles.
1998	Twelfth biennial conference, SCL, on Expanding the Horizons of Caribbean Language Research, St Lucia.

Due Respect

Society for Caribbean Linguistics Occasional Papers, 1973–1998

1. Peter Roberts. Speech of 6-year-old Jamaican children (transcriptions).
2. Ian Robertson. Dutch Creole in Guyana: Some missing links.
3. Ian Hancock. Creole features in the Afro-Seminole speech of Bracketville, Texas.
4. Ian Robertson. Dutch Creole speakers and their locations in Guyana in the nineteenth and early twentieth centuries.
5. Ian Robertson. A preliminary word list of Berbice Dutch.
6. Richard Allsopp. Africanisms in the idiom of Caribbean English.
7. Ian Hancock. Further observations on Afro-Seminole Creole.
8. Walter Edwards. Sociolinguistic models and phonological variation in Guyana.
9. Robert Le Page. Projection, focusing, diffusion or steps towards a sociolinguistic theory of language.
10. Pauline Christie. Assertive 'no' in Jamaican Creole.
11. Ian Hancock. English in St Helena: Creole features in an island speech.
12. Donald Winford. Phonological variation and change in Trinidadian English: The evolution of the vowel system.
13. Hazel Carter. Evidence for the survival of African prosodies in West Indian Creoles.
14. Claire Broadbridge. Some devices for focus in Trinidadian.
14. Ian Robertson. Redefining the Creole continuum: Evidence from Berbice Dutch.[1]
15. George Huttar. A Creole-Amerindian pidgin of Suriname.
16. John Rickford. Standard and nonstandard language attitudes in a Creole continuum.
18. Alison Watt Shilling. Black English as a Creole: Some Bahamian evidence.
19. McVey Graham, Jr. Caribbean French Creole survey.
20. George Huttar. Notes on Kwinti, a Creole of Central Suriname.
21. Charles De Bose. *Be* in Samaná English.

22. Jon Amastae. Complements of factive and inceptive verbs in Dominican French Creole.
23. Gertrud Aub-Buscher. African survivals in the lexicon of Trinidad-based French Creole.
24. Hubert Devonish and Walter Seiler. A reanalysis of the phonological system of Jamaican Creole.
25. Peter Roberts. *Have* and *be* in Caribbean Creoles: Evidence of continuity from lexifier languages.
26. Dhanis Jaganauth. Time reference in two Creoles: The non-referential component.

The volume's broad focus also reflects the wide range of Le Page's interests in his study of Caribbean language and matters relating to it, although it does not parallel these. Some of the essays will inevitably be seen as more important than others because of their subject matter and/or originality and depending on the observer's particular orientation. It is also recognized that they vary widely with regard to level of treatment, but this is not undesirable in a work aimed at a wide readership, including not only specialists in the field, but also teachers, students and other interested persons. Indeed, the significance of the fact that the idea for the volume came from a group largely composed of non-linguists, the Institute for Caribbean Studies, UWI, Mona, has not been overlooked. As well as a list of symbols and abbreviations at the beginning of the book, a glossary of technical terms has been provided.

Note

1. In error, two papers were numbered 14. To compensate, 17 was not assigned.

References

Alleyne, M. 1971. Acculturation and the cultural matrix of creolization. In *Pidginization and Creolization of Languages*, edited by D. Hymes. Cambridge: Cambridge University Press.
———. 1980. *Comparative Afro-American*. Ann Arbor: Karoma Press.
Allsopp, R. 1996. *Dictionary of Caribbean English Usage*. Oxford: Oxford University Press.

Arends, J., ed. 1995. *The Early Stages of Creolization*. Amsterdam and Philadelphia: John Benjamins.

———. 1995. Demographic factors in the formation of Sranan. In *The Early Stages of Creolization*, edited by J. Arends. Amsterdam and Philadelphia: John Benjamins.

Bailey, B. 1966. *Jamaican Creole Syntax*. Cambridge: Cambridge University Press.

Baker, P., ed. 1995. *From Contact to Creole and Beyond*. London: University of Westminster Press.

Bickerton, D. 1975. *Dynamics of a Creole System*. Cambridge: Cambridge University Press.

———. 1981. *Roots of Language*. Ann Arbor: Karoma Press.

Bickerton, D., and A. Escalante. 1970. Palenquero, a Spanish-based Creole of Northern Columbia. *Lingua* 24.

Byrne, F. 1987. *Grammatical Relations in a Radical Creole*. Amsterdam and Philadelphia: John Benjamins.

Carrington, L. 1984. *St Lucian Creole: A Description of Its Phonology and Morpho-Syntax*. Hamburg: Helmut Buske Verlag.

———. 1992. Images of Creole space. *Journal of Pidgin and Creole Languages* 7, no. 1.

———. 1993. On the notion of Africanisms in Afro-American. In *Africanisms in Afro-American Language Variations*, edited by S.S. Mufwene. Athens, GA: University of Georgia Press.

Carrington, L., D. Craig, and R. Todd Dandaré, eds. 1983. *Studies in Caribbean Language*. Port of Spain, Trinidad: Society for Caribbean Linguistics.

Cassidy, F.G., and R.B. Le Page. [1967] 1980. *Dictionary of Jamaican English*. Cambridge: Cambridge University Press.

Christie, P. et al., eds. 1998. *Studies in Caribbean Language II*. Port of Spain, Trinidad: Society for Caribbean Linguistics.

Cooper, V. 1998. A study in seventeenth-century ethnolinguistics: The Angolas in the French colony of St Kitts. In *Studies in Caribbean Language II*, edited by P. Christie et al. Port of Spain, Trinidad: Society for Caribbean Linguistics.

DeCamp, D. 1971. Towards a generative analysis of a post-Creole speech continuum. In *Pidginization and Creolization of Languages*, edited by D. Hymes. Cambridge: Cambridge University Press.

Devonish, H. 1989a. *Talking in Tones*. London: Karia Press, and Christchurch, Barbados: Caribbean Academic Publishers.

———. 1989b. Language variation theory in the light of co-occurrence restriction rules. *York Papers in Linguistics* 13.

———. 1996. Vernacular languages and writing technology transfer. In *Caribbean Language Issues Old and New*, edited by P. Christie. Kingston, Jamaica: The

Press, University of the West Indies.

Edwards, W. 1975. Sociolinguistic behaviour in rural and urban communities in Guyana. PhD diss., University of York.

Escure, G. 1980. Decreolization in a Creole continuum: Belize. In *Theoretical Orientations in Creole Studies*, edited by A. Valdman and A. Highfield. New York: Academic Press.

Fontaine, M. 1991. *Dominica's Diksyonnè*. Roseau, Dominica: The Folk Research Institute.

Gibson, K. 1982. Tense and aspect in Guyanese Creole: A syntactic, semantic and pragmatic analysis. PhD diss., University of York.

Hall, R.A., Jr. 1966. *Pidgin and Creole Languages*. Ithaca: Cornell University Press.

Holm, J., with A. Shilling. 1982. *Dictionary of Bahamian English*. Cold Spring, NY: Lexik House.

Hymes, D., ed. *Pidginization and Creolization of Languages*. Cambridge: Cambridge University Press.

Jansen, B., et al. 1978. Serial verbs in the Creole languages. *Amsterdam Creole Studies II*. Amsterdam: University of Amsterdam.

Jennings, W. 1995a. The first generations of a Creole society. In *From Contact to Creole and Beyond*, edited by P. Baker. London: University of Westminster Press.

———. 1995b. Saint Christopher: Site of the first French Creole. In *From Contact to Creole and Beyond*, edited by P. Baker. London: University of Westminster Press.

Kouwenberg, S. 1994. *A Grammar of Berbice Dutch*. Berlin: Mouton de Gruyter.

Le Page, R.B. 1957–58. General outlines of Creole English dialects in the British Caribbean. *Orbis* 6 and 7.

———. 1960. An historical introduction to Jamaican Creole. In *Creole Language Studies I: Jamaican Creole*, edited by R.B. Le Page. London: Macmillan.

———. 1964. *The National Language Question*. Oxford: Oxford University Press.

———. 1966. Foreword. In *Jamaican Creole Syntax*, by B. Bailey. Cambridge: Cambridge University Press.

———. 1968a. Problems to be faced in the use of English as the medium of instruction in four West Indian territories. In *Language Problems of Developing Nations*, edited by J. Fishman. New York: Wiley.

———. 1968b. Problems of description in multilingual communities. *Transactions of the Philological Society*. Oxford: Blackwell.

———. 1984. The need for a multidimensional model. Paper read at the fifth biennial conference of the Society for Caribbean Linguistics. University of the West Indies, Mona, Jamaica.

———. 1989. What is a language? *York Papers in Linguistics* 13.

———. 1992. "You never can tell where a word comes from": Language contact in a diffuse setting. In *Language Contact: Theoretical and Empirical Studies*, edited by E.H. Jahr. Berlin: Mouton de Gruyter.

Le Page, R.B., and A. Tabouret-Keller. 1985. *Acts of Identity*. Cambridge: Cambridge University Press.

Lewis, A. 1970. A descriptive analysis of the Palenquero dialect. Master's thesis, UWI, Mona, Jamaica.

Mazama, A.K. 1998. The nature of language contacts in Guadeloupe during slavery: Sociological and linguistic evidence. In *Studies in Caribbean Language II*, edited by P. Christie et al. Port of Spain, Trinidad: Society for Caribbean Linguistics.

Mondesir, J. 1992. *Dictionary of St Lucian Creole*. Berlin: Mouton de Gruyter.

Mufwene, S.S. 1986. Universalist and substrate theories complement each other. In *Substrata versus Universals in Creole Genesis*, edited by P. Muysken and N. Smith. Amsterdam: John Benjamins.

———, ed. 1993. *Africanisms in Afro-American Language Varieties*. Athens, GA: University of Georgia Press.

Muhleisen, S. 1993. Attitudes towards language varieties in Trinidad. Master's thesis, Free University of Berlin.

Parkvall, M. 1995. The role of St Kitts in a new scenario of French Creole genesis. In *From Contact to Creole and Beyond*, edited by P. Baker. London: University of Westminster Press.

Patrick, P. 1999. *Urban Jamaican Creole: Variation in the Mesolect*. Amsterdam and Philadelphia: John Benjamins

Pollard, V. 1983. The social history of Dread Talk. In *Studies in Caribbean Language*, edited by L. Carrington et al. Port of Spain, Trinidad: Society for Caribbean Linguistics.

———. 1994. *Dread Talk: The Language of the Rastafari*. Kingston, Jamaica: Canoe Press.

Rickford, J.R. 1980. Analyzing variation in Creole languages. In *Theoretical Orientations in Creole Studies*, edited by A. Valdman and A. Highfield. New York: Academic Press.

———. 1987. *Dimensions of a Creole Continuum*. Stanford, CA: Stanford University Press.

Roberts, P. 1988. *West Indians and Their Language*. Cambridge: Cambridge University Press.

Robertson, I. 1979. Berbice Dutch: A description. PhD diss., University of the West Indies, St Augustine, Trinidad.

Schwegler, A. 1992. Future and conditional in Palenquero. *Journal of Pidgin and Creole Languages* 7, no. 2.

Sebba, M. 1987. *The Syntax of Serial Verbs*. Amsterdam and Philadelphia: John Benjamins.

Singler, J. 1995. The demographics of Creole genesis in the Caribbean: A comparison of Martinique and Haiti. In *The Early Stages of Creolization*, edited by J. Arends. Amsterdam and Philadelphia: John Benjamins.

Tabouret-Keller, A., et al., eds. 1997. *The Vernacularization of Literacy: A Re-evaluation*. Oxford: Clarendon Press.

Taylor, D. 1961. New languages for old in the West Indies. *Comparative Studies in Society and History* 3.

Valdman, A., and A. Highfield, eds. 1980. *Theoretical Orientations in Creole Studies*. New York: Academic Press.

Winford, D. 1993. *Predication in Caribbean English Creoles*. Amsterdam and Philadelphia: John Benjamins.

Young, C. 1973. Belize Creole: A study of creolized English spoken in the city of Belize, in its cultural and social setting. PhD diss., University of York.

Youssef, V. 1996. Varilingualism: The competence underlying codemixing in Trinidad and Tobago. *Journal of Pidgin and Creole Languages* 11, no. 1.

Section One

Creole and English:
In the Society and in the School

Introduction

The relationship between English and Creole, as well as their relatively practical orientation, provides the link between the essays in this first section of the volume. Although the basic facts presented here are familiar to Caribbean linguists, at least, they are unlikely to have been seriously considered by a large section of the targeted readership. This fact justifies their inclusion here, despite their tangential relationship with linguistics as a discipline. Further, they reflect Le Page's own concern with the implications, for teachers in the Commonwealth Caribbean, of the linguistic situation in which they operate.

Carrington's opening essay reviews the status of Creole in the Caribbean region as a whole, on the eve of the twenty-first century, with direct reference to specific areas of language use. Its broad Caribbean focus contrasts with the Jamaican bias of the related section of the General Introduction. Carrington goes beyond simple description of the facts to advocate that close examination of the current situation in the various territories should replace the customary impressionistic statements, especially in the light of recent social changes.

The concern with education is more directly reflected in the remaining essays in the section. Simmons-McDonald addresses the question by overtly recognizing the distinction made in second language acquisition theory between the Chomskyan notion of competence and proficiency, defined as language development in the classroom. In a careful analysis, she highlights the need for teachers to be conscious of the implications of the fact that Caribbean learners acquire competence in a "heterogeneous and sociolinguistically

Section One – *Creole and English: In the Society and in the School*

complex environment" and of the differences between the codes generally used in the wider society and the one which is taught in school. The call is not new, but an important aspect of her presentation is the documentation she provides from her own fieldwork in St Lucia. Here children acquire competence in the French-lexicon Creole and/or an English-lexicon vernacular, as well as what she describes as a different kind of competence (and also a different kind of proficiency) in St Lucian Standard English.

Craig, revisiting the question of language policy, contrasts recent materials for teaching Standard English to Creole speakers with what he sees as the more positive developments of the 1970s and 1980s which, in his view, showed greater awareness of the fact that English was not the learners' first language. He recalls his own discussion, almost two decades ago, of the theoretical possibilities open to educational planners, and expresses concern about their failure to consider either these or specific recommendations which have come more recently from the English Panel of the Caribbean Examinations Council in response to continuing low levels of achievement in English.

The contributions by Pollard and Bryan, like Simmons-McDonald's to some extent, take the reader right into the classroom. Bryan examines the interaction between Jamaican Creole and English in classroom discourse. She provides evidence of codeswitching by both teachers and pupils and identifies ways in which teachers exploit the different codes in order to "get their classrooms to work". Pollard confines her investigation to problems relating to one of the basic rules of English, traditionally labelled subject–verb concord. She blames the high incidence of hypercorrection within and outside classrooms in Jamaica on some misleading formulations of this rule. By highlighting the interrelationship between the learners' interlanguage in the classroom and usage in the wider society outside the school, an issue also raised by Simmons-McDonald, Pollard's essay identifies one source of the variation which exists in the Jamaican community. Finally, Taylor's essay discusses the need for recognizing Caribbean English as a legitimate variety. While accepting the relevance of the concept of Standard English for the educator, she stresses the need to re-examine the traditional assumption that the model for English in the Caribbean is necessarily British English and refers to the history of attempts to define Standard English in Britain itself, to the problem of extreme conservatism and also to the influence of American English.

Chapter 1

The Status of Creole in the Caribbean

Lawrence D. Carrington

The end of the second millennium is a good time to review the state of languages whose birth can be dated within the latter half of this epoch.[1] The literature on the status of Creole languages has traditionally examined two features of their presence in our societies:[2] first, the functional distribution of the languages in various social domains, and, second, the attitudes of various categories of users towards the use of the languages. By and large, the social domains of use that have been examined have been determined by assumptions that place the languages of the society into relationships of polarity. Thus, the assessment of the status of Creole languages has been by reference to their coexistence with languages having established standard varieties. In the case of the Caribbean, those comparisons have been with major European languages that have themselves been lexical sources for Creoles of the region. An important part of the determination of status has been the degree of penetration of the Creoles into those areas of the public domain that have been traditionally dominated by the standard languages. The domains used as measures of penetration are frequently the following: politics and government, education, the media, and the performing and literary arts. There has been no recent survey of the use of Creole languages in the Caribbean region and such a survey is absolutely required. The more recent studies of the kind have been limited in their coverage either to a particular Creole language group, to an individual language, or to an individual country. For instance, my own study (*Creole Discourse and Social Development*, 1988) was directed only at the French-lexicon Creoles of the region. Mühleisen's thesis ("Attitudes towards Language Varieties in Trinidad", 1993) focused on Trinidad only, and Durizot-Jno-Baptiste's book (*La Question du Créole à L'École en Guadeloupe*, 1996) was concerned with Guadeloupe alone. Several other recent studies contribute pieces of information to our knowledge of the status of Creoles, but the data collection procedures and the analytical frameworks have not been governed by common considerations. Summary statements on status, however carefully they may be phrased, will be approximate and lack the level of accuracy necessary for planning. There is urgent need for a survey that targets all the varieties in the region with a common set of broadly conceived data-collection criteria and amply designed analytical frames of reference.

Government and Politics

Haiti is the only country in the region that identifies its Creole language as a national language within its constitution. Haitian is a variety of Greater Antillean French-lexicon Creole and its constitutional recognition dates from the end of the Duvalier period. Subsequent administrations have all consolidated its position. Dominica proclaims the existence of its language (Lesser Antillean French-lexicon Creole) in the country's coat of arms (*Apwé Bondié se Latè*), but there is no supporting statement in its constitution. Quite the opposite, both Dominica and St Lucia (where Lesser Antillean is also the vernacular Creole) state constitutional provisions that require ability to use English as a prerequisite for election to the House of Representatives or nomination to the Senate. Until May 1998, Standing Order 6(1) of the House of Representatives of St Lucia required that English be the language of address to the House. It has now been revoked and replaced by a new order: "The proceedings and debates of the House, inclusive of the records of such Proceedings shall be in the English Language, provided that a Member may offer occasional explanation in Kwéyòl."

Constitutional statements about language status do not apply to any other cases in the region. However, in several states there is informal provision for the use of Creole languages and official practices in a number of domains demonstrate their political importance. If the constitution is not the herald of the Creole languages in the region, it is the political campaign that announces their political importance. The official use of Papiamentu for government-to-people communications in Aruba and the Netherlands Antilles is a notable instance. Throughout the region, those who seek elected office must prove their popular bona fides by displays of bilingualism, including competence in the vernacular Creole language. The requirement is not ritual, because representatives must be able to communicate with their constituents. The irony is that most of their constituents expect them to maintain the linguistic status quo by not changing the dominance of the official language in the sectors of public respectability such as the education system.

The Education Sector

The education sector has been the traditional battleground for those who have strong views on the relative status and usefulness of the Creoles and standard languages. The history of the spread of general education from the metropole to the colonies and from the upper classes to the masses has determined the norm that education be available in the official language of a country. From the standpoint of educational theory, there has been a contrasting concern that it is pointless using a language that they do not understand as a vehicle for the instruction of children. That position had variable effect over the centuries and Creole languages have been used by various educational agencies, especially churches and missionary societies, as media of instruction. The churches have always understood what other educators have failed to grasp, namely that people learn best in their own languages, and so have been major users of the Creole vernaculars for religious education. In the Danish Virgin Islands, Moravian Brethren used the Dutch Creole of the enslaved for religious instruction. In all of the countries where French-lexicon Creole has been a vernacular, the Roman Catholic Church has taught its catechism through that medium, a practice that still obtains in contemporary Haiti. Within recent years, the Bahai'i have prepared religious material in French-lexicon Creole for use in Dominica. The importance of the use of vernaculars among religious groups has had important scholarly outcomes. These have taken the form of the development of writing systems, dictionaries and grammatical descriptions, a long-established contribution of churches and missionaries to the languages of the Caribbean. Sranan of Suriname owes much to the work of early missionaries and to more recent work by members of the Summer Institute for Linguistics (SIL), a Texas-based evangelical group devoted to the translation of the Holy Bible into every language of the world. Before long, St Lucia will have a Holy Bible in St Lucian arising from many years of excellent linguistic work by David Frank, a member of the SIL. The Roman Catholic Church itself has taught its catechism through materials prepared in French Creole. Jamaica, too, is the beneficiary of work by religious groups in the form of a Holy Bible prepared in Jamaican Creole, available on audio cassettes.

Despite the success of Creoles in creating Christians, they have generally remained outside the gates of the formal school systems. Although the debates about the usefulness of Creoles for educational purposes have been current for most of this century, it is the movement towards political independence of former colonies within the last forty years that has been one of the important stimuli for the discussion. At the end of each round of the debate, even if there is a gain for the Creole languages, their use is restricted to auxiliary functions. Teachers, schools or educational districts, in accordance with whatever practical limits the vocal sector of the population will tolerate at the relevant time, then idiosyncratically implement the provisions. At present, teachers and virtually all education systems in the region recognize the importance of an acculturation period for beginners in schools. Accordingly, almost everywhere concessions are made to the fact that significant proportions of students entering the school systems do not have sufficient working knowledge of the official languages to benefit from their use as the media of instruction. Within the formal school systems, the limited use of instruction through Creole languages has always been seen as a bridge to instruction through the official language. In some cases, the transition has been made after perfunctory periods; in others, it has been after prolonged usage with varied, even though always inadequate, results. The concessions vary from case to case; sometimes they are rational and in other cases irrational. For example, the 1983 concessions made by law in the case of the French Caribbean departments approved experimental use of Creole for instruction in areas of the curriculum with a cultural bias at the secondary rather than the primary level. On the other hand, the official provisions for the use of Papiamentu in its zone of influence are for the initial levels of schooling. Similarly, the concessions made in Trinidad and Tobago in the 1975 syllabus were at the primary level of schooling, the same level at which Haiti's education reform of nearly two decades sought to instrumentalize its language.

In discussing the education sector, a clear distinction must be made between instances in which a policy prescribes and supports the use of Creole as a medium of instruction, and cases in which it is the personal decisions of individual teachers or general practice that results in the use of a Creole language as a de facto medium of classroom interaction. The former case is real only when there is supporting written material for a content of some kind to be presented in the language. Such cases are rare and are currently operational only in Haiti, Aruba and Curaçao. A recent study by Hubisi Nwenmely (1996) provides us with an account of the teaching of the French-lexicon Creole of St Lucia and Dominica in metropolitan London with references to related activities in the islands themselves. This is not by any means the first case of a training programme for teaching Creole in an environment where it is not a working language. Departments of linguistics in the Caribbean, the United States and the United Kingdom, continental Europe and elsewhere have offered several programmes at university level. The difference in Nwenmely's case is that the London programme described by her was mounted to satisfy a social rather than an academic need, a need for affirmation of identity in an alien environment. The programme she described has been accorded educational credit by the London Open College Federation.

Her study is important for our present purposes because it treats the teaching of a Creole in a metropolitan setting, traditionally the most influential source for educational innovation or mimicry in the Caribbean. It presents a challenge to the educational authorities in St Lucia and Dominica by demonstrating a successful accredited course for teaching the same language that they shy away from in their own home-based educational systems.

Another important area in the education sector is the attitude of the region's major school examination body for the part of the region where English is the official language. The Caribbean Examinations Council has a policy by which only the content of a subject is the focus of marking. Consequently, it is only in the examination of English that students' scripts attract penalties for inappropriate language use. The policy affects the extent to which teachers in non-language areas reinforce the language variety modelled in the study of English at the expense of Creole varieties. Thus, although the school systems in the countries where English is the official language may not be formally using Creole varieties for instructional purposes, they are less actively resisting its use than in earlier periods of the history of education in the same areas.

Writing Systems and Technical Supports

Writing systems have been developed for all of the Creoles of the region. In most of the countries, this has been so for decades. Haitian has in fact gone through several official writing systems and has finally stabilized its current system without further change over the last fifteen years. The system for Sranan has been stable and unchallenged for a prolonged period. In the case of Papiamentu, slightly different conventions exist in Aruba and Curaçao, but the differences do not affect the mutual comprehensibility of the systems. In the case of the Lesser Antillean French Creole, scholars have agreed on a common writing system since the mid-1980s. A writing system for Jamaican has been available since the publication of the *Dictionary of Jamaican English* in 1967.

The extent to which the writing systems are known to the mass of the population differs from case to case and is strongly determined by the level of literacy in the country concerned. Thus, the writing system of Haitian may be known among the literate who also use French, but is not available to the vast majority of the population, who do not. The absence of provision for the teaching of literacy through the Creole languages means that only persons who have been made literate through the official languages can have access to the vernacular language in writing. The point is critical for correctly assessing the commitment of the states concerned to the development of their Creoles. Without a policy for the development of literacy through the use of Creole, the provisions for the use of the language at any level are premised on the acquisition of literacy through the official language. This is in many senses a self-defeating process.

The writing systems are supported by dictionaries that are available for an increasing proportion of the Creoles of the region. There are several dictionaries of good quality for Haitian, and dictionaries for Papiamentu and Sranan have been available for quite a long time. There is a historic volume for Jamaican, more than one work for Guadeloupean, a major one for St Lucian, a less ambitious volume for Dominican, and a major volume in preparation for Trinidadian. Bahamian also profits from a dictionary dating back to the early 1980s. Studies of the grammar of the Creoles of the region abound but few complete studies are written for nontechnical users. This is a serious shortcoming because it reduces the efficacy of editing printed material by persons who are not very conversant with linguistic concepts and terminology.

The Print Media

Despite the limited popularity of the writing systems and reference resources, Creole languages have penetrated the media throughout the region. In the print media, their longest established use has been in humour and in such literary work as newspapers have published over the last hundred years or so. Papiamentu has had the longest history of use as a conventional medium for written news. Haitian too has been established in that role, even though the size of the literate population of the country limits the potential for general advantage through the use of the language. Periodicals published by church organizations have been the longest-standing regular publications of this type in Haiti. French-lexicon Creole in the French Departments and in the CARICOM states of St Lucia and Dominica has also been used as a limited medium of news reporting. Most commonly, this has taken the form of modest inclusions within newspapers that are mainly printed in the official language or of periodical magazines with regular features incorporating pieces in the Creole language.

An interesting development can be noted in the case of contemporary Jamaica where verbatim quotations from witnesses of current events and incidents are increasingly included in the body of the reports by journalists. What is more, the inclusions are in front page items, not in features buried in the columns as entertainment for the reader. It is also noteworthy that the persons interviewed do not appear to shift their speech in the direction of English in response to the interview. Creole quotations from persons such as teachers, who would be expected in the traditional analyses to speak English, could be interpreted to mean that they do not feel constrained by the circumstances to be the hypocritical role model.

Until recently, the *Jamaica Observer* carried a column called "(W)uman Tong(ue)", written in Jamaican Creole by Carolyn Cooper, a member of the Department of Literatures in English at the University of the West Indies. On a regular basis, the column featured parallel texts written in the Cassidy–Le Page spelling and in what Cooper called "chaka-chaka spelling". This latter spelling system is particular to Cooper, who considers it to be more readily understandable than the Cassidy–Le Page system. It is difficult to tell without a careful analysis whether Cassidy–Le Page is indeed the reference point for the majority of those writing in Jamaican or whether the spellings in use are as idiosyncratic as Cooper's. Even if further study shows Cooper to have been without a large following, reference to the column may well keep the door open for an eventual review of the writing systems of Jamaican.

The Performing Arts and Literary Publishing

The Caribbean stage has long been a forum in which Creole languages have enjoyed prominence. The developments that have taken place towards the end of the century have essentially been in the kind of themes for which the use of Creole is considered acceptable and even necessary. The thematic range long ago transcended the farce and comic material that was originally the staple application accepted by the society. In general, the same literary perspectives that have been declared in writings in the official languages of the region are present in the material produced in the vernaculars. Drama of the most serious contemporary type is presented in the region's Creoles. Poetry in the vernaculars has changed shape, and writers and performers whose quality cannot be challenged are broaching every level of literary exploration. Although there is an increasing production of novels, they are less commonplace than short stories. As far as the use of Creoles in writing is concerned therefore, it is literary publication rather than the day-to-day press that is advancing the public evolution of Creole languages in their several societal functions.

Radio and Television

The use of Creole languages in radio broadcasts is much more widespread than it is in print. This is not surprising since Creoles have always had wider acceptance as spoken rather than written media, the latter presupposing the existence of a writing system and wide knowledge of it in the society. In programming that does not involve the reading of text, there is high use of local vernaculars. This is especially so in the field of popular entertainment, where almost all radio personalities explore the full range of the varieties available in their societies as they would in face-to-face communication. Music-based shows offer a wide variety of exposure to the Creoles, not only in the lyrics of songs, but also in the patter of the hosts.

The popularity of call-in talk shows, both for entertainment and for discussion of contemporary issues, has increased the proportion of air time in which Creole languages are heard on radio. Callers engage the hosts of the shows in their own language and the latter respond in like fashion. The result is prolonged dialogue, frequently on topics of a sophisticated nature. Significantly, many of the discussions between a caller and a host prompt calls from other listeners who pick up the same topics, but not necessarily in the same variety of speech as the previous callers. The importance of this point is that it demonstrates the extent to which the population may be focusing on the content rather than the medium of communication.

Formal news broadcasting in which the presenter reads from a script maintains the pattern of dominance of official languages, although inserts of verbatim clips may contain vernacular speech. Even so, the presentation of formal news broadcasts in Creole vernaculars is much more common than, say, ten years ago. Thus, in St Lucia and Haiti, for example, news broadcasts in Creole are well-established features of the broadcast day. However, this is not the case in the rest of the CARICOM region, where English is the official language. In the Papiamentu zone, it is a virtual norm.

The final factor which accounts for the growth in the radio use of Creoles is the dramatic increase in the number of broadcasting stations in the Caribbean region, due to the development of FM broadcasting. In every one of the countries of the region, there is competition to fill the several niches of popular appeal with a resultant increase in the number of programmes, advertisements and other communications that station operators consider must be broadcast in Creole. The motive force for the growth of broadcasting is not the language itself, but rather the marketing considerations which require that one reach every potential buyer of products in the society. Market forces drive the shift to the language of the listener.

Equally powerful is the development of religious stations and religious programming in which the vernacular Creole language is a major medium of proselytizing. This is especially the case in the French Creole zones. However, in the areas where English Creoles are the vernaculars, an opposite tendency seems to dominate the religious broadcasts. Americanized versions of English are the preferred variety for religious programming.

The television medium differs from radio in that more of the video material is of foreign (mainly North American) rather than of local origin. Since the use of the local Creole vernaculars on television is restricted to locally generated programming, the relative proportion of Creole used on television is lower than on radio. Curiously enough though, the formal news broadcasts are time slots in which there is frequent and prolonged use of Creole. The structure of the news programmes includes live coverage of many events and incidents in which interviewees speak their natural variety of Creole.

The most significant aspect of these developments is that the pressure to shift one's speech in the direction of a standard official language for communication in public (radio and television) appears to have diminished. It means that speakers may now have reduced inhibitions about the public use of their vernaculars and, equally importantly, are making less negative evaluations of those who use varieties that are richer in Creole elements than their own.

The Music Industry

A special note is necessary on the music industry. The Caribbean music industry is essentially based on Creole – French Creole and English Creole, especially Jamaican and Trinidadian. Zouk, kadans, reggae, dub, dance hall, calypso and soca dominate the region to the extent that dialect boundaries are being lowered, especially among the more youthful aficionados. The spread of these forms of music throughout the world shifts the level of international acceptability of the vernaculars and feeds back into the region values that change the profile of the users.

Some Issues That Arise

I wish to turn now to a number of issues that arise from this sketch of the status of Creoles in the Caribbean at the end of the twentieth century. First of all, we need to note that the status of the Creoles has been measured by the degree to which they have penetrated the domains of the official language. In particular, the measure has included the extent of the use of Creole in writing. The measure may itself be flawed because it assumes a priori that the domains in which the standard language has traditionally dominated are the preferred domains for the acquisition of status. What if they are not?

The assumption that Creoles acquire status as they penetrate the domains of the official language is part of an established pattern of the measurement of success in Creole societies. For instance, the progress of the formerly enslaved and indentured has been determined by the extent to which they have replaced the planter class in the latter's spheres of action: success by occupation of the "enemy's" space! However, we must be prepared for the possibility that the occupation of the enemy's space may no longer be the most useful index of status. Creole societies may have evolved sufficiently beyond the desire to replace the planter that the measures of status have to be revised.

Let us return to some of the interpretations that I placed on the data presented earlier. In reference to the use of Creole in Jamaica in radio and television interviews, I suggested first that the pressure to shift one's speech in the direction of a standard official language for communication in public appeared to have diminished. The second related proposition was that speakers' inhibitions about the public use of their vernaculars had decreased. A different interpretation is possible. Persons who use their Creole vernacular in interview-type situations on radio and television may still be operating within the established social patterns; that is, public self-presentation requires them to shift their speech in the direction of the official language. However, their shift may be taking them away from one variety of Creole to another, rather than moving their language out of the range of Creole. In other words, they have exercised a traditional choice of variety and it is their public-shifted variety that is in use, but that variety does not belong to the English band of the society's range. They may still be operating with the negative stereotype against Creole but are unable to get any closer to the standard official language.

The third proposition I made was that people were making less negative evaluations of others who used varieties richer in Creole elements than their own and were focusing on content rather than the medium of communication. More careful analysis at the level of discourse may be necessary to determine whether the attitudes embedded in dialogue across language varieties are even, or whether they are biased in one direction or the other. In other words, we need to determine whether those callers who are operating in English are reacting genuinely to the content of the submissions made by Creole speakers or whether they continue to be affected in their interaction by the medium of expression. The opposite case would also have to be examined.

Another issue that must be raised is whether the society has really changed its views on Creole or whether it is a change in the social structure of the Caribbean that has altered the data on language use. Within the last thirty years, several Caribbean states have undergone major social and demographic disruption. The events in Trinidad in 1970, followed by the oil boom in that country, changed the relationship between the traditional social structure and the employment structure of the country. Similarly, Jamaica's experiment with democratic socialism climaxed in the 1970s with major emigration of significant numbers of the middle classes and other skilled cadres of citizens, an event that transformed the structure of Jamaica's civil service, educational services and private sector. Guyana also underwent dramatic changes in the middle of its society when its economy floundered in the least successful days of the Burnham and Hoyte administrations. In such circumstances, our deductions are likely to be faulty if we determine the status of Creoles by referring to the language behaviours of the same occupational groups, language use in apparently identical social contexts, and by reference to a similar possible range of linguistic choices.

The democratization of education and the triumph of the capitalist ethic have allowed the Caribbean society to replace the escaped social groups with new cadres. If this is the new middle class, they have brought their language with them. It is to their credit that they have largely done so unselfconsciously.

Due Respect

At the beginning, I indicated that we need to have a proper survey of the use of languages in the Creole Caribbean. My last remarks should show how urgent this is. The issues I have raised must be among those that shape the design of the survey if we are to understand the true nature of the status of Creoles in this region.

Notes

1. An earlier version of this chapter was previously published in *Caribbean Quarterly* 45, nos. 2 and 3 (1999).
2. I am using the term *Creole* as a generic term to cover all the languages of the relevant type. Where a specific case is under discussion and where there is a readily recognized name for the Creole of the country, I use that distinctive name.

References

Carrington, L. 1988. *Creole Discourse and Social Development*. Ottawa: IDRC.

Cassidy, F., and R. Le Page. 1967. *Dictionary of Jamaican English*. Cambridge: Cambridge University Press.

Durizot-Jno-Baptiste, P. 1996. *La Question du Créole à L'École en Guadeloupe*. Paris: L'Harmattan.

Mühleisen, S. 1993. Attitudes towards language varieties in Trinidad. Master's thesis, Free University of Berlin.

Nwenmely, H. 1996. *Language Reclamation: French Creole Language Teaching in the UK and the Caribbean*. Clevedon: Multilingual Matters.

Chapter 2

Competence, Proficiency and Language Acquisition in Caribbean Contexts

Hazel Simmons-McDonald

In this chapter I attempt to discuss some issues related to second-language acquisition and the development of competence by speakers in the Caribbean. I shall also examine interaction and feedback as exemplified in a particular teaching style with a view to making some preliminary comments on the ways in which classroom practice may constrain the learning of Standard English and the development of proficiency or literacy-related skills. I begin by reviewing the notion of competence as set out in Chomsky's theory of language. I then go on to consider Carrington's (1989) model for first-language acquisition in a Caribbean setting, then to discuss some aspects of second-language acquisition (L2) with more frequent reference to the St Lucian context. Finally, I present some data from the speech and writing of students at primary and secondary levels, as well as some classroom process data and discuss why it is difficult for speakers in the contexts considered to develop proficiency in the variety that is required for school use.

    I want to begin by making a distinction between competence and proficiency. The term *competence* is used in the early formulations of grammar theory by Chomsky (1965) to mean the "speaker/hearer's knowledge of the rules of (a) language". Chomsky (1980a: 59) explains grammatical competence as "the cognitive state that encompasses all those aspects of form and meaning and their relation, which are properly assigned to the specific subsystem of the human mind that relates representations of form and meaning". In the literature, *competence* is often used to refer to the knowledge of language developed by a learner in naturalistic settings, for example, in the case of a child who is acquiring a first language (L1) in the home, and it is also sometimes used synonymously with *proficiency* to refer to the knowledge of language that a learner develops within the classroom. In the literature on second-language acquisition, where some prefer to make a distinction between acquisition in naturalistic environments and learning in the classroom, the term *proficiency* is used distinctly from *competence* to refer to language development in the classroom, more specifically to the development of literacy skills. In this chapter, I maintain that distinction and use *proficiency* in the latter sense.

There are several possibilities for children acquiring language in a Caribbean context. Carrington sets out a typology which attempts to capture the different environments for first-language acquisition in the Caribbean. He states that the target language for the speaker is ill-defined because "of the intensely variable nature of the input and because of the absence of exactly pertinent grammatical descriptions" (Carrington 1989: 65). He claims that Caribbean environments differ from homogeneous environments such as the middle- and upper-middle-class environments in North America, where the majority of the early research on child language development was conducted. He refers to the latter as "sterile" in comparison to the heterogeneous and sociolinguistically complex environment of the Caribbean. It is that heterogeneity which makes it difficult to determine the variety that the child is acquiring. In any context the child may be exposed to a variety of lects.

Carrington proposes a typology which describes six situations. The first (Type I) is called "consistent monolingual" and it refers to an acquisition setting in which speakers acquire a single code. Shifts in style, register and situational variety are "linguistically" within the grammatical system of that code. Carrington claims that this kind of acquisition setting is rare, yet one does find instances of it, such as in homes in remote rural areas in St Lucia in which French Creole is the language of choice and children acquire competence in that variety.

Carrington considers the second situation, "leaky monolingual" (Type II), to be more common. In this setting those who interact with the child use a single code, but the child is exposed to another code from other sources such as radio and does not have the pragmatic contexts from that added source for interpretation. Examples of such a situation would be found in those households in urban areas in which a variety of St Lucian English is the dominant code used, yet children might hear French Creole on the radio and, on occasion, television. Yet the latter variety would not be used to address the child, nor would it be used as the natural medium of communication among members of the household.

Carrington calls the third situation "monolingual with secondary input" (Type III), which refers to the presence of another code in the environment other than that used to communicate with the child primarily, but, for this second code, the child has the pragmatic support which will allow for interpretation. It means that a child in this situation can actually acquire both codes, but one is likely to be more dominant than the other. In the fourth situation, "special case in multi-code environment" (Type IV), others in the child's environment have access to and use several codes, but they make a conscious decision to use only one code with the child. It is also possible for a child in this situation to acquire not just the code that others use to interact with it, but any of the other codes that are used in the environment, as long as there is the pragmatic support that allows the child to derive meaning. Upon reflection, my acquisition of English and French Creole occurred in such an environment; although French Creole was never used directly in interactions with me, it was spoken by others around me at different times, and it was used for the telling of folk stories and some jokes. I consider it to be one of my first languages although it is not the dominant one.

There is little distinction between Carrington's Types IV and V ("routine case in multi-code environment"). In the case of the latter, community convention (as opposed to a household decision) determines that one code is the more appropriate to be used. However, this does not mean that other codes are not used in the presence of the child, which means that more than one code can be acquired (as in Type IV). The sixth situation (Type VI), which Carrington calls "open access", is one in which those who interact with the child will use more than one code for interaction. In this case, depending on the consistency with which these codes are used, the child is likely to acquire more than one lect. It is also the situation in which it is more difficult to "pin down" the target. According to this typology there are learners in the Caribbean who may have acquired Standard English only as their first language or dialect or a Creole only or a dialect of English or a vernacular, but this would be uncommon. The more common occurrence is that learners acquire more than one code, may be dominant in one and could probably understand the others; that is, they may have varying competence in the other codes. The linguistic complexity of the acquisitional environment would make a study of the child's acquisition not as straightforward as one might expect.

It is nevertheless very important for schools to be aware of the varying competence of their five-year-old charges. Several of the children actually acquire a vernacular variety of English as their L1; they are competent in that variety. They come to the school situation with an instantiation of a variety of English which differs, in some respects, from the standard variety which they need to learn for school purposes, and the school is the place where they will have most exposure to Standard English. They face the task of having to become literate in the Standard and to develop some measure of oral proficiency in that code for specific tasks. However, the degree of difference between the grammars of the varieties in question probably means that the learners have to reinterpret some principles as they attempt to acquire competence and develop proficiency in the L2. Researchers (see, for example, Craig 1967; Le Page 1968) have observed that where a variety of the dialect is close to the standard variety, learners (and in some cases teachers) have difficulty in determining the differences in some grammatical structures of the varieties.

The issue of second-language (or dialect) learning in the formal context of school is complex. One pertinent question that has been asked is, "Does a second language learner begin to learn a second language from scratch?" The second language learner already possesses a first language. The situation for language learners with an L1 with the same lexical base as the L2 will be different from that for speakers with an L1 which has a different lexical base (as in the case of speakers of French Creole). The vernacular speakers already have an instantiation of a variety of English which varies in some ways from the standard variety, whereas the French Creole speakers have a French-lexicon Creole, which differs in grammar and lexicon from the L2.

To capture the difference between the first- and second-language learner, Cook (1988) posits S_1 rather than S_0, Chomsky's initial state for L1 learners (Chomsky 1980a: 37), as the initial state for second language learning and S_1

as the terminal state of language for the L2 learner. In reality, S_1 represents the language competence with which the learner comes to the L2 learning situation. Typically, the final state described for second-language learners has been the language to be learned, the target language (TL), but it is known that few learners ever reach native fluency in the L2. The notion of an interlanguage which described the language of second-language learners as they progressed in the learning of L2 is discounted by Chomsky, who favours the view that only the complete knowledge of language counts.

Speakers in the Caribbean who acquire a particular lect of English, for example Jamaicans who acquire a mesolectal variety of Jamaican, actually acquire competence in that lect; they are not considered to have acquired "partial knowledge" of English. Several speakers achieve competence in other lects and can shift from the acrolectal variety (Standard Jamaican) to the basilectal variety depending on context and situation. In such cases it is perhaps more appropriate to consider that these speakers have *multicompetence*; that is, they have achieved competence in a variety of lects which differ from the standard lect in various ways. Their competence in each lect is complete. As Rickford (1983) points out, a dialect speaker does not forget or discard a lect once he or she goes on to acquire another lect. However, in the case of second-language acquisition, learners will typically discard forms from their interlanguage once they have figured out that these forms are not acceptable in the code that they are acquiring. In a process that Stauble (1977) describes as "the replacement of forms and the restructuring of underlying units", L2 learners achieve "closer approximations" to the TL An instance of this is the acquisition of negation by L2 learners of English who all seem to go through the same stages in the acquisition of *no* and *not*, a process which also seems to parallel the L1 acquisition of negation (see, for example, Bloom 1970; Cazden et al. 1975; and Simmons-McDonald 1988 for French Creole speakers).

Simmons-McDonald (1992, 1996) showed that French Creole speakers who were learning English in the school setting rejected early interlanguage forms, as did other speakers of L2 reported in the literature. However, interlanguage forms that were identical to structures in the vernacular variety commonly spoken in their communities were not discarded. Instead, the learners used these forms productively in their speech. In most cases, their

S_1 was a variety of St Lucian English vernacular which many children, in what were formerly dominant French Creole-speaking communities, now acquire as L1. I argued (1988, 1996) that, for these children, proficiency in English could best be achieved if they were taught Standard St Lucian as a separate code (using second-language teaching methodology) and not by correcting their L1 (the vernacular variety), which was common practice in the classrooms that I observed.

Chomsky's distinction between competence and proficiency becomes important when we focus on the school setting, the location in which children who are speakers of French Creole or St Lucian vernacular will develop competence (and proficiency) in the standard. The idea that competence acquired naturally may be different from competence acquired in instructed situations is interesting, because it suggests that classroom activities somehow do not lead to the acquisition of language that is "equal" to that acquired in naturalistic settings. More properly speaking, the difference seems to rest in the distinction between competence and proficiency, and the samples that I present in the next section suggest this also. Whereas children seem to develop some fluency in the oral use of a vernacular variety that varies in closeness to the standard in school, their written work reveals a level of proficiency which indicates that they have not developed literacy in the L2, so the fact that as many as 40 percent of children achieve zero on minimum standards tests and Common Entrance examinations is alarming, but not surprising.

This may very well result from the way in which they are introduced to the L2 when they first come to school and the way in which they continue to be taught throughout the primary school. Ovando and Collier (1998: 93) make the point that social and academic language development represents a continuum and that they are not separate, unrelated aspects of proficiency. Chomsky (1972) claims, "One does not learn the grammatical structure of a second language through explanation and instruction beyond the most rudimentary level for the simple reason that no one has enough explicit knowledge about this structure to provide explanation and instruction." Yet the approach used to teach French Creole speakers who have not acquired any English at all is through literacy in the L2, the rote learning of the alphabet and the use of basal readers.

In the next section I present some data from (1) speech samples of French

Creole speakers who were acquiring English as a second language in school, (2) written samples of these speakers taken from the Common Entrance examination and of other students writing the CXC school-leaving examinations, and (3) samples of interactional exchanges from selected classrooms in the primary school. The speech samples are taken from a corpus which was collected as part of a longitudinal study on the acquisition of English.

Cummins (1980) presents a model of bilingual proficiency which consists of a core grammar and the specific surface features of first and second languages. This core grammar is likened to Chomsky's notion of universal grammar (UG), but it also ties in with the notion of a multicompetence which was mentioned in the foregoing section. McLaughlin's (1991: 23) suggestion that a single language system underlies the language of the bilingual child is similar to Cummins's idea. McLaughlin explains that if a child has balanced exposure to the languages being acquired in early childhood, the child develops both languages simultaneously as first languages and, although children may typically go through a stage of language mixing, "especially lexical mixing", the rules of the two languages become differentiated. The attainment of bilingual proficiency means simply this, that the learner can differentiate between the grammars of the languages and can switch codes depending on the appropriateness of situation and context.

Children who acquire a second language sequentially within the con-text of the classroom face the task of constructing the grammar of the second language on the basis of the input to which they are exposed (for example, the teacher's speech, textbooks, their interactions with speakers of the language) and the kinds of feedback which they receive. Children within the Caribbean fit the following three main profiles, which roughly represent a reduced characterization of the Carrington model:

1. Those who acquire English as a first language and who probably have some receptive (and productive) competence in a vernacular variety;
2. Those who acquire an English lexicon-based Creole or a vernacular as a first language;
3. Those who acquire a Creole with a lexical base different from English (for example, French Creole) and who are learning English as L2 in the classroom.

In each of these cases the learners are expected to develop proficiency in English for academic success, which is measured by the yardsticks of the Common Entrance promotional and CXC school-leaving examinations. The language of these examinations and of the texts which are used is the formal language which Calfee and Freedman (cited in McLaughlin 1981: 27) describe as "highly explicit, context free, logical and expository". Ovando and Collier (1998: 93) cite Thomas and Collier (1989: 27), who use the phrase "academic language" to refer to the language which children require for success in school. They explain that this language refers to "a complex network of language and cognitive skills and knowledge required across all content areas for eventual successful academic performance at secondary and university levels of instruction". This is distinguished from the child's language, which is described by Cummins (1980) as "highly implicit, context bound, intuitive and sequential informal language". Elsewhere (Simmons-McDonald n.d.), I discuss issues related to learners who fit Profile 1, so I will not discuss them in any detail here, except to say that although these learners have competence in the standard variety, many of them (like those in Profiles 2 and 3) do not always exhibit control in their written work (they make literacy-related errors which indicate varying levels of proficiency). Winch and Gingell (1994: 177) have attributed most of the errors made by learners in these profiles to "a misunderstanding of the relationship between speech and writing". Some of the errors they identified are those that indicate an inability to handle the features of formal English, and they are identical to errors made by native speakers of English attending school in the United Kingdom. The types of errors they listed fell into the following categories: (1) context dependent, (2) topicalization, (3c) genre difficulties, (4) repetition, and (5e) errors due to ambitious constructions (p. 178). The following examples taken from the writing of CXC candidates contain instances of (3), (4) and (5).

1. *But she is known for her quick adaptations to such situations as she quickly overcomes these problems and is good example to be taken of, as she is good at seeing the good side of bad situations and of bad people.
2. *Mrs Brown was a very prompted and hard working teacher. Everyone of her student has shown great success in life from her.

3. *Remember that with all these years backing us, we are the originators, we are fortunate to have some of the greatest teachers of our time, they have been around for many years, they know the 'tact' to teaching which give us the 'act' of learning; fellow students we should be bonded as one, as unity as one in Tranquillity.
4. *I now recommend that you dwell into the nominations as quick as possible because time is quite short.

These examples represent what Winch and Gingell (1994) call "overambitious constructions". The writers of these sentences are clearly attempting a register and diction over which they have not achieved control, so that redundancy and inappropriate lexical choices (as well as awkward phrasing, which relates to unfamiliarity with idiom) result. In the two examples which follow, the problem is primarily literacy related rather than one of fluency.

5. *This time I was *incomplete* shock after listening to the results that were being expelled from the principal's mouth.
6. *There were swallows circling above me, catching the delicious fly's with their scooped beaks.

If (5) and (6) were spoken a hearer might wonder about the use of *expelled* (5) and *scooped* (6), but would have no difficulty understanding the message since he or she would be likely to interpret *incomplete* as preposition + intensifier and *fly's* as the plural of *fly* (*flies*) and not the genitive form. Winch and Gingell (1994: 177) identify such errors as resulting partly from "a misunderstanding of the relationship between speech and writing". Mistakes such as these require a different kind of treatment from those evident in the samples (presented below) of younger learners. The fifteen- and sixteen-year-old student has the formal operational capability of paying attention to form and, if taught the appropriate strategies, can revise to create a better written product. Use of process approaches to the teaching of writing and the inclusion of strategies for revision of all components of the product can help these learners overcome some of these problems. In the case of younger learners, who probably fit Profiles 2 and 3, the problem is both an acquisition and a literacy learning problem.

Calfee and Freedman (cited in McLaughlin 1981: 27) suggest that the child who is learning English as a second language in the formal situation of the classroom has more difficulty than the native speaker in coping with tasks in English because he or she is "both learning a second language" and "learning a second language for school use". Cummins (1980) refers to the ability to use the formal language of the classroom, which is needed for literacy functions, as "cognitive academic language proficiency" (CALP) and he contrasts this with the learner's use of language for communication purposes which he refers to as "basic interpersonal communication skills" (BICS), or what Ovando and Collier (1998: 93) refer to as social language.

Speakers who are acquiring English as a second language in the classroom have BICS in their L1, but as soon as they enter the first class of primary school they are required to begin to use CALP-related skills in English, which they do not speak. The jump from BICS in French Creole to CALP in Standard English is an unrealistic expectation, particularly in a context in which the scaffolding that should be provided in immersion situations is nonexistent. The instructional practices used with nonnative speakers of English in the first year of school not only violate acquisitional principles but they have negative long-term effects on the learners' oral and written production. Elsewhere (Simmons-McDonald 1996), I suggest that in the case of native speakers of French Creole at least, it makes sense to teach literacy in the child's native language even as classroom practice is tailored to facilitate the acquisition of the L2 before literacy in the latter is introduced. Research done elsewhere (see Ovando and Collier 1998: 94) shows that students may experience both cognitive and academic difficulties if "a certain academic and literacy 'threshold' is not reached in L1" (Ovando and Collier 1998: 94). A programme which focuses on the learning of English as a second dialect for native speakers of St Lucian English vernacular is also likely to be more beneficial to those learners.

The approach that is used with five-year-olds in most classrooms is the old approach of teaching the letters and sounds of the alphabet, then introducing phrases and short sentences in basal "readers". The input in English to which the children are exposed is highly structured and limited primarily to explanations about classroom routines and subject tasks. One-on-one exchanges between the students and the teacher are rare, so they do not get many opportunities to practise the L2 in communicative contexts that are likely to promote fluency in the variety. The children learn very quickly the vernacular variety that is widely spoken by their peers on the playground.

The following samples come from two compositions of eleven-year-old children who wrote the Common Entrance examination. The children were native speakers of French Creole when they entered school. Sample sentences are taken from the compositions in meaningful units and numbered. A gloss is provided for forms that are not readily transparent.

7. Sample A
   a. I want you to come to my Baday ('birthday') pate on May 11 ...
   b And if you can breen ('bring') yo mothe ('mother') and farthe ('father') wesh ('with') you and you can breen ha frand ('friend') wesh you on day of my Baday we drink and eat and play.
   c. My morthe Ben the cack ('cake') she pot the cack on the tabal ('table') she pot the candal on the cack and she lait the candal.
   d. She tol me to Bol ('blow') the candal. Wan ('when') I fenec ('finish') bol the candal she cot ('cut') the cack and gev ('gave') me and frand pec ('piece') of cack.
   e. Wan we fint eat the. We go and wash the dces ('dishes') and go and woch ('watch') t v and go to Bad ('bed').
   f. Wan we wa cp ('wake up') in the monin ('morning') me and the faro ('friend'?) go and Bay Brad ('buy bread') been ('bring') the Brad home gev my morthe the Brad and gev my a cup of te ('tea') and a pec Brad and go to school and gev me my lanch ('lunch').

8. Sample B
   a. Ones a pon a time my family tole ('told') me we are go to a trepe to vifote ('trip to Vieux Fort').
   b. I was so exsted adut ('excited about') it.
   c. And we left. At home when it was nine thirty we arive vifote at leven. Meicet ('minutes') to twelfe we went at the old XX mile ('mill') in sforie ('Soufriere').[1]
   d. I wented to bave ('bathe') and my mother told me. I coled ('could') not bave I wan ont ('was not') happy agane and on wa bak ('way

back') we stop at a sp mok et ('supermarket') an we bote meny fines ('bought many things').

e. I eta ('eat a') and cecken ('chicken') and it gaiv me beley eke ('belly ache') and family brot ('brought') me to the hopetal ('hospital') and they gave me an tollate ('toilet', 'showed me to a toilet'/'let me use a toilet') and I was fleing ('feeling') myselfe comfotabl ('comfortable') ones more.

It is clear from the examples in the above that the learners have acquired the word order of the basic sentence of the L2. If these samples were read they would sound like fluent vernacular to the listener. The problem is that these learners have difficulty in representing sentence boundaries in writing, for example, 8c, (*And we left. At home when it was nine thirty we arive vifote at leven*), and 8d (*I went to bave and my mother told me. I coled not bave I wan ont happy agane*). In the latter example, *wan ont happy agane* ('was not happy again' = anymore), *ont* is an example of transposition of letters, but *wan not* is what the phrase probably sounds like in fast vernacular speech. Nevertheless, the learners are able to use the irregular past tense and, as in 7d (*she tol(d) me*), 8d (*my mother told me*), and 8e (*and family brot me . . . and they gave me*). An instance of overgeneralization of the regular past tense, however, as in 8d, *I wented to bave*, suggests that this learner has not achieved full control of this structure. There is evidence that they can use the regular past although this is not consistently represented. The discourse, in both cases, shifts between present and past time, although one gets a sense of focus on topic in each case. The composition titles were given in the test and, in the case of 8, the learner used a heading, *Compusion – My ideas of a good family*. This "story" focuses on a particular family outing.

The data indicate that both learners are at early developmental stages in their spelling and there is evidence of use of a semisyllabic system as in 7f, *wa cp* ('wake up') and 8d *wa bak* ('way back'), *sp mok et* ('supermarket'). They are also attempting to spell words on the basis of the sound representations of letters. These strategies are not dissimilar to those used by young learners who also employ invented spelling systems before they have learned the appropriate phonetic-graphemic correspondences (see Bissex 1980; Rosencranz 1998). Bissex (1980: 35) refers to Read (1971), who made the observation that children do not know "the set of lexical representations and the system of phonological rules that account for much standard spelling; what they do know is a system of phonetic relationships that they have not been taught by their parents and teachers". The children from whom these samples were taken would have been exposed to at least seven years of classroom instruction before taking the Common Entrance examination. They would also have been introduced to literacy in the L2 upon entering school. Clearly, such an approach has not been effective in developing proficiency in the L2. It has been suggested by McLaughlin (1981: 28) that "proficiency in a second language in a school setting is predicted to depend largely on previous learning of literacy-related functions of language". McLaughlin goes on to state that the literacy-related functions of language, which are the CALP skills identified by Cummins, "are seen to be distinguishable empirically from the use of language for natural communication". The fluency that is apparent from reading these samples aloud strongly suggests that the children are writing as they speak, and they are trying to impose the conventions of formal written English, which they have not mastered, on their writing, a variety of the vernacular.

The following samples from vernacular speakers are similar to some of the structures used in 7; for example, 7c and 7e can be compared, respectively, with 10 and 11, in which the event is recounted in the present.

9. I have a car dat [jaitin] an a car dat doesn [jait] = 'lighting'/'light'.[1]
10. drink . . . I drink, I don' know what they call it again [B].[2]
11. I was give you a pig aready.
12. My bake was wet . . . I break it in two an den and den when . . . when Mary Anna was put her cup in my lunch kit da tea fall dong in my lunch kit.

One of the differences is that in the written samples (see 8 in particular) there is a consistent effort to sustain use of the past and to indicate boundaries in the written discourse that occur naturally in oral production. This also indicates some effort on the part of the older learners to impose the literacy conventions on their writing, but they do not seem to know how to represent a sentence unit in writing.

The spontaneous speech samples of the French Creole speakers show some vernacular features which suggest that the learners are acquiring this variety as L2. The samples were taken towards the end of the children's first year in Class 1 of the primary school.

13. When I'm ahm . . . when I am . . . mwen pa byen mewn mayad ('malad'), mwen mayad an shay mwen ka bwè medsin . . . when I sick . . . I have fing . . . lafièv ('fever').

    'When I'm . . . I'm not well I'm sick, I'm very sick I drink medicine . . .'

14. My baday ('birthday') I go an take. I go an take a banana . . . I no eat da banana.

    '(I went for) my birthday present . . .'

15. Da doctor say um i . . . i not bleedin a [jɔt] ('lot') so I . . . I . . . you can come back to school.

16. Look a pig i. A kochon. Boy take . . . ki manyè ou ka tape en patwa . . . in English . . . pig Yeah, sé pig ki non'y An dat is a cow yes . . . a . . . look a pig too.

    'Look a pig (tag) A pig. Boy take . . . how come you are taping in patwa . . . in English . . . pig say pig. Yeah it's pig that is its name . . .'

Although these examples contain several features of the vernacular, they also contain forms that are typical of the early stages of acquisition which have been found in the language of other learners. In (14), for example, the use of the negative particle *no* in nucleic structures (for example, *I no eat*) is a feature common to both first- and second-language acquisition. The tendency of second-language learners to memorize chunks of formulaic language which they have not yet the ability to analyse is also evident in (15) in the learner's reproduction of the words of the doctor. The occurrence of codeswitching to the L1 (French Creole) does suggest that the learners are using it as a springboard to access the L2. The structure of sentences in these examples (for example [14], *My baday* ['birthday'] *I go an take; I go an take a banana*) is similar to the structure of French Creole. Isaac (1986: 29) suggested that there is a variety of St Lucian English which is "a calqued form of the French Creole" or an "anglicized equivalent of the French Creole" which "shares properties with other Creoles". She also suggests that there is a cline from this level which is "markedly remote from the target language (Standard English) to a variety nearest the standard". The frequency of French Creole structures with English words slotted in and the reliance on French Creole words suggest that these young learners are relying on the L1 as they attempt to learn English. In the next section I present some data from selected Class 1 classrooms and discuss the approaches used to teach young learners.

Feedback and Interaction in the Language Classroom

Although there are few carefully structured studies that attempt to examine the effects of feedback on language learning, there are several process studies that examine the ways in which teachers treat the errors of second-language learners (Allwright 1975; Bruton and Samuda 1980; Chaudron 1986, among others). Research on the Caribbean situation also discusses the type of errors second-language learners are likely to make (Carrington 1969; Isaac 1986) as well as the limitations of error correction as a method of teaching (Craig 1976; Simmons-McDonald 1996). Other studies examine the type of feedback that teachers give and preferences for error correction (Cathcart and Olsen 1976; Chaudron 1977, 1983, 1986; Long 1977; Long and Sato 1983). Still other studies examine the type of teacher behaviour and interaction patterns in second-language classrooms (Allwright 1984; Aston 1986; Delamont 1976; Flanders 1970; Gaies 1977; Nystrom 1983; Politzer 1970; Wells 1981, among others).

Many studies done in the Caribbean have focused on error analysis following from Corder's (1967) distinction between errors and mistakes and the cognitivist position on the significance of learner error. Process-type studies on feedback and interaction in Caribbean settings are few, but one or two have generated preliminary findings in these areas (Burton 1993; Simmons-McDonald n.d.).

One explanation that has been provided for the occurrence of error in learner language is that the learner's performance in the L2 is not automatic. Seliger (1977) and other cognitive theorists have emphasized the importance of practice in the development of procedural knowledge and its automatization by the learner as well as the need for a classroom environment that will allow the learner, to negotiate meaning in conversational exchanges and engage in the kinds of practice of the second language that will promote the development of implicit knowledge of that code. As noted earlier in this essay, it is through meaning-focused instruction that implicit knowledge is developed. Ellis (1990: 188) makes the observation that meaning-focused instruction is "likely to afford the learner an opportunity to listen and to perform a greater range of language functions than will form-focused instruction. However, form-focused instruction encourages the learner to pay attention to the formal aspects of language." Ellis makes the point that focusing on form in the second language classroom can "raise the consciousness" of the learner and help him or her to notice the gap between his or her language and the input (p. 193). However, this is not likely to be an effective approach for young learners who have difficulty dealing with abstractions. Other findings suggest that error correction may be ineffective if the learner has no perception of inaccuracy (Craig 1976) and that inconsistency and lack of clarity in the kinds of feedback given may result in ambiguity in the minds of learners. Classroom environments that are rich with opportunities for the second-language learner to engage in meaningful exchanges have been thought to be conducive to the learning of L2. Johnson (1988) presents four criteria that are necessary for feedback to have an effect on the elimination of error in learner language: (1) the learner must have a desire or need to eradicate the mistake; (2) the learner must be able to form an internal representation of correct behaviour; (3) the learner must know that his or her performance is "flawed"; (4) the learner must have opportunities to use the language in real conditions.

Most of the learners who speak an English vernacular variety may not be motivated to eradicate what are described as errors in their performance because that performance is not considered to be deviant in the wider community, where they can communicate effectively with others who use the same variety. The learners have competence in that variety and the object of their being in school is to learn a second lect and to become proficient in it (to learn effective literacy skills in D2). Chomsky's principles and parameters approach (Chomsky 1981: 3–4) suggests that the learning of such a lect can take place if the learner is successful in reinterpreting the relevant principles. As Carrington (1989) points out, the lack of descriptions of the various varieties makes it difficult for the researcher to determine the target. Such descriptions would also be useful to the researcher of second-language acquisition, since they would allow one to determine what principles would need to be reinterpreted by the learner. Because the learner's L1 (the dialect) cannot be considered to constitute a "partial knowledge of English", this notion of Chomsky's (1986: 16) is not relevant in this case. Teaching Standard English to L1 vernacular speakers cannot, therefore, be interpreted to mean the eradication of a lect (the vernacular) as many educators do. Rather, it means that we must assist the learner to develop multicompetence through acquisition of the second lect and to become proficient in the use of that lect by developing effective literacy skills in it. It is therefore not useful to continue to describe the learner's native language as "incorrect" and proceed with a teaching approach that has as its aim the eradication of the "errors" in that language. Such an approach will fail because the learner does not have the perception that his or her performance is flawed.

With respect to the second criterion presented by Johnson, the learner will only be able to "form an internal representation of correct behavior" if he or she can perceive the difference between his or her initial representation and the representation of the structure in the target language. This suggests that instruction has to enable learners to become aware of the differences in the structures. An approach that presents the D1 and D2 as two related systems that differ in some respects is more likely to bring learners to a perception of difference than one which says "the system that you use is bad and incorrect and you should learn to replace it with this other one".

Winer (1993: 195), writing about Caribbean immigrants in North America, suggests the following: "Any approach to the teaching of students whose first language is English Creole, recognized or not, must include knowledge about and acceptance of the language and its culture, contrasted specifically with English language and culture varieties." While the issue of culture may not be as significant for learners within the Caribbean, the teaching approach(es) to which they are exposed certainly are, and the suggestion of a contrastive approach is one that merits further exploration. However, there may not be one efficacious method which teachers can use to help learners perceive the differences between the codes. One would also have to consider, in the determination of the approaches to be used, issues such as the importance to and effects of form- and meaning-focused instruction on learners of varying age groups. Second-language acquisition and classroom process research in the Caribbean still have some way to go in responding to issues such as these.

Due Respect

The predominant patterns of interaction in most classrooms in the Caribbean do not provide the opportunities for the kinds of meaningful practice that French Creole and vernacular speakers need to help them develop fluency in the second language/dialect. Interactions are dominated by the teacher and learners are required to respond briefly for the most part. Consider the following example taken from Simmons-McDonald (n.d.).

17. a. Teacher: Read the subject again. (Entire class reads from the board as the teacher points.)
    b. Class: Language Arts.
    c. Teacher: Now I'm going to ask you a few questions to review what we did last week. What is she, is she a boy or a girl?
    d. Class: A girl. (In chorus.)
    e. Teacher: You did not listen to what I said to do. I said to stand, then I will call your name and then I will ask you. What is . . . ?
    f. Class: A girl.
    g. Teacher: But I have not asked the question yet, you must wait. You must listen. What is she, is she a boy or a girl? (Points to a student. Students stand, some murmuring.)
    h. Teacher: I said to stand up. Then I will call you to answer. Curlita.
    i. Student: A girl.
    j. Teacher: I want you to answer in a sentence.
    k. Student: She is a girl.
    l. Teacher: Louder, louder.
    m. Student: She is . . .
    n. Teacher: Say 'she' . . .
    o. Student: She is a girl.
    p. Teacher: Okay, everybody repeat her answer. (Entire class repeats.)

In (17), more time appears to be spent on emphasizing the correct routine that students must follow in answering a question. The practice they receive is to articulate short utterances which are reinforced through choral recitation. Burton (1993) found that in classrooms in urban and rural schools in St Lucia, the lessons were teacher-centred and learners had few opportunities for using long turns in conversational exchanges. The interaction patterns were typically one-to-many (teacher-to-class). The following data set comes from her study and is used with her permission.

18. a. Teacher: Again
    b. Class: Come.
    c. Teacher: Next.
    d. Student: Basket.
    e. Teacher: What did he say, class?
    f. Class: Basket.
    g. Teacher: Okay, tell them the sound at the end.
    h. Student: t-t-t
    i. Teacher: What did he say, class?
    j. Class: t-t-t

Most of the examples of interactions from these two studies follow this pattern of teacher orchestration and choral responses by the learners. The kind of feedback that is given depends to a large extent on the kinds of interactional exchanges that occur in the class. The teachers in the ongoing study regulate learner responses and more often insist on choral responses which do not elicit the kind of feedback from the teacher that would help the learners to reflect in meaningful ways on their output.

A preliminary analysis of the data from the Simmons-McDonald study indicates that, in many ways, classroom process does not foster the development of oral proficiency that is a crucial part of overall proficiency. Further, vernacular speakers are taught like native speakers who are fluent in the Standard. Those who speak a variety that is removed from Standard English would benefit from approaches that teach English as a second dialect. By the same token, the L1 of the French Creole speakers cannot be ignored when they first come to school. The development of proficiency and literacy skills in L2 is likely to be fostered if some literacy work in the L1 is done. Walker (1984: 165) cites Swain (1983), who pointed out that skills that are basic to academic progress are most easily learnt in L1. Walker points out that these skills are cross-lingual and can be applied to L2 also. He says "it is easier to learn to read in L1 and then to apply this skill to L2 than to learn to read and learn L2 simultaneously. Once the reading skill is automated through L1, more attention can be paid to the acquisition of L2." Ovando and Collier (1998: 94) report that "learners' academic skills, literacy development, concept formation, subject knowledge and learning strategies all transfer from L1 to L2 as the vocabulary and communicative patterns are developed in L2 to express . . . academic knowledge." The studies cited in Ovando and Collier also attest to the crucial importance of the development of literacy in the first language. Bollée (1994) reports that children in the Seychelles with French Creole as L1, who were taught literacy in the Creole before being taught literacy in Standard French and English, made significant advances in all three languages and performance in mathematics and other subjects was significantly better than when the native language of the children had not been taken into account.[3] Bollée cites an article from a local paper, *Seychelles Nation* (April 26, 1985: 2), which included the following comment: "As to the positive effects of the introduction of Creole on other subjects, teachers of mathematics reported 'very encouraging results', and the English section, an 'Excellent overall performance of . . . pupils in English'." Research has shown that when the children's native language is ignored the result is a subtractive bilingual situation and the written data (from the eleven-year-old students) presented in this chapter certainly support this.

The need for a bilingual programme is indicated in the case of the French Creole speakers. It seems to me that the question of access to UG would be important only if such information could provide insight into the development of methods that might promote multicompetence and at least dual proficiency in the classroom setting. After all, this should be the main objective of educational systems within the region, since it constitutes a viable alternative to the current approach, which results in a waste of valuable human resources. Further research, initially in the form of pilot studies that monitor the progress of students exposed to the use of Creole and the responses of vernacular speakers to a carefully designed second-language programme, in which the vernacular has a place, is needed. The study of linguistics would also benefit from linguistics research which focused on ideal speakers–hearers who display the competence evident in vernacular speakers within the region and similar situations elsewhere. It would be an encouraging step that would not only contribute to the further development of the discipline but would also begin to be more representative of the variety of human language and mind.

Notes

1. XX indicates illegible forms in the raw data.
2. This is a negative tag used in French Creole. It is a truncated form of *non* and is nasalized. The form *wi* is a tag used in positive sentences; it means 'yes'. The reduced form is *i*, which appears in 11.
3. The Seychelles model promotes proficiency in three languages: the French Creole, French and English.

References

Allwright, R.L. 1975. Problems in the study of the language teacher's treatment of learner error. In *On TESOL '75*, edited by M. Burt and H. Dulay. Washington, DC: TESOL.

———. 1984. The importance of interaction in classroom language learning. *Applied Linguistics* 5, no. 2.

Aston, G. 1986. Trouble-shooting in interaction with learners: The more the merrier? *Applied Linguistics* 7, no. 2.

Bissex, G.L. 1980. *Gnys at Wrk*. New Haven, CT: Yale University Press.

Bloom, L. 1970. *Language Development: Form and Function in Emerging Grammars*. Cambridge, MA: MIT Press.

Bollée, A. 1993. Language policy in the Seychelles and its consequences. *International Journal of the Sociology of Language* 102.

Bruton, A., and V. Samuda. 1980. Learner and teacher roles in the treatment of oral error in group work. *RELC Journal* 11.

Burton, C. 1993. An investigation into the nature of interaction occurring in Stage One (5+) English Language or Language Arts classrooms in two St Lucian schools. BA Caribbean Study, University of the West Indies.

Caffee, R., and S. Freedman. 1980. Understanding and comprehending. Paper presented at Center for the Study of Reading. Urbana, Illinois.

Carrington, L. 1969. Deviations from Standard English in the speech of primary school children in St Lucia and Dominica. *International Review of Applied Linguistics* 7, no. 3

Carrington, L. 1989. Acquiring language in a Creole setting. In *Papers and Reports on Child Language Development*, edited by Eve Clark. Stanford, CA: Stanford University.

Cathcart, R., and J. Olsen. 1976. Teachers' and students' preferences for correction of classroom conversation errors. In *On TESOL '76*, edited by J. Fanselow and R. Crymes. Washington, DC: TESOL.

Cazden, C., et al. 1975. Second Language Acquisition sequences in children, adolescents and adults. Final Report. Project No. 730744 U.S. Dept of Health, Education and Welfare. Harvard University.

Chaudron, C. 1977. A descriptive model of discourse in the corrective treatment of learners' errors. In *Second Language Learning: Contrastive Analysis, Error Analysis and Related Aspects*, edited by B. Robinett et al. Ann Arbor, MI: University of Michigan Press.

———. 1986. Teachers' priorities in correcting learners' errors in French immersion classes. In *Talking to Learn: Conversations in Second Language Acquisition*, edited by R. Day. Rowley, MA: Newbury House.

———. 1988. Foreigner talk in the classroom: An aid to learning? In *Classroom-Oriented Research in Second Language Acquisition*, edited by H. Seliger and M. Long. Rowley, MA: Newbury House.

Chomsky, N. 1965. *Aspects of the Theory of Syntax*. Cambridge, MA: MIT Press.

———. 1972. *Language and Mind*. New York: Harcourt Brace Jovanovich.

———. 1976. *Reflections on Language*. London: Temple Smith.

———. 1980a. *Rules and Representations*. Oxford: Basil Blackwell.

———. 1980b. On cognitive structures and their development. In *Language and Learning: The Debate between Jean Piaget and Noam Chomsky*, edited by M. Piattell-Pallmarini. London: Routledge and Kegan Paul.

———. 1981. *Lectures on Government and Binding*. Dordrecht: Foris.

———. 1982. *Some Concepts and Consequences of the Theory of Government and Binding*. Cambridge, MA: MIT Press.

———. 1986. *Knowledge of Language: Its Nature, Origin and Use*. New York: Praeger.

Cook, V.J. 1988. *Chomsky's Universal Grammar*. Oxford: Basil Blackwell.

Cook, V.J., and M. Newson. 1996. *Chomsky's Universal Grammar*, 2d ed. Oxford: Basil Blackwell.

Corder, P. 1967. The significance of learners' errors. *International Review of Applied Linguistics* 6.

Craig, D. 1967. Some early results of learning a second dialect. *Language Learning* 17.

———. 1971. Education and Creole English in the West Indies. In *Pidginization and Creolization of Languages*, edited by D. Hymes. Cambridge: Cambridge University Press.

———. 1976. Bidialectal education: Creole and standard in the West Indies. *International Journal of the Sociology of Language* 8.

Cummins, J. 1980. The construct of language proficiency in bilingual education. In *Current Issues in Bilingual Education,* edited by J. Alatis. Washington, DC: Georgetown University Press.

Delamont, S. 1976. *Interaction in the Classroom.* London: Methuen.

Ellis, R. 1990. *Instructed Second Language Acquisition.* Oxford: Basil Blackwell.

Flanders, N. 1970. *Analyzing Teacher Behaviour.* Reading, MA: Addison Wesley.

Gaies, S.J. 1977. The nature of linguistic input in formal second language learning: Linguistic and communicative strategies in ESL teachers' classroom language. In *On TESOL '77,* edited by H.D. Brown et al. Washington, DC: TESOL.

Gleitman, L. 1984. Biological predispositions to learn language. In *The Biology of Learning,* edited by P. Mailer and H. Turace. New York: Springer.

Isaac, M. 1986. French Creole interference in the written English of St Lucian secondary school students. Master's thesis, University of the West Indies.

Johnson, K. 1988. Mistake correction. *ELT Journal* 2.

Krashen, S. 1982. *Principles and Practice in Second Language Acquisition.* Oxford: Pergamon.

Le Page, R.B. 1968. Problems to be faced in the use of English as the medium of education in four West Indian territories. In *Language Problems of Developing Nations,* edited by J. Fishman et al. New York: John Wiley and Sons.

Long, M. 1977. Teacher feedback on learner error: Mapping cognitions. In *Second Language Learning: Contrastive Analysis, Error Analysis and Related Aspects,* edited by B. Wallace-Robinett and J. Schachter. Ann Arbor, MI: University of Michigan Press.

Long, M., and C. Sato. 1983. Classroom foreigner talk discourse: Forms and functions of teachers' questions. In *Classroom-Oriented Research in Second Language Acquisition,* edited by H. Seliger and M. Long. Rowley, MA: Newbury House.

McLaughlin, B. 1981. Differences and similarities between first- and second-language learning. In *Native and Foreign Language Acquisition,* edited by H. Wintz. New York: Academy of Sciences.

Nystrom, N. 1983. Teacher-student interaction in bilingual classrooms: Four approaches to error feedback. In *Classroom-Oriented Research in Second Language Acquisition,* edited by H. Seliger and M. Long. Rowley, MA: Newbury House.

Ovando, C., and V.P. Collier. 1998. *Bilingual and ESL Classroom Teaching in Multicultural Contexts.* Boston: McGraw-Hill.

Politzer, R. 1970. Some reflections on 'good' and 'bad' language teaching behaviours. *Language Learning* 20.

Read, C. 1971. Pre-school children's knowledge of English phonology. *Harvard Educational Review* 41.

Rickford, J. R. 1983. What happens in decreolization. In *Pidginization and*

Creolization as Language Acquisition, edited by R. Anderson. Rowley, MA: Newbury House.

Rosencranz, G. 1998. *The Spelling Book: Teaching Children How to Spell, Not What to Spell.* Newark, DE: International Reading Association.

Seliger, H. 1977. Does practice make perfect? A study of interaction patterns and L2 competence. *Language Learning* 20.

Simmons-McDonald, H. 1988. The acquisition of English negation by speakers of St Lucian French Creole. PhD diss., Stanford University.

———. 1996. Language and education policy: The case for Creole in formal education. In *Caribbean Language: Issues Old and New,* edited by P. Christie. Barbados, Jamaica, Trinidad and Tobago: The Press UWI.

———. N.d. Input and interaction in the classrooms of primary schools.

Stauble, A. 1977. An exploratory analogy between decreolization and second-language learning: Negation. Master's thesis, University of California.

Stern, H.H. 1983. *Fundamental Concepts of Language Teaching.* Oxford: Oxford University Press.

Swain, M. 1983. Understanding input through output. Paper presented at the tenth University of Michigan Conference on Applied Linguistics.

Thomas, W.P., and V.P. Collier. 1997. *School Effectiveness for Language Minority Students.* Washington, DC: National Clearinghouse for Bilingual Education.

Wallace-Robinett, B., and J. Schachter, eds. 1983. *Second Language Learning: Contrastive Analysis, Error Analysis and Related Aspects.* Ann Arbor, MI: University of Michigan Press.

Walker, A. 1984. Applied sociology of language: Vernacular languages and education. In *Applied Sociolinguistics,* edited by P. Trudgill. New York: Academic Press.

Wells, G. 1981. *Learning through Interaction.* Cambridge: Cambridge University Press.

Winch, C., and J. Gingell. 1994. Dialect interference and difficulties with writing: An investigation in St Lucian primary schools. *Language and Education* 8, no. 3.

Winer, L. 1993. Teaching speakers of Caribbean English Creoles in North American Classrooms. In *Language Variation in North American English Research and Teaching,* edited by A. Wayne and C.D. Lance. New York: Modern Language Association.

Chapter 3

Language Education Revisited in the Commonwealth Caribbean

Dennis R. Craig

Twenty years ago, in the inaugural lecture for the professorship in language education at the University of the West Indies (Craig 1980), I indicated that two main alternatives in language education at the beginning of schooling were available to West Indian countries.

First Alternative
Conduct all of the early education of the child, including initial instruction in reading and writing, in the home language. Select one of the following alternatives for treatment of English:
  Either (1) introduce English as a second language at some later stage after the child has acquired literacy in the home language or (2) introduce English as a second language at the very beginning, with the understanding that reading and writing skills acquired in the home language will be transferred to English whenever appropriate.

Second Alternative
Continue in school the oral use of the child's home language. Introduce English as a second language at the very beginning and link the acquisition of reading and writing to the learning of English. If required, reading and writing skills acquired in English can be transferred when necessary to the home language.

It is interesting to review the issues in language education that were current at that time, to consider what has happened in the discipline and in its applications since then, and to reflect on the 1998 situation.[1]

By the end of the 1970s, the descriptive and theoretical studies of West Indian Creole languages, such as those of Cassidy, Le Page and DeCamp, which had appeared since the 1950s and of which detailed references are given in Craig (1976), had begun to have two results, both of which underlie the language education alternatives suggested above. The first of these results, since it was the one that became most early evident, was a perception that the newly available descriptions of Creole and related languages had created a possibility for the more effective teaching of standard languages to Creole and other vernacular speakers. Some of the West Indian-relevant evidence of this perception (see Craig 1976 for precise references) includes work on the North American social-dialect situation, and is represented in the following efforts:

- Allsopp's early series on "The Language We Speak", in *Kyk-Over-All* up to 1953, and "The English Language in Guyana", in *English Language Teaching*, 1953;
- Beryl Bailey's "Teaching of English Noun–Verb Concord in Jamaica" and "Some Problems in the Language Teaching Situation in Jamaica";
- Elsa Walton's, "Learning to Read in Jamaica";
- John Figueroa's promotion of language education activity at Mona in the 1960s;
- Shuy's editorship of *Social Dialects and Language Learning* in 1964;
- Bill Stewart's editorship of *Nonstandard Speech and the Teaching of English* in 1964;
- Ralph Fasold's "Isn't English the First Language Too?" and "What Can an English Teacher do about Nonstandard Dialect?";
- Baratz and Shuy's editorship of *Teaching Black Children to Read*;
- Craig's work between 1964 and 1976, Lawrence Carrington's and other work in Trinidad, work in Guyana, such as that of Basil Armstrong, George Cave, Belle Tyndal and Walter Edwards, and

works of other persons in the Caribbean which, together with the references above and all others preceding 1974, can be seen listed in *Bidialectal Education: Creole and Standard in the West Indies* (Craig 1976, as indicated above).

Concurrently with work such as the preceding on Creole and nonstandard language, the Bernstein studies of the early 1960s were suggesting that lower social-class acculturation and, with it, the nonstandard language of the lower social classes, predisposed their subjects to lower levels of cognitive functioning than standard language and an upper social-class acculturation. The latter thesis evoked a rebuttal in Labov's (1969) "Logic of Nonstandard English", which was a demonstration of the basic linguistic truism that there is no one-to-one relationship between linguistic form and cognitive functioning, and that all languages have a capacity to provide representations for all levels of cognitive activity.

Labov's demonstration had a big role to play subsequently in producing the second result that derived from the study of Creole and related nonstandard language, and more will be said about that shortly. It also, to a lesser extent, lent support to the efforts of language educators to use the newly available linguistic descriptions of Creole and nonstandard language as a means of arriving at more effective procedures for teaching English to speakers of the latter languages.

And there were other developments, too, that fuelled the drive for a more effective teaching of English and literacy to Creole- and vernacular-speaking children. One of these developments was the demonstration by psychologists of the importance of early stimulation in the intellectual development of children. The argument from this premise justified "Headstart" in North America and is reflected in the Caribbean in the programme funded by the Van Leer Foundation and conducted by D.R.B. Grant, beginning in the late 1960s. Semaj (1984: 3.7 and 3.8) makes an interesting reference to the latter programme.

Another development was the heightened international interest in the learning and teaching of foreign or second languages. The interest was stimulated by advances in language laboratory technology, and the ferment that grew out of the interfacing of audiolingualism, situational teaching and the new cognitive approaches that had replaced traditional grammar–translation strategies in language teaching. Ellis (1990), reviewing the underlying theories in these developments, characterizes them as "behaviourist learning theory" to distinguish them from the later development of "naturalistic learning theory" that came in the 1970s and 1980s and that are particularly associated with the work of Krashen (1976, 1982).

Preceding the last-mentioned development, a factor which helped to push language education in the Caribbean and elsewhere was the relatively easy availability of funding. With the conscience of the world awakened by the civil rights, equal opportunity and similar movements, welfare funds on both sides of the Atlantic were channelled more heavily into education – most of it language education – than ever before or ever after. We may note, for example, that straddling the decade between the late 1960s and late 1970s, there were the Schools Council and other educational projects in Britain that focused heavily on the language problems of West Indian immigrant children; in the United States, there were the numerous funded projects that produced all of the North American works already mentioned and several others. Also in the course of that decade, focusing heavily again on language, there were the UNESCO RLA 142 Project in Jamaica and other Caribbean countries, the Carnegie Project, which did significant work in Guyana, the Ford Foundation Project that produced the Jamaican Language Materials Workshop Primary Education Materials and gave an early impetus to the *Dictionary of Caribbean English Usage* (Allsopp 1996), and the USAID Primary Education Project across most of the Commonwealth Caribbean.

From the very earliest attempts to apply the findings of Creole language studies to the teaching of the related standard languages to Creole speakers, it had been recognized that normal foreign or second-language teaching procedures were likely to be ineffective because, to most Creole speakers, the related standard language, though not a mother tongue, was not a completely foreign language either. Reference to this fact is to be found in the earliest works of Beryl Bailey (already mentioned), for example, and evidence that a parallel to this fact also exists in the relationship between French and the French-based Creoles is probably to be seen in the claim of Pradel Pompilus (1973) that Haitian Creole speakers attempting to learn French experience certain difficulties not experienced by speakers with other mother tongues.

This matter of the difficulty of teaching a related standard language to Creole or nonstandard speakers, and the relevance to it of the discussion on linguistic variation, interlanguage and mesolectal phenomena are considered at some length in my 1983 article, "Teaching Standard English to Nonstandard Speakers: Some Methodological Issues". I mention it since space precludes any further discussion of these matters here, but they are exceedingly important since, by the end of the 1970s, controversies over possible ways of resolving the issues had led to a profound pessimism about whether Standard English can be successfully taught to speakers of related Creole or nonstandard English. The reflection of this pessimism, even before it reached its peak, can probably best be seen in some of the essays in the 1974 anniversary issue (edited by Alfred Aarons) of the *Florida Foreign Language Reporter:* Richard Day's "Can Standard English Be Taught? or What Does it Mean to Know Standard English?"; Melvin Hoffman's "It's Getting Harder to Tell the Scorers without a Placard"; Thomas Kotchman's "Standard English Revisited, or Who's Kidding/Cheating Who(m)?"; and William Stewart's "The Laissez-faire Movement in English Teaching: Advance to the Rear?"

The growth of this pessimism did not by any means put an end to the creation of well-conceived materials and procedures for teaching Standard English; it was a parallel development. It coincided, for example, in the decade between the mid-1970s and 1980s, with the creation of the Timehri Readers and Workbooks in Guyana, the already mentioned Language Materials Workshop Series in Jamaica, the University of the West Indies/USAID materials all over the West Indies, and the establishment of an English as a Second Language (ESL) Group in the North American TESOL Organization, which was chaired by Lise Winer, then based in Trinidad, and later by Don Wilson from the University of the West Indies at Mona, Jamaica.

But the thrust of these developments of the late 1970s and early 1980s was effectively blunted by a set of adverse circumstances. One of these circumstances was that the English as a Second Dialect (ESD) interest group in TESOL disappeared under the superior weight of persons who were more interested in ESL than ESD (Murray 1997: 1), and the attempt to use special materials for teaching English to Creole and nonstandard speakers in North America, as in the West Indies, has since been persistently weakened by several factors.

In the West Indies, one of these factors is the continuing dominance in education, even among persons who would attempt to deny it, of an English-as-the-mother-tongue tradition. Education officers, teacher trainers, school teachers (who were themselves trained under the latter tradition) cannot put into practice, without themselves undergoing a thorough retraining, the step-by-step classroom procedures that are necessary in ESL/ESD teaching. The result is that ESL/ESD materials and methodologies are often illogically compared with those of mother tongue teaching and, on the basis of that comparison, condemned as being "unstimulating", "lacking in depth and maturity of language", and "stilted and unnatural" (Craig 1996). Creole- and nonstandard-speaking children, the vast majority of the West Indian school population, are still being expected to learn to read English sentences which they would understand only partially, if at all, if they heard those sentences spoken. Secondary school–age children, who have failed to gain entry in schools but can really operate at a secondary level, are expected to learn English through using Cecil Gray's *Language for Living* and *English for Life*, both admirable books for those who already possess at least an initial competence in English as the mother tongue. Even though textbooks other than the latter have grown in popularity since 1990, the mother tongue orientation of those texts is similar to that of their predecessors, but with a more direct focus on the types of questions students may expect in the secondary school examinations.

On the other hand, with the remarkable exception of Longman's Sunstart Reading Series, which follows a controlled approach to the presentation of language structure, textbooks like the New World English Series (Craig and Walker-Gordon 1981), following such an approach, have failed to become popular. One reason could be that the methodologies, as well as consumer appeal of the series, have not been progressively updated and promoted, but the weight of mother tongue traditions in teaching cannot be completely separated from those reasons. So far as methodology is concerned, nevertheless, a more direct and in-depth approach to the training of teachers, as is provided in Craig (1999), which will be discussed shortly, probably holds the solution to the problem.

Another factor that has militated against the effective application of measures for increasing the competence of Creole and nonstandard speakers in the related standard language is uncertainty in Ministries of Education and other policy-making agencies about the direction in which language education ought to go. This uncertainty often becomes realized as ambivalence, vacillation, frequent shifts of policy to match the frequent shifting of government ministers, and so on. Policy is often not determined on sound logical and professional grounds which will outlast political change. Examples of this may be seen in the shifts that have taken place over the years on the issues surrounding the use of Creole in early education in countries as diverse as Jamaica, St Lucia, Dominica, Grenada and Belize.

In this situation, for example, attempts such as those of Kephart(1984), the Belize Kriol Project(1995) and Rickards (1995) to use Creole for initial literacy or to improve the proficiency of older nonliterates in schools have not evoked much enthusiasm within the official practice of education. At the same time, the alternative of teaching English as a second dialect or language from the beginning of schooling has not been generally adopted either, despite the emergence since the 1980s of newer descriptive works such as those of Roberts (1988), Pollard (1993), and Solomon (1993), which also include guidelines for teachers. And, although in different parts of the Caribbean there are institutions, such as the St Lucian Folk Research centre, the National Kriol Council of Belize, and Creole-promoting interests, such as the Jamaican ones mentioned by Shields-Brodber (1997), that are actively engaged in the instrumentalization of Creole, the activities of such institutions and interests are not indicative of any choice of alternatives in educational policy, but serve, rather, to increase the urgency for such choices to be made.

This brings us back to the second of the major results, referred to earlier, that derive from the study of Creole languages. This second result is the accumulation of evidence on the adequacy of Creole and related nonstandard language. It was this accumulation of evidence that led a US Federal Court in 1979 to rule that Black elementary school children had a right to be educated in the Black English dialect. But, as Geneva Smitherman, who led the children's evidence in the case, reminds us, in her article (1983), which bears the same title as Hubert Devonish's well-known book (published in 1986), "Language and Liberation", the Court also reaffirmed the institutional obligation of school systems to teach children "to read in standard English of the school, the commercial world, the arts, science and professions".

The latter reaffirmation of the US Federal Court is often lost or forgotten. When it is remembered, however, and proposals are made for its implementation, what often results is much vagueness and confusion. Smitherman's 1983 proposal, coming four years after the 1979 Federal Court judgement, is a case in point. She proposed as follows:

> Although standard English is the dominant language of instruction and in general use in the social domain, this does not preclude . . . the development of a language policy in the Black community to protect our own interests. A common language, which we possess, is one of the defining characteristics of a nation. We need to raise this objective reality to a level of national consciousness and an explicitly articulated policy. There are several possibilities whereby this policy might be put into practice. We might recognize the functionality of standard English while simultaneously acknowledging its limitations for us as a people. Or we might propose a trilingual language policy, [which would include] Black English, standard English, and a third language that would permit dialogue between us and "Third World" people. And I am sure there are other possibilities that will emerge from our collective consciousness and wisdom. To bring this policy into being in a rational and scientific manner will require language scholars and other humanists and social scientists among us to engage in a new kind of research enterprise. The paradigm governing this new research must be such that it links theory and practice and thus generates research that will lead to the goal of liberation. (Smitherman 1983: 23)

In the Caribbean, Devonish's proposals, coming three years after those of Smitherman, were much clearer:

> The language policy being proposed for the education system is a bilingual one. Creole would be the initial medium of education, the medium by which literacy is acquired, as well as a subject to be taught. English would be introduced as a second language as early in the education system as is thought sound from an educational standpoint.
>
> The language planning proposals put forward earlier scrupulously

avoided the suggestion of Standard Creole being developed and imposed on the population for official use . . . (1986: 120–21)

Devonish's proposals for initial literacy in Creole correspond with one of the two alternatives I have myself suggested. But apart from the mentioned problem of a "Standard Creole" for use in printed materials, selection of that alternative faces the formidable problem of engineering the social, if not political, revolutions that are necessary in order to implement the proposals, and, with the passage of time, the possibility of such engineering seems to be getting increasingly remote. The reason for this is that the rapid mixing of language varieties that is taking place all over the Caribbean, and that Shields-Brodber (1997) has described for Jamaica, is, in effect, creating a convergence of Creole and the local standard variety of English. And this convergence is making it less possible for a discrete Creole to be used in literacy, as the first alternative requires.

The intractability of the problem of implementing proposals such as the two preceding, however, is perhaps best illustrated in the North American situation. Thirteen years after Smitherman's proposals, North American education systems were no nearer to interpreting them, much less implementing them, unless we regard the beginning of the implementation as being evidenced by the December 1996 resolution of the Oakland California School Board which "shocked the world", as Todd (1997) remarked. The board resolved that African American children should be taught in Ebonics, otherwise known as African American Vernacular English (AAVE), and that funds be set aside for a teaching programme in Ebonics. The aim of the board, as subsequently evaluated, was obviously to give "Ebonics", following Williams (1975) who coined the term, the status of a foreign language, so that the education of Ebonics/AAVE speakers would receive the same level of funding as bilingual education programmes in the United States.

In the wake of this development, there have been many commentaries, recommendations and evaluations, of which one of the most comprehensive collections is in Perry and Delfit (1998). Many of the pedagogical suggestions in the latter revert to procedures that were first enunciated in the 1960s and 1970s for teaching ESD. This fact is indeed given a tacit acknowledgement in Smitherman (1998–99), where the *Bridge Readers* of Simpkins and colleagues

(1975) are approvingly referred to. The fact, however, is explicitly acknowledged in Rickford (1998), which stresses the same point as Smitherman, but goes further to indicate, in view of the obvious needs of Ebonics/AAVE speakers targeting English and literacy, the relevance of second-dialect teaching approaches developed in Europe and the Caribbean in the 1960s and 1970s. With reference to the Caribbean, nevertheless, while mentioning some of the seminal works on descriptions of Creole and the general educational implications of those descriptions, Rickford omits to mention the practical applications subsequently developed and described earlier in this chapter and in Craig (1976, 1983).

From all of the preceding, at the end of the 1990s the indications are that language education in the Creole-related vernacular situations in both North America and the Caribbean continues in a state of crisis. The reason for this is not difficult to find, as will be presently suggested.

The decade of the 1980s, and continuing into that of the 1990s, has not brought into the general field of second-language teaching any developments that, isolated and applied as a discrete set of procedures, can be particularly efficacious in teaching a related standard language to Creole or other vernacular speakers on a worldwide scale. Communicative Language Teaching (CLT) procedures have proved to be inadequate for developing required proficiencies in normal second and foreign language situations (Kumaravadivelu 1994; Celce-Murcia et al. 1997), and those procedures have long been known to be even more inadequate in Creole and other vernacular situations where the structural overlap between the target and the learner's already possessed repertoire facilitates a high level of communicative competence (Craig 1983, 1998, 1999).

Nevertheless, in the context of the many controversies and professional uncertainties associated with the language education of vernacular speakers (see, for example, Aarons 1994), the most efficacious principles for the education of the latter speakers have hardly had a chance to be applied, without significant erosion, on a consistent, long-term basis. The specific needs of vernacular-speaking learners of a related standard language continue to be often ignored, and CLT, or related approaches such as "Whole Language", which undoubtedly have a place in the vernacular speaker's acquisition of standard language proficiency (Craig 1999), have often been elevated, detrimentally to vernacular speakers, to the status of being the only necessary set of procedures. This elevation of CLT and related approaches has generally been facilitated by their obvious relationship to mother tongue teaching approaches and the already mentioned traditional dominance of the latter.

In the period spanned by the dominance of CLT, there have been some other developments, nevertheless, which provide insights that can be beneficially included within the procedures for teaching a related standard language to vernacular speakers. The relevant developments particularly concern the recognition of the importance of consciousness-raising activity (Sharwood Smith 1981; Schmidt 1990) and language awareness (Fairclough 1992). The importance of the latter factors lies in the fact that, moving beyond dialect awareness, as defined by Wolfram and Shilling-Estes (1995), they induce vernacular speakers to perceive contrasts between their own and the targeted standard which they would be unlikely to perceive through mere communicative interaction. This result then provides an essential base for the augmentation of vernacular speakers' motivation to acquire the target and to apply their own individual learning strategies (Oxford 1990; Green and Oxford 1995) to that end. The recognition of the importance of the latter factors is, in a way, a reassertion of the importance of cognitive factors in language learning. The specific needs of vernacular-speaking learners of a related standard language justify that increased attention be paid to those factors.

Relevant specifically to the Commonwealth Caribbean, the conclusion from all of the preceding is that there is a need to recover ground that has been lost in language education since the University of the West Indies/USAID Primary Education Project ended more than a decade ago. The existence of this need is substantiated by the complaints about low English language proficiency which come annually from the one regional institution, apart from the University of the West Indies itself, which has grown steadily over the period: the Caribbean Examinations Council (CXC).

These complaints come from the CXC in a situation where the economies and educational provision in the West Indian region are such that, according to World Bank statistics, the percentage of the relevant age cohort which reaches a level of schooling that would permit it to sit the CXC examinations, and the percentage of that cohort which passes the subject English at Grades I and II are as shown in Table 3.1.

Due Respect

Table 3.1

	CXC Stream	English Grade I/II
Antigua	55	28
Barbados	(55)	(25)
Belize	21	8
Dominica	25	7
Grenada		12
Guyana	26	3
Jamaica	32	8
St Kitts	43	18
St Lucia	21	9
St Vincent	35	13
Trinidad	65	24

Source: Extracted from World Bank 1993: 45, with the exception of Barbados, which is otherwise estimated.

What this suggests is that relatively inadequate proportions of West Indian children get a chance to experience genuine secondary education, and that 3 percent of the relevant age group will pass Secondary English at an acceptable level in Guyana, and varying proportions above that will pass in other countries, but hardly more than 25 percent even in the best of those other countries. In relation to the performance in English of candidates who sat the CXC examinations in 1992, the Panel of Examiners decided that the situation was so alarming that they needed to send a special report to the ministers of education in the region (see Appendix). The panel, it may be noted, had been repeating its alarm several years before 1992, and it has continued to do so since. There is evidence that the situation is getting worse in Commonwealth Caribbean countries, as Table 3.2 shows: the average percentage of passes in English for the years 1994–1996, when compared with the averages for 1988–1990, shows more instances of decline than improvement, although the changes in both respects are small.

There can be no doubt that the panel's recommendations were sound, and it would be interesting to see how West Indian governments would, if ever, attempt to implement the recommendations in the context of the two main policy alternatives that are open to them. At the moment, no West Indian government seems to be taking the fundamental look at language policy which the panel has advised, although Belize (1995) shows an inconclusive attempt

Table 3.2: The English language situation in the Commonwealth Caribbean: Percentage of passes for the CXC English-A examination, General Proficiency Levels I and II

Country	AV% 1988–90*	AV% 1994–96	Change over 9 yrs
Anguilla	n/a	43.95	
Antigua/Barbuda	48.26	52.15	+3.89
Barbados	52.6	51.12	-1.48
Belize	33.43	34.0	+0.57
British Virgin Islands	72.6	58.86	-13.74
Cayman Islands	n/a	78.77	
Dominica	34.63	36.16	+1.53
Grenada	22.7	25.85	+3.15
Guyana	12.4	14.92	+2.52
Jamaica	29.4	25.85	-0.47
Montserrat	72.76	66.95[1]	-5.81
St Kitts/Nevis	49.2	44.42	-4.78
St Lucia	45.0	37.36	-7.64
St Vincent/Grenadines	39.13	38.3	-0.83
Trinidad/Tobago	35.2	36.66	+1.46
Turks & Caicos Islands	n/a	44.29	

1. No candidates in 1996. Averages taken from 1994–95.
Sources: (a) *Compiled from OECS/ERS, Table 15; (b) CXC 1994–96 Annual Report on Administration of the Examination.

which has not been followed through. And, although most governments are striving within their means to improve their education systems, insufficient proportions of their efforts are being channelled towards the solution of their language-specific problems. Where efforts of the latter kind are being attempted, they tend to be under the influence of external funding agencies whose consultants generally have not had opportunities to acquire the necessary understandings of relevant vernacular situations. In Craig (1999) these issues are discussed, and a detailed programme provided for the training of language and literacy teachers at primary and secondary levels.

Note

1. An earlier version of this chapter was presented at the tenth biennial conference of the Society for Caribbean Linguistics, University of Guyana (1994).

References

Aarons, A., ed. 1974. Issues in the teaching of Standard English. *Florida Foreign Language Reporter* 12, nos. 1 and 2 (special issue).

Allsopp, S.R.R. 1996. *Dictionary of Caribbean English Usage*. Cambridge: Cambridge University Press.

Bailey, Beryl. 1963. Teaching of English noun-verb concord in primary schools in Jamaica. *Caribbean Quarterly* 9, no. 4.

———. 1964. Some problems in the language teaching situation in Jamaica. *Social Dialects and Language Learning*, edited by R. Shuy. Champaign, IL: National Council of Teachers of English.

Belize. 1995. The principles and practice of teaching English as a second language. Module 2 of the course in *The Teaching of the Language Arts*. Writer: Dennis Craig; Consultant: Lynda Moguel; Course Coordinator: Rosalind Bradley. Belize Teachers' College, Belize.

Belize Kriol Project. 1995. *How fi Rite Bileez Kriol (How to Write Belize Creole)*. Belize City: Belize Kriol Project.

Bernstein, P. 1961. Social structure, language and learning. *Education Research* 3.

———. 1962. Social class, linguistic code and grammatical elements. *Language and Speech* 5.

Celce-Murcia, M., et al. 1997. Direct approaches to L2 instruction: A turning point in Communicative Language Teaching. *TESOL Quarterly* 31, no. 1.

Craig, D. 1976. Bidialectal education: Creole and Standard in the West Indies. *International Journal for the Sociology of Language* 8. Reprinted in J.B. Pride, (ed.), *Sociolinguistic Aspects of Language Learning and Teaching*. Oxford: Oxford University Press.

———. 1983a, 1986. *New World English*, Books 3 and 4. London: Longman Group.

———. 1983b. Teaching Standard English to nonstandard speakers: Some methodological issues. *Journal of Negro Education* 52, no. 1.

———. 1996. English language teaching: Problems and prospects in the West Indies. In *Education in the West Indies: Developments and Perspectives, 1948–98*, edited by D. Craig et al. Mona, Jamaica: Institute of Social and Economic Research (ISER), University of the West Indies.

———. "Aafta yu laan dem fi riid an rait dem kriiyol, den wa muo?": Creole and the teaching of the lexifier language. Paper presented at the fourth international Creole Language workshop, March 19–21, 1998. Florida International University, English Department Creole Language Program.

———. 1999. *Teaching Language and Literacy: Policies and Procedures for Vernacular Situations*. Georgetown, Guyana: Education and Development Services Inc.

Craig, D., and G. Walker-Gordon. 1981. *New World English,* Books 1 and 2. London: Longman.
Devonish, H. 1986. *Language and Liberation: Creole Language Politics in the Caribbean.* London: Karia Press.
Ellis, R. 1990. *Instructed Second Language Acquisition.* Oxford: Basil Blackwell.
Fairclough, N., ed. 1992. *Critical Language Awareness.* London: Longman Group.
Gray, C. 1968. *Language For Living.* London: Longman Group.
———. 1980. *English For Life.* London: Thomas Nelson and Sons.
Green, J., and R. Oxford. 1995. A closer look at learning strategies, L2 proficiency and gender. *TESOL Quarterly* 29, no. 2.
Kephart, R. Literacy through Creole English: Report of an applied project. Paper presented at the conference of the Society for Caribbean Linguistics, University of the West Indies, Mona, Jamaica, 1984.
Krashen, S. 1976. Formal and informal linguistic environments in language acquisition and language learning. *TESOL Quarterly* 10.
———. 1982. *Principles and Practice in Second Language Acquisition.* Oxford: Pergamon.
Kumaravadivelu, B. 1994. The postmethod condition: (E)merging strategies for second/foreign language teaching. *TESOL Quarterly* 28, no. 1.
Labov, W. The logic of nonstandard English. In *Twentieth Annual Round Table: Linguistics and the Teaching of Standard English to Speakers of Other Languages or Dialects,* edited by J. Alatis. Washington, DC: Georgetown University School of Languages and Linguistics.
Murray, D. 1997. TESOL speaks on Ebonics. *TESOL Matters,* June/July 1997.
OECS/ERS. 1991. Foundation for the future: OECS education reform strategy. Organization of Eastern Caribbean States (OECS) Secretariat. Castries, St Lucia.
Oxford, R. 1990. *Language Learning Strategies: What Every Teacher Should Know.* New York: Newbury House/Harper and Row.
Perry, T., and L. Delpit, eds. 1998. *The Real Ebonics Debate.* Boston: Beacon Press.
Pollard, V. 1993. *From Jamaican Creole to Standard English.* Brooklyn, NY: Caribbean Resource Center, Medgar Evers College, City University of New York.
Pompilus, Pradel. 1973. *L'Étude Comparée du Créole et du Français.* Port au Prince: Éditions Caraïbes.
Rickards, S. 1995. The language of patois. *ROSEGRAM,* May 1995. Jamaica: Reform of Secondary Education (ROSE) Secretariat, Ministry of Education.
Rickford, J. 1998. Using the vernacular to teach the standard. Revised version of remarks delivered at the California State University at Long Beach (CSULB) conference on Ebonics, March 29, 1997. In *Conference Proceedings,* edited by DeKlerl. (Available on website – http://www.stanford.edu.rickford'papers/ Vernacular to teach Standard html)

Roberts, P. 1986. *West Indians and Their Language*. Cambridge: Cambridge University Press.
Schmidt, R. 1990. The role of consciousness in second language learning. *Applied Linguistics* 11, no. 2.
Schneider, E., ed. 1997. *Englishes around the World*. Vol. 2, *Caribbean, Africa, Asia, Australasia: Studies in Honour of Manfred Görlach*. Amsterdam and Philadelphia: John Benjamins.
Semaj, L. 1984. *Child Development in the Caribbean: An Annotated Bibliography, 1962–82*. Mona, Jamaica: Regional Preschool Child Development Centre.
Sharwood-Smith, M. 1981. Consciousness raising and the second language learner. *Applied Linguistics* 11.
Shields-Brodber, K. 1997. Requiem for English in an English-speaking country: The case of Jamaica. In *Englishes around the World*, vol. 2, edited by E. Schneider. Amsterdam and Philadelphia: John Benjamins.
Simpkins, G. et al. 1975. *Bridge: A Cross-Cultural Reading Test Field Report*. Boston: Houghton Mifflin.
Smitherman, G. 1983. Language and liberation. *Journal of Negro Education* 52.
———. 1998–99. "Dat teacher be hollin at us." What is Ebonics? *TESOL Quarterly* 32, no. 1 and 33, no. 1
Solomon, D. 1993. *The Speech of Trinidad: A Reference Grammar*. St Augustine, Trinidad: School of Continuing Studies, UWI.
Todd L. 1997. Ebonics: An evaluation. *English Today* 51, no. 13.
Thornbury, S. 1998. Comments on Celce-Murcia, Dornvei, and Thurrell: Direct approaches in L2 instruction: A turning point in CLT? *TESOL Quarterly* 32, no. 1.
Williams, R. 1995. *Ebonics, the True Language of Black Folks*. St Louis, MO: Institute of Black Studies.
Wolfram, W., and N. Shilling-Estes. 1975. Moribund dialects and the endangerment canon: The case of the Ocracoke brogue. *Language* 71, no. 4.
World Bank. 1993. *Caribbean Region: Access, Quality and Efficiency in Education*. Washington, DC: World Bank.

Appendix

*Statement from the English Panel on Candidates' Performance in the English A Examination, Caribbean Examinations Council Western Zone Office (1992)**

The CXC English Panel is concerned about what appears to be a continually deteriorating level of performance of the students of the Caribbean in written expression as well as in the comprehension of expository writing and literature. This inadequacy is already manifesting itself in the performance of our students in the workplace, and in tertiary level institutions including UWI, which has now found it necessary to introduce a programme of Remedial English for first year students who have failed to pass a proficiency test.

Studies throughout the Caribbean indicate the following causes:

1. English language programmes at both the Primary and Secondary level which are uncoordinated, do not take cognizance of the language environment in which the students live and speak and do not give sufficient opportunities for structural learning of the patterns of English nor the opportunity to utilize these patterns in a free and creative manner.
2. A lack of preparedness on the part of the teachers at the Primary and Secondary levels for the task of teaching English in the Caribbean situation.
3. The lack of a serious language component at either the Teachers' College level or the UWI Diploma in Education level which would serve to upgrade the teaching bodies to enable them to meet the demands of our peculiar situation.

The Panel is of the view that, unless strong action is taken immediately, our student bodies, including the naturally gifted in the Sciences and Technology as well as in the Arts, will find it difficult to cope with the demands of an academic programme which requires them to read and write extensively in the English Language. The Panel is also convinced that this situation cannot be rectified by merely paying attention to the final two years of the Secondary School Programme. It requires a total integrated and dedicated programme of study beginning at the infant level and continuing through Secondary School. Ministries of Education are therefore urged to take steps to address this problem in their own territories, and where possible, through the coordinating facilities provided by the CARICOM Secretariat, to work with neighbouring governments who are experiencing problems of the same type. Particular emphasis should be placed on the following:

1. The teachers: Upgrade the teachers' language knowledge and pedagogical skills through in-service courses and the development of a formal English course for Teachers' College level and the Diploma in Education programme.

2. Proper monitoring of the teaching of English in the school system with a view to providing advice to teachers and gaining further insights into the teaching situation so as to be able to develop appropriate remedies and techniques.

3. The development of a linguistically and pedagogically sound teaching programme appropriate to the territory and to the different levels of competence demonstrated by the student body. The development of systems of evaluation at crucial points in the student's development so as to determine:
   i. the efficacy of the programmes proposed; or
   ii. the need for remedial action.

4. The introduction of methods or strategies that would provide the student with the opportunities for expression, both orally and in writing, with the emphasis on the former in the earlier years, and for reading materials appropriate to their age group, reading levels and interests.

The Panel wishes to indicate that there are two aspects of examination utilized by other cognate subject areas, which because of the large numbers involved and the cost associated with it, cannot be utilized by the English Examining Committee. These are: an oral examination and SBA (School Based Assessment). The Panel believes that the advantages of these two examination strategies can be obtained by Ministries of Education if they are introduced on a territorial basis and conducted by panels of teachers and curriculum officers of the country. CXC should be asked to provide assistance on a consultancy basis; certification made by the individual Ministries may be authenticated by CXC, even though this will not form part of the official CXC certificate at this time.

The Panel urges the Council to request Ministries to consider the gravity of the situation described above and take the action as recommended.

* This statement has been slightly modified by the author.

Chapter 4

Defining the Role of Linguistic Markers in Manufacturing Classroom Consent

Beverley Bryan

Classrooms are interactional spaces where discourses are formed and reformed according to the social, cultural and linguistic resources available to the participants (teachers and students). In this chapter, within the context of language choice, I want to examine the use of Jamaican Creole as one of the languages of Jamaican classrooms, and to focus in particular on how it is employed to foster agreement about the shape and direction of the discourse of the classroom.

To begin this process, I want to discuss how some classrooms work. To do that, I am first going to describe some small pieces of discourse from two Jamaican classrooms. The classes described below were two out of many observed, after the teachers had been interviewed about their aim in teaching English, the methods they used, and the influences to which they were subject. Such inquiry yielded much information about how these teachers relate to Jamaican Creole (JC) on the personal and institutional levels. The discussion about this relationship begins with the classroom observations.

Lesson One

This is an inner city Kingston school which, at the time, received children who had not been placed in high schools by the now defunct Common Entrance placement test. The class is referred to as a "remedial" Grade Eight (Year Two)

Due Respect

class, insofar as all the children are very poor readers, operating at no more than the Grade Three level. In this case the lesson is centred on a story called "The Blow", written by the teacher to compensate for the shortage of material at the children's level. It is about two hundred words long and is presented to the children in the teacher's handwriting on a sheet of paper. The story is about an unlucky gambler on whom misfortune fell.

The teacher repeats the title "The Blow" ['ðər 'blo:] and points to it stuck on the board.

1. T1: *What does it* [the title] *mean?*
2. S1: *Laik in a futbal mach an im nok out.* ('It's like in a football match and he's knocked out.')
3. T1: *He got knocked out of the football match . . . yes.*
4. S2: *Wisl bluo Mis.* ('A whistle blows, Miss.')
5. T1: *Blowing of a whistle.*
6. S3: *Yu get a bluo in yu yai an yu kyaang si gud.* ('You might get a blow in your eye and you can't see well.')
   (The hands are shooting up very fast as the children call for the teacher's attention.)
7. T1: *OK. OK . . . last one.*
8. S4: *Im waif lef im.* ('His wife left him.')
   (The children get so excited that the teacher has to stop the class to give them a quiet interlude when they close their eyes, listen to sounds and control their breathing. When they return to the lesson, the teacher directs them to read the story that is pinned on the board. The children begin to read in chorus.)
9. *The Blow.* ['ðər 'blo:]
   (The teacher laughs. When they have finished the story, the teacher asks them about its meaning.)
10. S5: *Im neva rich.* ('He wasn't rich.')
11. S2: *Im waan pie piis piis.* ('He wanted to pay bit by bit.')
12. S3: *Im a go waanti.* ('He'll soon need it.')
13. T1: *Huol aan.* ('Hold on!'/'Wait a minute!')
    (The teacher stops the class and holds to her bosom the

hands of three students in the front row. She asks the whole class to stand and breathe deeply and calmly. This lasts for about three minutes before they return to the discussion of "The Blow".)

14. S1: *Im laas im hous* ['He's lost his house.']
15. S2: *Im laif mashop* ['His life's messed up.']

Lesson Two

This is another Grade Eight class which is considered by the school to be functioning at Grade Three level, but it has students with a range of abilities.

16. T2: *We're going to do proverbs. Have you heard the word before?*
17. S1: *In the Bible, Miss.*
18. T2: *What does it* [the word *proverb*] *mean?*
19. S2: *A wise saying.*
20. T2: *It's a figurative saying. It's not literal. It means something else. Can you give me an example?*
21. S3: *Hai siit kil Miss Matty.* ('High seat killed Miss Matty.')
    (Teacher puts this example on the board; more examples are coming.)
22. T2: *You know I don't take chorus answers. Please raise your hand.*
23. S4: *Chikin meri aak de nier.* ('The chicken merry, hawk is near.')
    (Laughter. The teacher puts the contribution on the board: *Chicken merry, hawk is near.* Chorus of *"Miss, Miss"* as hands go up.)
24. S5: *Who laughs last laughs the best.*
    (Many hands and cries of '*Nuo man . . . me Mis.*')
25. S6: *Beta liet dan neva.* ('Better late than never.')
    (Teacher puts this on the board.)
26. S7: *Kyaang kech Kwaku, yu kech im shot.* ('If you can't catch Kwaku, [at least] catch his shirt.')
27. S8: *Wan wan koko ful baaskit.* ('One coco at a time will fill the basket.')

28.	T2:	*Can you explain these?*
29.	S3:	*"Hai siit . . ." means you want to live big Miss, but you can't.*
30.	S4:	*Chikin meri, aak de nier. Somtaim wen yu tiif, poliis de nier, Mis.* ('Sometimes when you steal, the police are close by, Miss.')
31.	T2:	*Sometimes you are stealing and the police might be near. Somebody is on the floor, please give him a chance. Are you listening?*
32.	S1:	*Yes, Mis wi kyan hier . . .* (The teacher asks for some English proverbs and gets)
33.	S2:	*Rome was not built in a day.*
34.	S9:	*Every cloud has a silver lining.*
35.	S1:	*Don't count your chickens.* (The teacher writes these on the board and adds, "Opportunity knocks but once" to the list. Towards the end, she rounds off the lesson by asking the students to read and explain one of the English proverbs they were looking at.)
36.	T2:	*Come, Simone, the rest of us stop writing and listen.* (Simone declines and a boy tries.)
37.	S9:	*A gunman gets an opportunity to go to foreign to study. He turns it down. A week later he get shoot and die.* (Some laughter at *"get shoot and die"*.) (The class is dismissed with homework.)

The classroom observations illustrate a number of points I want to make about how we understand the way in which classrooms operate in environments where more than one language contend with each other.

Translation and Codeswitching

The aspects of language choice I am pointing to could be described as codeswitching and translating. Both have been discussed in many other places. Malakoff and Hakuta (1991), for example, differentiate between translation and codeswitching. They acknowledge that both should be considered bilingual language skills available to children and adults alike. Translation, the focus of their work, is seen, typically, as a strategy used to enhance communication to monolingual speakers of the target language by the reproduction of an equivalent utterance. It is recognized as a natural linguistic skill and one necessary in a bilingual environment. They discuss the importance in translation of generating meaning, recognizing that translation does not work by a word-for-word or necessarily a phrase-by-phrase correspondence. Syntactic and lexical restructuring is often necessary before reformulating.

Malakoff and Hakuta (1991: 146) also discuss codeswitching and suggest a more intensely psychosocial role for this type of language behaviour: "Codeswitching is used for signalling group boundaries, conveying emphasis, role playing, establishing sociocultural identity." Myers-Scotton (1993) is primarily concerned with the motivations for codeswitching but spends considerable time reviewing the developing body of literature on the subject. Included in her discussions is some attention to the functions of codeswitching. She looks at the seminal work of Gumperz in charting the field of research in this area. In the Caribbean, attention to this phenomenon has included the significant explorations of Le Page and Tabouret-Keller (1985), where language choice is an individual act used to make connections with others within the community.

> [W]e see speech acts as acts of projection: the speaker is projecting his inner universe, implicitly with the invitation to others to share it, at least insofar as they recognize his language as an accurate symbolization of the world and share his attitude towards it. By verbalizing as he does, he is seeking to reinforce his models of the world, and hopes for acts of solidarity from those with whom he wishes to identify. (Le Page and Tabouret-Keller 1985: 181)

In Jamaica, several researchers have investigated the phenomenon of codeswitching in the language classroom. Pollard (1978) looked at the phonology, syntax and situation required for codeswitching. She considered also the implication of such behaviour in providing insights for the classroom, especially in developing activities such as role playing. Shields (1987) differentiated between codeswitching and style-shifting, seeing the former as moving between two linguistic systems while the latter moved within a single one. Like Malakoff and Hakuta and Le Page and Tabouret-Keller, she attaches great psychosocial significance to switching: "A speaker's choice of one over another grammatical system is not done in vacuo but informed by a network of complex factors, the norms of which are shared by the participating actors" (Shields 1987: 112).

Shields's discussion of the motives for codeswitching also enters into the continuing debate about the reasons for the practice, relating to the importance of situation or topic (situational switching and metaphorical switching) which was first posed by Blom and Gumperz (1972). Myers-Scotton tries to untangle the issues by suggesting that metaphorical switches have something to do with the presentation of self in relation to the topic. Another dimension is added to the issue with Kachru's (1978) introduction of the term *codemixing*, which is differentiated by its attention to intrasentential behaviour, and the insertion of linguistic items from one code to another with the social motivation of asserting familiarity with the discourses of power and authority.

In the lesson extracts cited above, there are clearly evident instances of codeswitching and translation. Instances of codemixing will be explored later on. In examining the classes observed, the first points relate to the language of the teachers. Both teachers use English, the target language, to interact with the children:

1. T1: *What does it mean?*
20. T2: *It's a figurative saying. It's not literal. It means something else. Can you give me an example?*

There is a good deal of translating going on, with the teacher attempting to parallel the students' responses in English.

2. S1: *Laik in a futbaal mach an im nok out.* ('It's like in a football match and he's knocked out.')
3. T1: *You got knocked out of the football match, yes.*
4. S2: *Wisl bluo Mis.* ('A whistle blows, Miss.')
5. T1: *Blowing of a whistle.*

As we can see, the translation is not always literal. For example, *Laik in a futbal mach an im nok out* is not directly paralleled by "You got knocked out of the football match." The teacher seems to be presenting specific structures for the students to copy, for example, "You got knocked out" and "blowing of a whistle". In this respect, these examples are not typical of the Malakoff and Hakuta model. Although they are translations from source to target, they are not made for the benefit of monolingual speakers of the target language. The teachers recognize the children's limited proficiency in English, and translate with an emphasis on structures needed to allow greater access to that language.

29. S4: *"Chikin meri, aak de nier". Somtaim wen yu tiif, poliis de nier, Mis.*
30. T2: (rephrases) *Sometimes you are stealing and the police might be near.*

Significant though, was her own use of Creole. Look, for example, at the

Huol aan . . . huol aan. ('Hold on!'/'Wait a minute!')

The teacher uses a Creole expression, recognizable as such from its phonology. This might be a momentary slip, but it is certainly an example of codeswitching. Elsewhere throughout the lesson (Lesson One) she has maintained the use of English. The slip comes when she and the students become excited about the interaction. It is an emotional moment of intimacy when she clasps the hands of the children joyfully to her bosom.

Moving now to the students' language, we see that they often use Creole.

10. S5: *Im neva rich.* ('He wasn't rich.')
11. S6: *Im waan pie piis piis.* ('He wants to pay bit by bit.')

They also used English:

16. S1: *In the Bible, Miss.*
17. T2: *What does it mean?*
18. S2: *A wise saying.*

Due Respect

The latter is a formal question-and-answer situation, when the content of the exchange is formal:

37. S9: *A gunman gets an opportunity to go to foreign to study. He turns it down. A week later he get shoot and die.*

They can also successfully switch between English and Creole:

29. S3: *Hai siit . . . means you want to live big, Miss but you can't.*

Additionally, the students are very enthusiastic about the content of the lessons and empathize with the predicament of the characters presented in the material:

23. S4: *Chikin meri, aak de nier.*
(Laughter. Teacher puts the contribution on the board: *Chicken merry, the hawk is near.* Chorus of "*Miss, Miss*" as hands go up.)
24. S5: *Who laughs last laughs best.*
(Many hands and cries of "*Nuo man . . . me Miss.*") (Lesson Two)

and

S5: *Im neva rich.* ('He wasn't rich.')
S2: *Im waan pie piis piis.* ('He wanted to pay bit by bit.')
S3: *Im a go waanti.* ('He soon need it.')
(Lesson One)

I shall now examine the notion I have been discussing of consent in classrooms, thinking about some of the ways in which teachers get classrooms to work. Where there is joint accommodation to the project to be accomplished, I am suggesting that a specific language act such as codeswitching is one of the means by which this is achieved. I am also suggesting that we look more closely at the function of codeswitching and other forms of language behaviour as they appear in the classroom. The motivations we unearth might help us understand more clearly how specific language choices serve to impede or clarify the discourse necessary for bilingual and multilingual classrooms.

Markers of Agreement

The use of language in these specific ways I have termed "markers of agreement", and I would consider codeswitching and translating to be two such markers of agreement. They refer to the kind of accommodation practised in the classroom, the ways of speaking and interacting. It refers to those communications where the language of the student and that of the teacher are used to foster consent about the kind of practice that takes place in schools, the kind of practice that helps the child, in some cases, to "learn school". Drawing on the insights of Brice Heath (1983), the concept of "learning school" is part of that cluster of notions relating to consent, and it is one that is becoming familiar to educational ethnographers who examine the contention that schools and classrooms are cultures into which children must be initiated (Bryan 1996). Foster (1992) reviews some of the research literature in this area of culture and education. She focuses on the interactional style of Black teachers, which she sees as an important factor in mediating classroom discourse for African American children. She notes how these teachers can help to link the classroom discourse with communication patterns that are familiar to the students. Callender's research in England (1997) takes this further, suggesting that the style of the interaction might be something which is particular to Black talk. Her review of the literature on Black communication style points to the significance of the call–response patterns she observed in British classrooms. She cites Smitherman's co-signing and repetition as two examples of African-derived communication patterns available to Black teachers. Smitherman outlines five specific call–response patterns: co-signing (agreeing with the speaker), encouraging (urging the speaker to continue), repetition (using the same words as the speaker), completer (completing the speaker's statement), on T (emphatic agreement to an apt contribution).

I am suggesting that the notion of "markers of agreement" can be aligned to the idea of a Black communication style and some of these instances are introduced above, as they relate to Jamaican classrooms. For example, co-signing, which confirms or endorses a speaker's view, is found in the teacher's response to students as she translates:

4. S2: *Wisl bluo Mis.*
5. T1: *blowing of a whistle.*

There is also an example of repetition in Lesson Two:

20. T2:   *It's a figurative saying. It's not literal. It means something else. Can you give me an example?*

I would suggest that the following:

13. T1:   *Huol aan!* ('Hold on!'/'Wait a minute!')

and the attendant pause to cool the fervour of the lesson is an on T response, indicating that the respondents are completely in line with the appropriate response. These examples of language behaviour, however, now need more detailed analysis as to their operation in the classroom, especially the language classroom.

Teachers' Language

The first markers of agreement, linguistic means of working towards consent, can be seen in the teacher's language. In translating, she is reproducing an utterance in English for those who might have difficulty with the target language rather than the source language, going against the spirit of a typical translation, according to Malakoff and Hakuta. When she switches to Creole, we are reminded that for many teachers, too, English is a second language and one which is used solely on public occasions. The teachers are more comfortable in Creole, a language they share with the students, and are therefore able to understand some of the problems the students face. It is the main, underlying connection between the students and the teachers. The teacher in Lesson One shows that she understands, accepts and can handle Creole. Reference has already been made to recent literature about how bilingual teachers, who know the child's mother tongue, can help the child to "learn school" (Davis and Golden 1994). Joint patterns of communication and joint understandings about language help the child to accommodate to the culture of the classroom.

Because she can and does use the vernacular language and can perhaps call on a Black communication style, the teacher's maintenance of, and support for English within the classroom, takes on a different tone. She is indicating something about how important she sees English within the classroom, as the official language of the school. She is also presenting what she sees as a model for her students to emulate. Her classroom language, the structures she offers as models, can be seen as recognition that the students need to be inducted into alternative ways of speaking, rather than a better way. The role of English is clear and limited, relegated to the specific purposes which it is possible for them to achieve.

In accepting the students' language and carrying out the translating, the teachers are also structuring the discourse to increase consent and help in the acquisition of a second language. In noting how the teachers translated for the children, I am reminded of Davis and Golden's (1994) observation of how bilingual teachers in Afro-American communities use the language they have in common with the children, not just to engage them, but to move them into the second language, English. Here is recognition that the language learner has to be helped by moving him or her from the known to the unknown. This strategy was particularly evident in the lesson on proverbs (Lesson Two). The topic is a familiar one and, as a linguistic artefact, is part of the oral culture of the children. In this lesson the teacher moved away from the well-known idea of biblical proverbs, "wise sayings", to Jamaican proverbs such as *Kyaang kech Kwaku, yu kech im shut* to *A gunman gets an opportunity to go to foreign to study. He turns it down. A week later he get shoot and die*. The facility in moving between two languages is an important part of this mutual engagement, this initiation into the culture of the school.

Students' Language

With the students' use of language, we see the response to markers of agreement and how they worked with them. Much of this is not explicit, but the interaction reveals how the classroom is working on that joint project. They used Creole among themselves, spontaneously and unselfconsciously. And the teachers made no attempt to change that. However, in the formal public discourse, they often attempted to use the acrolect, but, if they were unsuccessful, the teacher translated for them. So several different kinds of language were operating in the classrooms at the same time but in different ways. The students often indicated their awareness of English as an appropriate language. When it was being attempted by one of their peers, they derisively marked unsuccessful efforts with laughter, for example,

37. S9: ... *A week later he get shoot and die.*

Superficially, this might seem a harsh response, but the tone as witnessed in other classes, was always mocking, as though they were sharing an ill-fitting garment, occasionally worn but easily discarded. It can be seen as laughing at the practice as much as laughing at the speaker. They were demonstrating their lack of concern about their lack of English, as, for them, the language served no purpose but to answer teacher's questions. Significantly, the teacher did not try to translate such an utterance. It is possible that she, unlike the students, did not notice the error, indicating her own limited competence. However, it is much more likely that she did not believe that it warranted an intervention. She would only translate complete Creole contributions, perhaps concluding that other contributions were attempts at English that should not be over-corrected.

In one class, "The Blow" (Lesson One), the students mimicked the teacher's English and she laughed with them, because she was acknowledging the contradictions of the project called "learning English". The students accepted the preoccupation with English and the teacher accepted that some students did not or could not produce it. It is this assumption which allowed the task to be seen as a shared venture, disentangled from notions of individual failure. There seemed to be an atmosphere of trust, of going along with the teacher's project and giving her priorities the benefit of the doubt. Such is the nature of the consent.

The classroom interaction could be seen on one level as being quite unsophisticated, with a lot of teacher questions that were knowledge-focused rather than expressive.

16. T2: *We're going to do proverbs. Have you heard the word before?*
17. S1: *In the Bible, Miss.*
18. T2: *What does it mean?*
19. S2: *A wise saying.*
20. T2: *It's a figurative saying. It's not literal. It means something else. Can you give me an example?*

Certainly the first three turns suggest what Cazden (1988) called the teacher's "unmarked" discourse structure in the classroom initiation/response/evaluation (IRE). The teacher asks a question, gets an answer, then comments, sometimes implicitly, before nominating another speaker. However, this would be a very superficial reading of these two lessons. In both instances, the responses are much more symmetrical, with as much student response as teacher participation. Teachers and students have been schooled in the same cultural practices, using a common discourse. They can move along together in their understanding and the students demonstrate that they have a lot to contribute. The use of indigenous content is also relevant here, with the use of proverbs in one instance and the recognizable moral tale of the gambler in another. All of the participants, as churchgoers, would know the proverbs of the Bible, as well as the common examples from Jamaican folklore.

The culture of the church is evident in these communications and this is underscored by the use of questions as a motivational tool. Callender (1997) also confirms the contribution of the church to an African-derived Black communication style found in diaspora communities. The inspirational tone is clearly a favoured interpretation of the style, as can be seen in the rhythm of both classes. In Lesson Two (on proverbs) the interaction ricochets back and forth, with questions, answers and counter-answers Many children want to "testify" to the extent that in the remedial class the teacher has to cool their fervour with a break, and then later in the lesson she clasps the hands of those in front of her to her bosom, in joy at their contribution. This is highly interactive teaching.

Lesson Three: A London Classroom

To underscore the point about how codeswitching and other language choices serve as markers of agreement, I am now going back to look at the use of JC in a related, yet distant classroom in urban London. Teachers here who teach children from a Jamaican Creole background were asked the same question about their aim in teaching English, the methods they used and influences to which they were subject. A section of an observation made subsequently, reveals how JC is used.

Due Respect

The Lesson

This is a Grade Eight class, embarking on some silent reading with a Caucasian class teacher and an Indian support teacher brought in as bilingual support. The school refers in its brochures to dealing with children from forty different language backgrounds. In this class, apart from the English-speaking Londoners, there are children from many different countries, including Portugal, Eritrea, Vietnam and Jamaica, to name a few.

The reading class is becoming very restless. There are two Black male students (S1 and S2) sitting with a Vietnamese boy (S3) nearby.

38.	S1:	*See Rockers on Channel Four last night?*
39.	S2:	*Oh yea, dat woz rof.*
40.	S1:	*I can't do this, sir. Can I do it for homework?*
41.	S2:	*I don't like this rubbish.*

The Indian teacher is a Hindi speaker and the fact that he speaks English as a foreign language is slightly evident in his pronunciation. He attempts to take charge of the class by sending out all three boys. The Vietnamese boy gets very upset and says:

42.	S3	*He's mad yanuo. He have a mashop eye. He duon even know English.*

One of the Black boys (S2) points to the other (S1). He says:

43.	S2	*Shut up styar! Taak tu im styar, not just me.*

The lead teacher and the rest of the class pay little attention as the Indian teacher marches them out.

There is now an increasing body of literature which might throw some light on the language behaviour observed in this classroom. For example, research by Rosen and Burgess (1980) described JC's interaction with scores of other languages in London, including the local variety of English. They referred to this new variety as London Jamaican (LJ). Hewitt (1986) showed its appropriation by Caucasian adolescents as the way in which the language was used to negotiate interracial friendships.

Focusing on the West Midlands, Sutcliffe (1992) referred to the same variety as British Jamaican Creole (BJC), and noted how far it had moved from rural Jamaican speech. The results of JC's migration to England were confirmed in Sebba's (1993) description of the structure of LJ. He saw LJ as a language of identity, acquired in adolescence, and used for codeswitching, usually with family and friends, "chatting patois". In Rampton (1995), JC was only one of the languages that adolescents use to connote difference. Rampton took further the work of Hewitt and explored, in the British Midlands, the complexities of "crossing" for adolescents of Indian and Pakistani descent who interacted with children of English and Caribbean backgrounds. Codecrossing, as Rampton puts it, is within the domain of metaphorical switching and involves "the use of language varieties associated with social or ethnic groups that the speaker does not normally 'belong to'" (Rampton 1995: 14). Language choice is ascribed a much more significant ideological load than the one given by Malakoff and Hakuta. It is seen as presenting a view of linguistic identity as "socially defined and interactionally negotiated" (Rampton 1995: 339).

These authors' contributions mark the beginning of work towards exploring Creole continuities outside Jamaica. My own observation, recorded above, recognizes this work, but in entering the classroom, I seek to reflect further on the significance of "markers of agreement". It is to make the point that culture and context determine how the language is to be used; when JC is transported to the London classroom, something quite different from what transpired in the Jamaican classroom is enacted. Where teacher and students do not share the language, the boys adopt the "Jamaican" talk as a way of exhibiting bad behaviour.

43. S2:   *Shut up styar! Taak tu im styar, not just me.*

This is a good example of London Jamaican codeswitching discussed earlier in Sebba's (1994) work and the use of the lexical item *styar* gives the flavour rather than the substance of the language. In this case the item is an old one, rarely used, which underscores the linguistic load that this one word is carrying in this interaction. In this example it is used by a Black boy who may or may not be from Jamaica. Hewitt (1986) had warned us that the speaker's actual country of origin did not matter, as LJ was common property by an adolescent's language. Rampton's youths could cross also from one variety to another, irrespective of race. What was surprising, in this instance, was the behaviour of boys from ethnic backgrounds other than the Caribbean, in this case, S3, a refugee from Southeast Asia, whom we shall call Chen.

42. S3:   *He's mad yanuo. He have a mashop eye. He duon even know English.*

Chen's choice of language here is a particularly apposite example of the argument being developed here about markers of agreement. It could be seen as an inversion of Kachru's codemixing. By the insertion of linguistic items to accommodate to what he defines as power and authority, Chen understands that he is operating in a culture, the discourse of which he has had to learn. He knows which kind of language, which practices will allow him to communicate the self he has internalized from the actions around him. Within Rampton's discussion of code alteration, this utterance might be seen as a form of codecrossing, carrying the symbolic resonance of the disjuncture between speaker and voice.

He expresses his difference through appropriation of ways of speaking meant to connote defiance. Language is the weapon used to exclude the teacher and show him or her lack of respect. The encounter is made all the more ironic because it is an Indian teacher, another migrant, who is involved. And one of Chen's charges, in LJ, is that the Indian teacher does not know English. Something is radically wrong and it is not a simple language deficit. What is clear is that there was no specific discourse acknowledged as appropriate for the teacher–student interaction, no accepted markers of agreement. What in the Jamaican classroom was the language used to foster consent and a common identity had become part of a Black oppositional style, used to disturb accepted meanings.

Concluding Remarks

The observation of the London classroom shows that the differences in context exposed notable differences in the responses to Jamaican Creole. The markers of agreement had been inverted in the London setting, to illustrate the importance of context in reading their significance. So, even though it is crucial to understand the language, the focus has to be on the different meanings languages can carry, meanings which are forged through political and cultural processes such as migration. It follows, therefore, that the focus on language in the classroom also has to be about how a language becomes significant in terms of its history and origins, and its meaning potential to its users. This naturally leads to a consideration of its social and cultural significance, its status to its users and factors leading to variation in style. More important are its relations of power (hegemony) with other languages in the community, which in this case would be English. The implications are for language classrooms that require richer and deeper understandings of language as historically and socially constructed.

I am also saying that such understandings about language are conveyed in the classroom by explicit and implicit markers of agreement in the discourse of classroom communication. These kinds of understandings might come from the fact that teachers and students speak the same language and share a voice. They are therefore able to engage at many different levels: sharing personal experience about such things as the value of the language, its use in different settings and its cultural forms. Such commonality is not always possible, but just as important as sharing the same language is the possibility and the need for the children and the teachers to share understandings about language use. Included in this would be the understanding of the differences between the language of the school and the language of the home, the varieties available, the personal meaning a particular language variety might have and, most importantly, the language's community value. Such insights apply to Creole as much as any other language to be acquired. These understandings of the possibilities of bilingualism help to create the context or conditions for children to learn school.

References

Blom, J., and J. Gumperz. 1972. Social meaning in structure: Code-switching in Norway. In *Directions in Sociolinguistics,* edited by J. Gumperz and D. Hymes. New York: Holt, Rinehart and Winston.

Bryan, B. 1996. Learning school: Cross-cultural differences in the teaching of English. *Changing English* 3, no. 2.

Callender, C. 1997. *Education for Empowerment: The Practice and Philosophies of Black Teachers.* Stoke-on-Trent: Trentham Books.
Cazden, C. 1988. *Classroom Discourse.* Portsmouth, NH: Heinemann.
Chambers, I. 1994. *Migrancy, Culture and Identity.* New York: Routledge.
Davis, K., and Golden J. 1994. Teacher culture and children's voices in an urban kindergarten. *Linguistics and Education* 6.
Foster, M. 1992. Sociolinguistics and the African American community: Implications for literacy. *Theory and Practice* 31, no. 4.
Gumperz, J., ed. 1982. *Discourse Strategies.* Cambridge: Cambridge University Press.
Heath, S.B. 1983. *Ways with Words: Language, Life and Work in Communities and Classrooms.* New York: Cambridge University Press.
Hewitt, R. 1986. *White Talk, Black Talk: Inter-racial Friendship and Communication among Adolescents.* Cambridge: Cambridge University Press.
Kachru, B. 1978. Code-mixing as a communicative strategy in India. In *International Dimensions of Bilingual Education,* edited by J. Alatis. Washington, DC: Georgetown University Press.
Le Page, R., and A. Tabouret-Keller. 1985. *Acts of Identity.* Cambridge: Cambridge University Press.
Malakoff, M., and K. Hakuta. 1991. Translation and metalinguistic awareness. In *Language Processing in Bilingual Children,* edited by E. Bialystock. Cambridge: Cambridge University Press.
Myers-Scotton, C. 1993. *Social Motivations for Codeswitching: Evidence from Africa.* Oxford: Oxford University Press.
Pollard, V. 1978. Codeswitching in Jamaican Creole: Some educational implications. *Caribbean Journal of Education* 5, nos. 1 and 2.
Rampton, B. 1995. *Crossing: Language and Ethnicity among Adolescents.* London: Longman.
Rosen, H., and T. Burgess. 1980. *Language and Dialects of London School Children.* London: Ward, Lock Educational.
Sebba, M. 1993. *London Jamaican.* London: Longman.
Shields, K. 1987. Language variation in the classroom. PhD diss., University of the West Indies.
———. 1989. Standard English in Jamaica: A case of competing models. *English World-Wide* 10, no. 1.
Smitherman, G. 1977. *Talkin' and Testifyin': The Language of Black America.* Boston: Houghton Mifflin.
Sutcliffe, D. 1992. *System in Black Language.* Clevedon: Multilingual Matters.

Chapter 5

"A Singular Subject Takes a Singular Verb" and Hypercorrection in Jamaican Speech and Writing

Velma Pollard

Winford, writing about language use in the Anglophone Caribbean, provides a suitable starting point for any discussion of hypercorrection in that context, when he says:

> ... the majority of the population, whose native language is some form of Creole, typically have only limited command of SE, and in many cases limited opportunity or motivation to use it. Particular situations may demand that speakers shift their speech in the direction of SE, but the nature and extent of such shifting varies considerably according to the social background of the speakers. (1994: 44)

The attempt of the Creole speaker who is not bilingual, to make the shift to which Winford refers, is fraught with difficulties in direct proportion to her or his exposure to English. What results includes, in most instances, hypercorrection. Crystal (1980: 176) says that linguists use the term to refer to "movement of a linguistic *form* beyond the point set by the variety of *language* that the speaker has as his target", that the speaker goes "too far" and produces a variety which "does not appear in the standard" (1980: 176). Patrick and McElhinny (1993: 4) describe linguistic hypercorrection in Jamaica within a sociolinguistic framework and focus on phonological adjustments considered prestigious. They define as "qualitative hypercorrection", what happens when "a prestigious sound occurs in places where standard speakers would not natively use it". Patrick (1997: 45) adopts the folk label Speaky-Spoky to describe a type of qualitative hypercorrection occurring when "non-elite speakers generalize prestigious linguistic forms to inappropriate environments, producing utterances which the grammar of the elite would not generate".

Hypercorrection is, of course, a common feature of second language learning (see, for example, Preston 1989: 116; Ellis 1994: 205). Given the fact that English, the prestige language, is a second language for many speakers in the Commonwealth Caribbean, the high incidence of hypercorrection in their speech is not surprising

Unlike Patrick and McEhinny's study, this chapter does not address phonological hypercorrection. It treats grammatical hypercorrection, the overgeneralization of a syntactic or a morphosyntactic rule. Isolated for special attention is the present tense singular of the English verb and its representation by Creole speakers offering their best English. In a society where Jamaican Creole is the language of the street and, frequently, of the home, the classroom is sometimes the only place where children hear English more or less consistently. School is the place where parents expect their children to learn English, the language which will allow them to function effectively in prestigious situations. But much of the teaching of English in Jamaican schools has been, and continues to be, teaching *about* English, and it fails, as a result, to achieve the expected results. Even today the learner is asked to memorize a significant number of rules of English grammar, for example. The emphasis placed on language in use in teacher-training institutions is not always maintained in the teaching situation. Outside of institutional support, teachers tend to revert to classroom practices they remember from the classrooms of their youth. English is remembered as a collection of rules. The rules, as they are taught, are frequently misleading, especially those which have to do with the English verb. This chapter contends that both the partial understanding of the way the English verb functions and the differences between it and the Creole verb, are largely responsible for the selection of inappropriate verb forms in school compositions and later in situations perceived to be prestigious.

The form of the English verb in the present tense varies only in one instance: when its subject is a third-person singular noun or pronoun. In the present tense, therefore, the English verb is often identical in form with the invariable Creole verb. It is the third-person singular, the locus of the contrast in form, which confuses the Creole-speaking learner. However, the fact that most reporting is about a third person (Peter, Mary, Mother, Father, he, she, it, etc.) makes for a certain frequency of use. The same error gets repeated over and over. The form of the third-person singular becomes a feature that distinguishes English from Creole in the minds of learners. Some teachers themselves are not clear about the forms of the English verb and do not understand, either, how the Creole verb functions. In fact, in spite of half a century of research and of workshops in schools and teachers' colleges, there are still today teachers, along with other opinion makers in the society, who describe Jamaican Creole as broken English and reject the notion of Creole grammar.[1] Any teaching strategy which involves a comparison of the verb forms of English and Creole, therefore, can only be as successful as are the efforts to change this opinion and to point them towards addressing analyses of the grammar of the two languages of the society in a serious way.

For the Creole speaker with limited knowledge of English, the form of the verb that contrasts with what is perceived as Creole becomes a prime agent for moving an utterance from Creole to what the user considers to be English. The popular ways of stating the relevant rule in school serve to confuse more than to clarify the issue. It is either said that a singular subject takes a singular verb or that subject and verb must "agree". The teacher who was confused by her or his teachers continues to confuse his or her own students as this "rule" is taught faithfully and unquestioningly in schools across Jamaica, from the earliest contact in the elementary school to the latest contact at the university. *Caribbean Junior English* 3 (1983: 69), for example, quotes the rule and gives the following examples:

> The boy plays football every Sunday.
> The boys play football every Sunday.

If the young learner should wish to extrapolate from such examples and personalize the sentence, she or he will surely feel that "I plays football every Sunday" is acceptable. On the same page of that text, there are complementary lists under the headings "Singular" and "Plural". The lists include "does/do" with no explanation for the thus anomalous "I do".

Rediscover Grammar with David Crystal (1988: 76) states: "The present tense uses the base form of the verb which changes only in the third person singular where there is an 's' ending." This is a version which makes sense as long as students have already grasped the concepts of number and person.

In some primary school classrooms in Jamaica today, roundabout explanations are put forward to allow singularity to reside in an "s", sometimes realized as a piece of cardboard of that shape shifted as the number of the conditioning noun or pronoun changes, and referred to as the "moveable 's'". An additional rule that has evolved is that the noun forms its plural by adding "an 's'" while the verb forms it by removing one. This latter sounds nicely balanced, but the question might well be asked: "Remove it from where?" If one begins with the first-person singular, there is no "s" to remove. To avoid confusing the student, the teacher needs to maintain a steady view of the grammatical position he or she is describing.

Teaching the present tense verbs in terms of "agreement" might be partly responsible for the extent of hypercorrection evident in the scripts written by Creole-speaking children and in the delivery of adult Creole speakers who wish to be considered to be speaking Standard English. In any event, overgeneralization, extending the "s" ending (which one expects for the third-person singular only) to inappropriate contexts, has become a mark of "English" to such an extent that artists exploit it in casting Jamaican characters whose linguistic ineptness they wish to underline. Louise Bennett, for example, a Jamaican poet who writes exclusively in Creole, has the ardent suitor in "Love Letta" (Bennett 1966: 201) write:

> Me Sweety Sue, I goes for you
> Like how flies goes for sugar.

In another poem (Bennett 1982: 68), she makes the female speaker at a wedding, a situation construed to require prestigious language, introduce her toast in the following way:

> Let I takes in hand wine glasses
> Let I fill it to the tip.

The title of the poem is "Speechify", one of the terms used to describe this kind of talk, And, in a real-life situation, a woman responding to the question "How many children do you have?" easily responds, "I has five of them."

While there are no statistics to support this claim, it is probably true that in the Creole-speaking environment, the form of the English verb with "s" is most called upon to indicate that a speaker intends to use English. It easily separates itself from Creole, since the Creole and the base form of the English verb are similar. Compare the following:

mi liv ya (Creole)
ai liv hier (English)
ai livz hier (hypercorrected form)

The speaker perceives the third of those utterances to mark her or him as one who has the ability to use an "other" and "higher" code in a stratified society where language (like clothes) indicates one's social status.

The society expects schooling to make a difference. The individual is expected to leave school with competence in speaking and writing English. Overgeneralization of the "s" form, however, continues to account for a large percentage of students' grammatical errors in primary school compositions, and persists sometimes after five years of secondary schooling. Since the error finds such strong reinforcement in community speech, teachers need to identify strategies to help students recognize it and make a conscious effort to eliminate it.

In remedial lessons in the secondary school, the first step might be to explain to students why the rule they have been taught ("a singular subject takes a singular verb"), when carefully applied, yields incorrect sentences. Students at that level are likely to have been in contact with another language, Spanish, for example. For their benefit, the teacher might contrast Spanish, in which the verb form changes whenever person changes, with English, where the form of the verb is nearly always the same.

At the primary level, the careful elicitation from the class of sentences which illustrate the present tense use of the verb, and the visual representation of those sentences on the blackboard, will help to underline the accurate usage. The elicited paragraph may read:

I *hate* milk. All the children in my class *hate* it.
We blow bubbles with it when nobody big is around.

Due Respect

Similarly, sentences in which the verb does change may be elicited as in the following:

> My sister's house *looks* very large to me.
> My nephew John *lives* like a king.
> He *sleeps* in a big bed in a large room. (Pollard 1993: 24)

Evelyn Beyer's poem, which follows, provides a fine contrast between the singular "I walk" and a variety of plurals, and it is a poem which young children find easy to memorize. There are other, more sophisticated, poems which can be used to illustrate the same point at more advanced levels. What is necessary is the will of the teacher to search for and find material for use in this enterprise.

> Jump or jiggle
> Frogs jump
> Caterpillars hump
> Worms wiggle
> Bugs jiggle
> Rabbits hop
> Horses clop
> Snakes slide
> Seagulls glide
> Mice creep
> Deer leap
> Puppies bounce
> Kittens pounce
> Lions stalk
>   But –
> I walk.

Poetry and prose passages are great allies in consolidating the work the teacher does towards greater accuracy in speaking and writing English. In fact the prescribed comprehension text is a ready and accessible resource. Some teachers still separate the comprehension exercise from the writing exercise and so miss the support the one can provide for the other. Perhaps teachers see the arrangement of the comprehension text as compelling and are unwilling to use the book creatively. Teachers would do well to list several passages and poems illustrating the same point in a teacher's note-book to be called upon as the need, identified in pupils' compositions, arises. Students will eventually be able to derive the rule, in their own words, from extensive observation of the language in use. They may then regard, as a polished rendition, Crystal's version quoted earlier: "The present tense uses the base form of the verb which changes only in the third person singular, where there is an 's' ending."

Second only to the third-person singular as a grammatical indicator of "English" in the repertoire of the Creole speaker is the past tense of the verb. Here is another instance where the English verb is sufficiently different from the base form to ensure that it cannot be mistaken for a Creole verb. Note the following exchanges between an English speaker (ES) and a Creole speaker (CS):

1. ES: *I have no water today.*
   CS: *I had. You can bring a bucket to get some this evening.*
2. ES: *Do you have any soursops?*
   CS: *Yes I had.*
        (ES, a prospective buyer, begins to walk away but looks back in time to see CS, the salesman, uncovering a table full of soursops.)

Note also the following utterances:

3. The nurses say they have something to *told* me. (Young mother at Jubilee hospital to a newspaper reporter)
4. I am to *wrote* everything from the board? (Grade Six pupil questioning teacher)

It is clear that the English verb, wherever it is identical in form with the Creole verb, runs the risk of not being considered English by the Creole speaker. The perception of what differentiates English from Creole seems to be part of the problem.[2]

As the call for the return of "grammar" to the teaching of English is renewed under pressure from teachers reaching for answers to the frustration they experience with poorly written English and failure at examinations, attention needs to be paid to details such as those mentioned earlier with regard to the third-person singular. Grammar never really left the Jamaican classroom even when teachers were being instructed in the use of more communicative methods of language teaching. At this time, however, teachers are openly insisting on it and researchers in language acquisition are revisiting the question of its treatment in the classroom. These two groups are not necessarily advocating the same methods.

The question of how best to present information about grammar must become a major concern, particularly of teacher trainers. Its presentation, usually through illogical rules, has embarrassed teachers and misinformed pupils over many decades. Unfortunately, in the Jamaican situation the children who try to use these rules to decide on their verb forms are usually the monolingual Creole speakers, children who can least afford to be confused, since there is no reinforcement for English in their home environment. Teachers with no idea of what else they might do place strong emphasis on rules in remedial English classes. Those children who speak English at home and those who are bilingual (English and Creole) may learn the rule by rote, but when they come to write tend to be informed, not by the rule, but by the sound of the word as they remember it, and write down what sounds right.

It is time to examine the English grammar that is being taught and, if necessary, rewrite the rules in less ambiguous terms so that the cause of accuracy may be effectively served. Within the last two decades, the place of grammar in the teaching of English has been the subject of considerable debate in the international community, particularly with regard to Second Language Acquisition (SLA).

Fotos was able to refer to several sources when she made the following comment: "A compelling body of evidence has accumulated recently supporting the position that formal instruction on language properties is related to the subsequent acquisition of those properties" (Fotos 1994: 323).

The resurgence of the case for grammar in the international community has been largely a response to the wave of enthusiasm for communicative language teaching (CLT), which had great currency during the decade of the 1970s. Celce-Murcia and colleagues see this resurgence as part of the "natural process of cyclical development" which L2 teaching approaches tend to undergo, each method evolving after the acceptance, application and eventual criticism of an earlier method (Celce-Murcia et al. 1997: 142). The criticisms, however, have not been without supporting evidence. Some of the best programmes in which CLT has been used have produced students who continue to write ungrammatical English after many years in the classroom. Williams mentions studies done on students in Canadian immersion programmes in which students make "impressive strides" in their language development but continue to make errors in morphology and syntax (Williams 1995: 13).

Commenting more generally on the use of CLT methods with their "emphasis on fluency and communicative success", Williams singles out gender assignment in French and the third-person singular in English as involving forms learners do not learn because they do not need them in order to communicate successfully in class. She also mentions the third-person singular as one of the forms that have been most resistant to teaching (15). The difference between the traditional way of teaching grammar, which fell into disfavour, and what is suggested within the literature now is that the latter allows formal instruction to be merged creatively with communicative language teaching.

Fotos, quoted earlier, describes the situation in this way: "In response to empirical findings which indicate that a return to some type of formal instruction may be necessary after all, several lines of research have recently emerged which are exploring ways to integrate instruction on problematic grammar forms within a communicative framework" (Fotos 1994: 323). Current literature on SLA has a great deal of information to offer the interested teacher. What grammar, how much and by what means will, however, still depend on the teacher's judgement and on her or his classroom research on particular student populations. In the case of Jamaica and other countries where the L1 of the majority of the students is a Creole language, especially where it is an English-related Creole, there are additional considerations, the chief of which might be the place of descriptions of the L1 in the teaching of English. The international community of researchers into Second Language Acquisition does not serve these countries in this regard, because the L1s with which they interact are languages with long scribal traditions, languages whose descriptions have been refined over many centuries. Simple descriptions of Jamaican Creole will have to be part of the packet offered Jamaican teachers in training, with notes on how these may be used alongside some of the more modern grammars of English.

The suggestions made earlier in this chapter are not meant to be exhaustive but to indicate the directions the classroom teacher might take. Grammatical hypercorrection will not disappear, but considerable inroads may be made towards the reduction of its use if school leavers are able to use the English present tense verb accurately and are clear about the use and meaning of the past tense forms in English.

Notes

1. As recently as September 1999, Chester Burgess, honorary director of the Jamaica Chamber of Commerce, writing in the nation's premier newspaper, had this to say: "The claim for having a grammar collapses in the light of day-to-day experience of Patois users knowing or showing little respect for number, person, case, or even gender."
2. Peter Roberts (1976: 12) seems to support this suggestion. He states: "A general tendency . . . is apparent and it is that the socially insecure (and aggressive) speaker tends to think that what he says normally . . . is not SE. In his attempts to produce SE therefore he deliberately changes to something else. The general rule is therefore that the nonnormal form is correct or SE."

References

Bennett L. 1966. *Jamaica Labrish*. Kingston: Sangster's Book Stores.

———. 1982. *Selected Poems*. Kingston: Sangster's Book Stores.

Burgess, C. 1999. Slave talk, Patois, Yahoolish, English. *Gleaner*, September 11.

Celce-Murcia, M., et al. 1997. Direct approaches in L2 instruction: A turning point in Communicative Language Teaching. *TESOL Quarterly* 31, no. 1.

Crystal, D. 1980. *A First Dictionary of Linguistics and Phonetics*. Boulder, CO: Westview Press.

———. 1988. *Rediscover Grammar with David Crystal*. Harlow: Longmans.

Ellis, R. 1994. *The Study of Second Language Acquisition*. Oxford: Oxford University Press.

Fotos, S. 1994. Integrating grammar instruction and communicative language use through grammar consciousness-raising tasks. *TESOL Quarterly* 28, no. 2.

Patrick, P. 1997. Style and register in Jamaican Patwa. In *Englishes around the World* 2, edited by E. Schneider. Amsterdam and Philadelphia: John Benjamins.

Patrick, P., and B. McElhinny. 1993. Speakin' and spokin' in Jamaica: Conflict and consensus in sociolinguistics. In *Proceedings of the Nineteenth Annual Meeting, Berkeley Linguistics Society*, edited by J. Guenter et al. Berkeley, CA: Berkeley Linguistics Society.

Pollard, V. 1987. Past time expression in Jamaican Creole. PhD diss., University of the West Indies.

———. 1993. *From Jamaican Creole to Standard English*. Medgar Evers College, Brooklyn: Caribbean Research Center.

Preston, D.R. 1989. *Sociolinguistics and Second Language Acquisition*. Oxford and Cambridge, MA: Basil Blackwell.

Richards, H. 1983. *Caribbean Junior English* 3. Revised with P. Mordecai and G.W. Gordon. Aylesbury: Ginn.

Roberts, P. 1976. Hypercorrection as systematic variation. Paper presented at first Conference of the Society for Caribbean Linguistics, University of Guyana, Turkeyen.

Williams, J. 1995. Focus on form in Communicative Language Teaching: Research findings and the classroom teacher. *TESOL Journal,* Summer.

Winford, D. 1994. Approaches to language use in the Anglophone Caribbean. In *Language and the Social Construction of Identity in Creole Situations*, edited by M. Morgan. Los Angeles, CA: Center for AfroAmerican Studies Publications.

Chapter 6

English in the English-Speaking Caribbean: Questions in the Academy

Monica Taylor

English language educators throughout the Caribbean, like their counterparts elsewhere, face the challenge of re-examining the assumptions underlying the existing notions of correctness and legitimacy. They must come to terms with fundamental questions relating to the ownership of English and the locus and legitimacy of the standards which define Standard English in any given time and place.

This chapter explores these and other sociopolitical aspects of English language education in the region, highlighting the danger of linguistic schizophrenia faced by the Caribbean educator attempting to establish a synergy between (socio)linguistic theory and classroom practice.

One of the most engaging debates concerning the teaching of Standard English since the 1980s has centred on the question of defining its boundaries. The debate has been most vigorous in the British educational system, as illustrated by, for example, Davidson (1994), McArthur (1994) and Crystal (1996). This has been of great interest to the Caribbean observer, for uninformed lay person and trained language educator alike have lamented the "decline of English" in the Caribbean and insisted on a return to "good", "proper", "correct" or "standard" English, always implying that this target was a palpable, safely preserved entity in the Mother Country against which one could check the local varieties for accuracy and "purity" whenever there were doubts. The debate has often been muddied by a failure to separate the issue of the strategic importance of English from the more technical questions concerning the locus of definition, ownership and legitimacy.

Concerning the importance of English, there is no dispute. Every generation has attested to the importance of this language that has rapidly spread across the world and assumed cultural and economic significance. Scholars such as Leathes (1913) and later Swales (1993) attest to the global imperative to be fully literate in English. While there is no controversy about the importance of English as an international lingua franca, the same cannot be said about the more thorny matters which English language educators must resolve from time to time in their professional lives.

The first of these thorny matters is the fundamental question of the ownership of English. Indeed, if people in the Caribbean are not perceived to own the English they speak and write, it is impossible for the educator to proceed as she or he ought, using the important notions of appropriateness and context. Braj B. Kachru (1991) speaks eloquently of the need to recognize the "'pluricentricity' and multi-identities of English", with its more than 700 million users across the globe. No longer can England be reasonably regarded as the centre of English, since a complex matrix of pluricentric Englishes is a more accurate representation of reality (Kachru 1988). This pluricentricity of English has also been acknowledged by some modern lexicographers, for example, those responsible for the *Encarta World English Dictionary* (1999). Tom McArthur, writing in the introductory pages of this dictionary, asserts that, "inasmuch as a language belongs to any individual or community, English is the possession of every individual or community that wishes to use it, wherever they are in the world . . ." (p. xxxii). In this spirit, the *Encarta* purports to be "the first dictionary to be able to reflect the new world status of English, bringing together all the main varieties in the language from the United States, Canada, Britain, Australia, New Zealand, Africa, Asia, the Caribbean, and the Pacific rim" (p. xi). But even as we acknowledge the pluricentricity of English, the notion of international intelligibility should be preserved.

Notwithstanding the fact that English has been in the Caribbean for more than three hundred years, many still balk at the notion of the Caribbean as a legitimate centre of English. The co-existence of an English-lexicon Creole alongside English in territories such as Jamaica has made it very difficult for many persons to argue lucidly about the status of English in the Caribbean. Ignorance and the natural trappings of social judgement typically collapse the language continuum toward its middle, leading to a lament that something called "broken English" is what remains of English in this part of the world. Some proponents of this view reject in principle the notion that there could be any centre of correctness other than Britain itself.

This is the position taken by some African scholars who, in many respects, face the same English language dilemma that confronts the Caribbean. Taking an approach that is entirely different from Braj Kachru's, a Ghanaian linguist, Ahulu (1994), confronts the issue with respect to English in Ghana and rejects the notion of a distinctive Ghanaian English. Using examples from English usage in India and Ghana, he proposes instead that various postcolonial countries share the same nonstandard usages. He proposes one Standard English or a notion of correctness that is common to all users of English. However, when one considers the living, responsive nature of language in society, the vast physical and cultural distances separating the 700 million users of English around the world, one is forced to leave in the realm of myth any such notion of a world Standard English purportedly "acting as a strongly unifying force among the vast range of variation which exists" (Crystal 1996: 14). The issue here goes far deeper than whether people say that British Standard English (whatever that is) is their yardstick.

But what exactly is Standard English? McArthur (1994: 12), discussing the English language dilemma in the British context, raises this intriguing question: "How do aspirants to Standard English know if they have truly got there?" An examination of some typical definitions will highlight a number of contextual considerations:

> [Standard English is] the variety of the English language which is normally employed in writing and normally spoken by "educated" speakers of the language . . . It refers to grammar and vocabulary but not pronunciation. (Trudgill and Hannah 1994: 1)

> [Standard English is] widely regarded as the speech and writing of the "well educated". But those who believe this often place geographical limits on just who the "well educated" are. Very traditionally minded people use a regional limit: well educated people in southeast England. Milder traditionalists have a national limit: people anywhere in Britain. Progressives and pragmatists tend to be expansive:

such people throughout the English-speaking world and maybe beyond it and maybe without the "well" . . . The further people move from a regional position, the more they accept variation in accent, intonation, pronunciation, grammar, spelling, punctuation and vocabulary. Indeed when they abandon the touchstones of capital and nation they are drawn willy-nilly towards multiculturalism . . . Standard English exists but it is fuzzy at the edges, and young people need to learn this fact along with everything else that can help them handle loaded social weapons. (McArthur 1994: 12–13)

We might say, in short, that Standard English is the kind of English which draws least attention to itself over the widest area and through the widest range of usage. It is particularly associated with English that is intended to have the widest reach, and in consequence is traditionally associated most of all with English in not just a written form but a printed form. In fact, standards of Standard English are determined to a far greater extent than most people realize by the great publishing houses. (Quirk and Stein 1990: 123)

These definitions and others emphasize the preeminence of the careful speech/writing of the "educated" as a frame of reference for norms existing in a given time and place. And as an extension of the "educated", the printed form exercises a tremendous influence as Quirk and Stein have pointed out. But McArthur's discourse points to the important issue of who defines the "educated". This question of definition has important implications for the Caribbean with its history of colonization and self-doubt. The peculiar history of the Caribbean has made its people reluctant to acknowledge their own worth. The dynamics of this history has resulted in what Görlach (1997) refers to as a "lack of historicity" embodied in a middle-class fear of being reminded of the painful past. This has resulted in a "safe" dependence on the norms of the colonizer for validation and status. This is a fear that often makes Caribbean people unwilling to accept the legitimacy of their own institutions, their own scholarship, tending always towards othercentric values.

The reality is that in every society that claims English as its own, there are grey areas regarding what constitutes Standard English because language is constantly changing (Wood 1981: iv). The words of Sir Bruce Fraser, who was responsible for the revision of the classic *Complete Plain Words* by Sir Ernest Gowers, point to some implications of this:

> This tempts me into moralizing about the duty of anyone who writes about the use of English for the general practitioner. He must, as I see it, have the courage of his convictions, but must not express them too dogmatically on points which fairly admit of a different opinion. He must avoid pedantry, and must also recognize that what seems obviously right to one man seems pedantic to another. He must offer resistance to undesirable innovations, but must not assume that every innovation is sure to be undesirable. He must respect the genius of the language, which includes a wonderful capacity for change. All this requires personal judgement, and every man's judgement is fallible. (1973: v)

Our educators, too, would do well to bear these considerations in mind as they approach their hallowed texts and other symbols of linguistic authority that they hold dear. For, in many instances, the greater our degree of psychological self-doubt, the more passionately we cling to perceived symbols of status and legitimacy, even in the face of disconfirming evidence.

If our educators embrace archaic notions of the Standard as palpable, preserved, unchanging model of what is "correct", they will continue to be consumed by a preoccupation with peripherals such as split infinitives and illegal terminal prepositions. When it is considered that generations of outstanding, educated writers and speakers have happily committed some of these common "errors", one wonders, along with Pyles and Algeo (1993), about the basis of their retention in the academy as "errors". Propensities of crusading grammarians notwithstanding, Standard English is most usefully conceived in terms of acceptability in particular circumstances, freed from the tyranny of archaic rules that are no less illegitimate than a breach of basic subject–verb agreement.

An understanding of the early evolution of the English language that some persons regard as a God-given standard facilitates a healthy attitude toward the notion of Standard English. The period 1100 to 1500 saw a great amount of dialectal diversity existing in roughly five broad geographical zones in Britain.

Until the late fifteenth century, authors simply wrote in the dialect of their native regions. Geoffrey Chaucer, for example, wrote in the London variety of the East Midland dialect. The speech of London, "essentially East Midlandish in its characteristics, though showing Northern and to a less extent Southern influences", became the foundation of a standard for all England, because "London had for centuries been a large (by medieval standards), prosperous, and hence important city" (Pyles and Algeo 1993: 141). What is often termed "Standard Modern English" had its roots in this London variety, the standard finally crystallizing through the efforts of grammarians such as Robert Lowth as well as lexicographer Dr Samuel Johnson in the eighteenth century.

While the educator is urged to recognize that linguistic standards are not sent down from heaven on stone tablets, there is an inevitable tension between this urging and some of the tools of the trade. Most, if not all, of us, encourage our students to rely on dictionaries to verify what is correct or acceptable. Yet, in a sense, by the time a lexicographer has managed to have the manuscript published, reality has already moved to another plane, at least with respect to some of the items listed. Dictionaries, nevertheless, have played an important role in fixing notions of what is correct. For example, the publication of Samuel Johnson's two-volume dictionary was hailed as "the most important linguistic event in the eighteenth century . . . for it to a large extent 'fixed' English spelling and established a standard for the use of words" (Pyles and Algeo 1993: 206). By no means untouched by the impulses of his time, Johnson attempted to exercise a directive function, "but had the good sense usually to recognize prior claims of usage over the arbitrary appeals to logic, analogy, Latin grammar, and sheer prejudice so often made by his contemporaries, even if he did at times settle matters by appeals to his own taste, which was fortunately good taste" (Pyles and Algeo 1993: 207).

In addition to the tensions generated by the reliance on dictionaries, conflicts also arise from the use of school grammars; many of the notions of correctness that are espoused today are based in large measure on ideology of the eighteenth century that regarded language as being of divine provenance and therefore of perfect beginnings. The view was that this perfect specimen was under constant threat of corruption and decay but for the saving diligence of wise men who established themselves as authorities, writers of dictionaries and grammars.

Due Respect

While many grammar books attempt a progressive approach to language description, some still perpetuate eighteenth-century standards. For example, Crystal (1996) and Burton (1984), who are responsive to the social reality of language in the present age, and also Kaplan (1995), who discusses the flaws in the logic of old justifications for rules such as the outlawing of the double negative, contrast with others such as Kirzner and colleagues (1995) who still promulgate eighteenth-century rules, such as the infamous split infinitive, and attempt to defend them with varying degrees of success.

Moreover, although the established authorities, the Fowler brothers, Sir Ernest Gowers and Sir Bruce Fraser, are credited with exposing and discrediting some common language misapprehensions in England (Sparrow 1980), closer examination of at least H.W. Fowler's achievements in *Modern English Usage* (1926), highlighted in the quote below from Gowers, indicates that Fowler's recommendations were not taken seriously enough, as some of the misapprehensions and "cobwebs", thought to have been swept away, were still present thirty-one years later. Many remain to this day.

> It was refreshing to be told by a grammarian that the idea that *different* could only be followed by *from* was a superstition . . . and that it was better to split one's infinitive than to be ambiguous or artificial . . . that it was nonsense to suppose that one ought not to begin a sentence with *and* or *but*, or to end with a preposition, that those who are over-fussy about the placing of the adverb only are the sort [sic] of friends from whom the English language may well pray to be saved, that it is a mistake to suppose that the pronoun *none* must at all costs be followed by a singular verb . . . that to forbid the use of *whose* with an inanimate antecedent is like sending a soldier on active service and insisting that his tunic collar shall be tight and high. (Gowers 1957: 10)

In a strange kind of cycle, educators, agents of change on the one hand, often find themselves, on the other hand, as proponents of eighteenth-century fossilizations that grow again like the fabulous hydra's heads even after they have been cut down. In 1977, Christie, while discussing attitudes to the emergence of a written Jamaican Standard English, declared:

> Many of us reject on principle any form which is at variance with the precepts of the traditional grammar books or with the inventory of the *Oxford English Dictionary*. The concept of Standard English, however, is always changing over space and time. (Christie 1977: 28)

The same admonition would be entirely appropriate today.

Even if Caribbean educators choose to say that their frame of reference is British Standard English, they have not escaped the Standard English dilemma; the British are also busy trying to clarify the parameters of that Standard. For them it remains "fuzzy at the edges". The development of a concept of Standard English grounded in Caribbean reality is therefore vital for the guidance of those of us who are entrusted with the task of shaping thoughts about language as well as teaching English language skills.

If we conflate the common core concepts posited by both Kachru (1988) and Allsopp (1996), the need for non-British loci of legitimacy becomes self-evident. The work of Kachru has been tremendously important in promoting the idea of legitimate centres of English beyond the British Isles,* while Allsopp has perhaps done most to promote a Caribbean locus of legitimacy for the English spoken by its people. Through his monumental *Dictionary of Caribbean English*, he has charted a path for the resolution of many standardization difficulties, particularly those related to lexicon (words and set phrases). Allsopp recognized that in many respects the present Caribbean English situation is similar to that which defined early United States nationhood when, for example, with the aim of promoting "the purity and uniformity of the English Language . . . in the United States", an American Academy of Language and Belles Lettres was formed in 1820 (influenced, no doubt, by the Académie Française, which had its origin in seventeenth-century France) and Noah Webster reportedly warned of the impotence of such an institution in the absence of their own dictionary to provide a standard (Allsopp 1983: 13). An additional factor though, that Allsopp and others have had to grapple with is that Caribbean English

> is lodged in a number of widely separated nation–territories with a traditionally very low intensity of contact between the mass of their populations. Demographic inferiority, economic and cultural

> insecurity (when compared with America, Canada and Britain) are strongly reflected in a lack of confidence in all territories in the validity of Caribbean English. (Allsopp 1983: 189)

In this context issues of standardization are difficult but not impossible to resolve. If we return for a moment to the earlier definitions of Standard English and note the pivotal role of educated speakers/writers, it is clear that, to the extent that the Caribbean region may be conceived as a distinctive region with distinct cultural practices, aspects of the English language are likely to evolve which, though respectable, are different from the norms which were in vogue when our grandparents went to elementary school under the auspices of Queen Victoria. There is then a legitimate Caribbean Standard English, which may be defined as

> the literate English of educated nationals of Caribbean territories and their spoken English such as is considered natural in formal social contexts. There being many such territories, each with its own recognizable "standard", Caribbean Standard English would be the total body of regional lexicon and usage bound to a common core syntax and morphology shared with Internationally Accepted English, but aurally distinguished as a discrete type of certain phonological features such as a marked levelling of British diphthongs and a characteristic disconnecting of pitch from stress as compared with British and American sound patterns. (Allsopp 1996: xlvi)

Unless educators accept the legitimacy of the Caribbean as its own locus of acceptability, they are likely to be caught in a web of linguistic schizophrenia occasioned by the mismatch between traditional British-centred prescriptivism and Caribbean reality.

Part of this reality is that the lines of demarcation, which many English language educators are wont to draw between British English and American English, for example, are not as clearly delineated as one would think. It is easy to dispose of some matters, such as the spelling of *centre* as opposed to *center*, but, in many instances, having fully absorbed the linguistic influences of our American neighbours, we develop formal repertoires which are as indebted to American as to British influences. In this regard the Caribbean educator is firmly caught in the British English (Br. Eng), North American English (NAm. Eng), Caribbean English melting pot.

In fact, many authorities on English across the world point to the constantly shifting borders between British and American English. An examination of a few examples will illustrate the fluidity of the boundaries which are often identified in school grammars and elsewhere. All the examples that follow in this section were taken from Trudgill and Hannah (1994). I have replaced their term "English English" with the more usual "British English".

1. Derivational Morphology

NAm. Eng tends to be more productive than Br. Eng in its use of derivational morphology but the NAm. Eng derivations tend to be borrowed quickly into Br. Eng., for example,

    -ify   (citify, humidify, uglify)
    -ize   (burglarize, decimalize, hospitalize, rubberize, slenderize)

2. *Auxiliaries*

    a. *shall* is rarely used in NAm. Eng. except in legal documentation or very formal styles.

British English	North American English
I shall tell you later	I will tell you later
Shall I drink this now?	Should I drink this now?
I shan't be able to come	I won't be able to come

    b. *should* in its hypothetical sense:

Older speakers and writers of Br. Eng:	I should enjoy living here if I could afford to do so.
NAm. and younger Br. Eng:	I would enjoy living here if I could afford to do so.

In 2a. and b., the educated Caribbean speaker is more likely to use the NAm./Br. Eng forms than the exclusively Br. Eng ones.

Due Respect

3. *Collocation*

Some verbs differ in the prepositions or prepositional adverbs they collocate with. Examples of these collocation differences are:

British English	North American English
to battle with/against (someone/something)	to battle (someone/something)
to check up on (something)	to check on (someone/something)
to fill in (eg a form)	to fill out (eg a form)
to meet (someone)	to meet with (someone)
to prevent (someone becoming . . .)	to prevent (someone from becoming . . .)
to protest at/against/over (something)	to protest (something)
to battle with/against (someone/something)	to battle (someone/something)
to stop (someone doing something)	to stop (someone from doing something)
to visit (someone)	to visit (with someone)

In a survey conducted by this writer, seventeen lecturers at UWI, Mona, were presented with the examples of collocation above, identified only as Option A and Option B instead of Br. Eng or NAm., and asked to identify for each set of expressions the option that represented their normal pattern of careful speech. Only one person, who was in fact British, checked one option (Br. Eng) consistently. The remaining sixteen (fifteen Caribbean and one Canadian), all chose a mixture of Br. Eng and NAm. Eng as their norm. A majority chose four or more NAm. Eng items. Eleven of the people surveyed were English Language Arts educators. These are persons who clearly belong to that important reference group called the "educated". The patterns used by these educated persons must therefore be taken into consideration in any determination of what constitutes Standard Caribbean English.

Perhaps the Caribbean as a whole is particularly receptive at this time. Christie (1989) cites the youthfulness of the population, combined with a greater sense of Caribbean identity and familiarity with the use of regionalisms in formal contexts, as factors likely to engender a positive attitude to new norms. While it is beyond the scope of this chapter to examine details of the corpus of a Caribbean standard, the following brief mention can be made of some of the most likely candidates for the Caribbean segment.

Lexical items

The most uncontroversial are names of regional flora and fauna, as well as terms associated with a range of cultural practices and other commonly used items, for example, *upliftment* 'uplift, enlightenment, improvement'.

Syntax

a. Some cases of repetition and fronting:

    She was tired, tired 'She was very tired'

    It's old that she's old 'Old, that's what she is'

b. Word order differences, for example,

    Last year this time 'This time last year' (Christie 1989).

Lexicosemantics

a. The use of the modal auxiliary *could* as an all-purpose item loosely indicating shades of possibility both past and present (Allsopp 1996);

b. Idioms, for example,

    cut your eye (at sb.) 'show a gesture of contempt by looking at a person and then closing one's eyes while turning one's face away sharply'

    keep a party 'have a party'

    make a lime 'have an informal social gathering to pass the time away in chat and banter'

However, conceding that the Caribbean is a legitimate centre of ownership of English does not mitigate the dilemma that educators must constantly face regarding the inherent "fuzziness" of Standard English. What is essential is an ongoing dialogue in the English language teaching community; educational administrators, teachers and publishers in the region need to share a common vision of what forms should be recognized as educational targets. Through this dialogue, stakeholders can establish a framework for ensuring that our pupils "communicate effectively and that they become confident and articulate users of Standard English" (Proposals of the Secretary of State for Education, April 1993, quoted by Keith Davidson).

Let us agree that Standard English must be grounded in the reality of the careful speech and formal writing of our educated citizens. Let us also agree that our Standard Caribbean English will share an essential common core with the other Standard Englishes of the world. But, in addition to that common core, it will accurately reflect the areas of systematic divergence where the community of the "educated" has agreed on what is acceptable in their careful speech and writing. Let those of us who inhabit the Academy, that is, the community of scholars including educators, commit and recommit ourselves to the education of teachers who are equipped with the linguistic knowledge and confidence to mediate the English language conflicts that present themselves from day to day. And by all means let us agree to continue the dialogue.

References

Ahulu, S. 1994. How Ghanaian is Ghanaian English? *English Today* 38, no. 10.
Allsopp, R. 1983. Cross-referencing many standards: Some sample entries for the *Dictionary of Caribbean English Usage* (DCEU). *English World-Wide* 4, no. 2.
―――. 1996. *Dictionary of Caribbean English Usage*. Oxford: Oxford University Press.
Burton, S.H. 1984. *Mastering English Grammar*. London: Macmillan.
Christie, P. 1977. The question of English and education in Jamaica. *Torch* 25, no. 3.
―――. 1989. Questions of standards and inter-regional differences in Caribbean examinations. In *English across Cultures–Cultures across English*, edited by O. García and R. Otheguy. Berlin and New York: John Benjamins.
Crystal, D. 1996. *Rediscover Grammar with David Crystal*. London: Longman.
Davidson, K. 1994. Double standards. *English Today* 38.10, no. 2.
Encarta World English Dictionary. 1999. New York: St Martin's Press.
Fowler, H.W. [1926] 1965. *Modern English Usage*. Oxford: Oxford University Press.

Görlach, M. 1997. Language and nation: The concept of linguistic identity in the history of English. *English World-Wide* 118, no. 1.

Gowers, Sir Ernest. 1957. H.W. Fowler: The man and his teaching. Presidential Address, English Association.

———. 1973. *The Complete Plain Words*. Revised by Sir Bruce Fraser. London: HMSO.

Kachru, B. 1988. The sacred cows of English. *English Today* 16.4, no. 1.

———. 1991. Liberation linguistics and the Quirk concern. *English Today* 25.7, no. 4.

Kaplan, J. 1995. *English Grammar: Principles and Facts*. Hemel Hempstead: Prentice-Hall.

Kirszner, L.G., and S.R. Mandell. 1995. *The Holt Handbook*. New York: Harcourt Brace.

Leathes, S. 1913. *The Teaching of English at the Universities*. Pamphlet no. 26. The English Association. Oxford: Oxford University Press.

McArthur, T. 1994. Language used as a loaded weapon. *English Today*, 38.10, no. 2.

Pyles, T., and J. Algeo. 1993. *The Origins and Development of the English Language*. New York: Harcourt Brace Jovanovich.

Quirk, R., and G. Stein. 1990. *English in Use*. London: Longman.

Sparrow, John. 1980. *Good English. The English Association: Presidential Address*. Oxford: Oxford University Press.

Swales, J. 1993. The English language and its teachers: Thoughts past, present and future. *ELT Journal* 47, no. 4.

Trudgill, P., and J. Hannah. 1994. *International English*. London: Edward Arnold.

Wood, F.T. 1981. *Current English Usage*. Revised by R.H. Flavell and L.M. Flavell. London: English Language Book Society/Macmillan.

Section Two

Aspects of Structure

Introduction

The contributions in this section, which deal with morphology, syntax and phonology, mostly imply that Creole structure is more complex than is generally suspected. Although Le Page's interest developed mostly in the area of sociolinguistics, his earliest work, as embodied in his groundbreaking survey in the 1950s (see Dedication), investigated and outlined the structural characteristics of what he then referred to as Caribbean dialects.

Kouwenberg and La Charité, in discussing reduplication in Caribbean lexically English Creoles, particularly Jamaican, argue that the contrast in meaning between Jamaican *yala-yala* 'yellowish' and other adjectives, suggested in Cassidy (1971: 72), is more apparent than real. They conclude that differences in the possible interpretations of reduplicated adjectives in Jamaican largely depend on the number of syllables in the "base" form. For them, reduplication is mainly used in that variety to mark what could be termed "inflectional categories" and is therefore not primarily a strategy for expanding the lexicon, as was claimed by Hancock (1980) and Alleyne (1980), for example. Their findings challenge the traditional view that Creoles lack morphology. Jaganauth analyses the grammaticalization of Jamaican *se*, comparing its functions and their development with those of related forms in Guyanese, Sranan and Saramaccan. In doing so, she identifies functions not previously noted. Next, Winford compares the tense/aspect systems of Guyanese, Sranan, Belizean and Jamaican. He sees his study as laying the foundation for fuller comparisons which could assist in clarifying relationships between Caribbean Creoles as well as their origins.

Devonish's is the only chapter dealing with phonology. His concern is with the relationship between the tonal systems of "Anglo-West African" and Sierra Leone's Krio. In a relatively lengthy discussion, he provides linguistic evidence that some tonal patterns in Krio were strongly influenced by varieties spoken in the Caribbean, rather than vice versa, as might have been expected in view of some of the claims made by historians.

References

Alleyne, Mervyn. 1980. *Comparative Afro-American*. Ann Arbor, MI: Karoma Press.
Cassidy, F. 1971. *Jamaica Talk: Three Hundred Years of the English Language in Jamaica*. 2nd ed. London: Macmillan Caribbean.
Hancock, Ian. 1980. Lexical expansion in Creole languages. In *Theoretical Questions in Creole Studies*, edited by A. Valdman and A. Highfield. New York: Academic Press.

Chapter 7

The Mysterious Case of Diminutive *yala-yala*

Silvia Kouwenberg and *Darlene La Charité*

Jamaican *yala* 'yellow' reduplicates to *yala-yala* 'yellowish', with an attenuated interpretation.[1] Given that attributes generally reduplicate with an intensifying semantic effect, the expected interpretation of *yala-yala*, analogous to that of reduplicated colour adjectives, such as *blak-blak* 'very black', *red-red* 'very red', *wait-wait* 'very white', and *griin-griin* 'very green', would be 'very yellow'. Instead, its reduplication appears to involve just the opposite: a lessened degree of the quality (Cassidy 1971: 72). In this essay, we will show that an intensified interpretation of *yala-yala* is in fact possible, and can be distinguished from the attenuated interpretation by its prosody. We will further show that the attenuated interpretation of *yala-yala* is a predictable instantiation of a reduplicative process which produces adjectives from bisyllabic bases, with semantic effects of approximation, similarity, attenuation, and so forth.

Caribbean Creole Adjective Reduplication

Reduplication is considered to be among the typical Creole strategies for expansion of the lexicon, others being compounding and morphological conversion (Hancock 1980; Alleyne 1980). Despite this assumption, there are few reduplicative processes which are widely shared among Creole languages. Furthermore, a survey of reduplication in Caribbean Creole languages shows that it is overwhelmingly used to mark what may be considered inflectional categories, rather than as a word-formation process (Kouwenberg and La Charité 1999). It cannot be maintained, therefore, that reduplication is a strategy for expansion of the lexicon.

In a sample of eight Caribbean Creole languages of diverse European lexical bases (including Dutch, English, French and Iberian languages), reduplication of adjectives is the only type of reduplication which we found to be shared by all of them. An example of a reduplicated adjective is given for each language in our sample in Table 7.1.[2]

Table 7.1

Language	Unreduplicated adjective		Reduplicated adjective	
Berbice Dutch Creole	kali	'small'	kali-kali	'very small'
Caribbean French Creole	salé	'salty'	salé-salé	'very salty'
Jamaican	blak	'black'	blak-blak	'very black'
Ndjuka	tuu	'true'	tuu-tuu	'emphatically true'
Negerhollands	wa	'true'	wa-wa	'really true'
Papiamento	chikí	'small'	chikí-chikí	'very small'
Saramaccan	langa	'long'	langa-langa	'very long'
Sranan	bisi	'busy'	bisi-bisi	'very busy'

Note: The label *Caribbean French Creole* is used here to refer generically to Caribbean varieties, as one of our sources, Valdman, *Le Créole,* purportedly represents a generic French Creole grammar, whereas Carrington, *St Lucian Creole,* describes St Lucian Creole. In using the label *Caribbean French Creole,* we do not mean to imply that French Creole languages of the Caribbean should not be distinguished.

It is evident from the data in Table 7.1 that the reduplication of adjectives yields consistent and predictable results across the group. In each case, the form is fully reduplicated.[3] The semantic effect is to emphasize or intensify the quality attributed by the adjective. Adjective reduplication is referred to in the literature on Creole languages as emphatic, intensifying, or augmentative. We consider this reduplication inflectional, since it preserves the semantic and categorial properties of its base. (See Kouwenberg and La Charité 1999 for further discussion.) In the following, we will look in some more detail at the properties of this reduplicative process in Jamaican.

Jamaican Adjective Reduplication

The intensifying or emphatic reduplication of adjectives is easily elicited from Jamaican speakers, and appears to be unconstrained by semantic class or phonological form. Thus, as the following examples show, it may apply to adjectives denoting colour (*blak*), shape (*raun*), size (*shaat*), texture (*rof*), disposition (*nais*), physical appearance (*priti*), and so forth. It applies to monosyllables (*fos*) and bisyllabic forms (*difren*), and it applies to complex adjectives (*miks op*). As can be seen here, it also applies to *yala*.

Table 7.2

Unreduplicated adjective		Reduplicated adjective	
blak	'black'	blak-blak	'very black'
difren	'different'	difren-difren	'very different'
fos	'first'	fos-fos	'very first'
miks op	'mingled'	miksop-miksop	'very mingled'
nais	'nice'	nais-nais	'very nice'
priti	'pretty'	priti-priti	'very pretty'
raun	'round'	raun-raun	'really round'
rof	'rough'	rof-rof	'very rough'
shaat	'short'	shaat-shaat	'very short'
ton	'torn'	ton-ton	'torn to shreds'
yala	'yellow'	yala-yala	'very yellow'

Based on the preceding, it appears that we need to consider *yala-yala* 'yellowish', listed in Cassidy (1957, 1971) and Cassidy and Le Page (1980), an exceptional form, contrasting with "normal" intensified *yala-yala* 'very yellow'. However, before we declare the discussion closed, there is yet another type of reduplication which is relevant to this issue: adjective-forming reduplication as opposed to simple reduplication of adjectives. When adjective-forming reduplication is considered, it becomes clear that the apparent ambiguity seen in the reduplication of *yala* is evidence that it marches to the beat of two different drums.

Jamaican Adjective-Forming Reduplication

The *Dictionary of Jamaican English* (Cassidy and Le Page 1980) contains about two dozen reduplicated forms which are adjectives, and which share the unusual property that they are formed by the addition of an augment /i/ to a monosyllabic base. Further work with native speakers proved that these forms are easily elicited and interpreted. This informant work further yielded many more forms which behave in a similar fashion. Moreover, a clear difference emerged between simple whole-word reduplications of monosyllabic forms and /i/-augmented reduplications. Consider the forms in Table 7.3. drawn from Cassidy and Le Page (1980), Gooden (2000) and informant work.

Table 7.3

	Unreduplicated form		(i) Whole-word reduplication		(ii) /i/-augmented reduplication	
A	bwai	'boy'	bwai-bwai	'a lot of boys'	bwayi-bwayi	'characteristically boyish'
	buk	'book'	buk-buk	'many books'	buki-buki	'bookish'
	hol	'hole'	hol-hol	'many holes'	holi-holi	'full of holes'
B	kot	'to cut'	kot-kot	'to cut repeatedly'	koti-koti	'much cut'
	dyuk	'to puncture'	dyuk-dyuk	'to puncture repeatedly'	dyuki-dyuki	'perforated, punctured'
	laaf	'to laugh'	laaf-laaf	'to laugh a lot'	laafi-laafi	'inclined to laughter'
C	blak	'black'	blak-blak	'very black'	blaki-blaki	'sooty, with black stains'
	fred	'afraid'	fred-fred	'very scared'	fredi-fredi	'timid, fearful'
	big	'big'	big-big	'very big, large'	bigi-bigi	'biggish (still growing)'

In (a) of Table 7.3, we present some examples of noun bases, in (b) verb bases, in (c) adjective bases. As can be seen, each of these can be input for two different types of reduplication: (i) simple whole-word reduplication; (ii) /i/-augmented reduplication. It should be noted at this point that unreduplicated /i/-augmented base forms either do not exist synchronically (cf. *buki, *laafi, *bigi, etc.), or are unrelated to the reduplicated form (cf. *blaki* female nickname, *holi* 'holy', altogether unrelated to either *hol* 'hole' or *holi-holi* 'perforated'), and therefore could not have provided input for /i/-augmented reduplication. Nor is it likely that such forms existed historically; in that case, we would expect to find at least some surviving forms. Recall that new /i/-augmented base forms are easily elicited, testifying to the fact that this formation is not a vestige of an older stage.

It is clear from the data in Table 7.3 that where simple whole-word reduplication (type [i]) is applied, an output form of the same category as the base is produced, be it noun, verb, or adjective. The semantic effect of reduplication is to denote multiplicity for objects (nouns), iteration or continuation for events (verbs), intensification or emphasis for attributes (adjectives). Cassidy (1971: 71) points to a common semantic core of repetition in all these interpretations, but "increased quantity" may be more accurate. (See Kouwenberg and La Charité 2000 for elaboration of the semantic properties of reduplications of this type.) We consider these whole-word reduplications to be inflectional.

Where /i/-augmented reduplication (type [ii]) is applied, on the other hand, the output is an adjective, irrespective of the input category. The semantic effect is to produce the attribution of the object (in the case of nouns), activity (in the case of verbs), or property (in the case of adjectives) denoted by the base as a characteristic attribute. We refer to these jointly as "X-like". The semantic and categorial changes are such that this process can be said to derive new lexical entries.

The adjectival status of these forms can be demonstrated by their acceptability in attributive positions, for instance, in (1) below, where *faaki-faaki* premodifies the noun *trel:*

1. *Yu fain laik siks faak on di shabl, so yu get di faaki-faaki trel go daung de*
   You find like six fork on the shovel, so you get this fork+ifork+i trail go down there.
   'You'll find about six prongs on the shovel, so you'll end up with this furrowed trail going down.'

The adjective produced by /i/-augmented reduplication lacks an emphatic or intensified interpretation, even where the input is an adjective. Thus, *blaki-blaki* may be used to refer to an object which has black stains, such as those produced by soot from fire, but there is no implication that these stains cause the object to be very black. In fact, one informant indicated clearly that where such an object is fully black (for instance, a pot blackened by soot), *blaki-blaki* is not appropriately used. Similarly, *fredi-fredi* is applicable to someone who is generally or frequently timid or fearful, but clearly not someone who is very fearful. In short, the implication is one of recurrence, not of intensity. This is similarly illustrated by reduplicated *griini-griini* in (2).

2. (after describing chemical ripening of bananas)
   Yu sii dis griini-griini luk pan dem
   You see this green+igreen+i look on them
   'You see them looking unripe in places.'

In each of the examples in Table 7.3, the base is a monosyllabic form. The addition of the /i/-augment evidenced in (ii) produces a bisyllabic base for reduplication. The result is a reduplicated form which is semantically as well as phonologically distinct from the output of whole-word reduplication of type (i). Compare, for instance, *buk-buk* (type [i]) and *buki-buki* (type [ii]). In addition, in the case of noun and verb bases, the forms are distributionally distinct: the categorial and distributional properties of the derived adjectives *buki-buki* and *koti-koti* differ from those of the reduplicated noun *buk-buk* and the reduplicated verb *kot-kot*, respectively.

Let us now look at cases where the base is intrinsically bisyllabic. We will first look at noun and verb bases. Table 7.4 provides some examples which are distinguished by the category of the input: nouns in (A), verbs in (B). We will consider adjectives below. Based on the semantic and categorial effects of reduplication, it is possible to distinguish between reduplications which effect an increase in quantity without changing the meaning or the categorial status of the base, and reduplications which derive adjectives, attributing the object or event described by the base noun or verb as a characteristic property. These reduplications thus display the same semantic effects as the type (i) and type (ii) reduplications of monosyllabic forms illustrated in Table 7.3.

Table 7.4

	Unreduplicated form		Type (i) reduplication		Type (ii) reduplication	
A	*maka*	'thorn'	*maka-maka*	'many thorns'	*maka-maka*	'having thorns'
	faya	'fire'	*faya-faya*	'many fires'	*faya-faya*	'hot, fiery, burning'
	sprekl	'freckle'	*sprekl-sprekl*	'many freckles'	*sprekl-sprekl*	'having freckles'
B	*bata*	'beat, batter'	*bata-bata*	'beat severely'	*bata-bata*	'battered'
	wigl	'wriggle, squirm'	*wigl-wigl*	'wriggle a lot'	*wigl-wigl*	'squirmy'
	laba	'blab, tell secrets'	*laba-laba*	'blab a lot'	*laba-laba*	'prone to blab'

We immediately see that /i/-addition does not apply to bisyllabic stems. Thus, whereas *holi-holi* 'perforated' can be derived from monosyllabic *hol* 'hole', **sprekli-sprekli* cannot be derived from bisyllabic *sprekl*. Nevertheless, a reduplication involving the same semantic and categorial effect as the /i/-augmented reduplications of Table 7.3 is possible. This suggests that the /i/-addition observed in Table 7.3 satisfies a prosodic constraint that the input to type (ii) be bisyllabic. Intrinsically bisyllabic nouns and verbs have two possible, semantically distinct, reduplicative interpretations, one the widely used interpretation of increased quantity (multiplicity, iteration) and the other a "characterized by" or "X-like" interpretation. Although segmentally nondistinct, these can be distinguished by their different distributional properties; whereas type (i) reduplication does not affect category, hence produces nouns and verbs, type (ii) reduplication derives adjectives. Thus, for instance, an informant used utterance (3) in describing certain types of mangoes which, different from others, are characteristically dotted with black spots. Reduplicated *sprekl-sprekl* here appears in a position in which nouns and verbs are not accepted.

3. *Som a dem baan sprekl-sprekl*
   Some of them born *freckl-freckl.*
   'Some of them are characteristically spotted.'

We will now turn to the reduplication of bisyllabic adjectives. As is the case for bisyllabic verbs and nouns, the application of type (i) and type (ii) reduplication to bisyllabic adjectives produces segmentally identical forms. Moreover, their application produces distributionally nondistinct outputs. Type (i) reduplication maintains the adjective class of the input, and type (ii) reduplication derives an adjective. As a result, the output forms of both type (i) and type (ii) reduplication are adjectives. However, the meanings produced are potentially opposite, as is clearly the case for *yala-yala* in Table 7.5.

As can be seen in Table 7.5, type (i) and (ii) reduplication of *yala* 'yellow' produces segmentally and distributionally nondistinct forms: intensified 'very yellow', and attenuated 'yellowish', respectively. Only the latter interpretation is listed in Cassidy (1957, 1971) and Cassidy and Le Page (1980). We found, however, that not all speakers accept the attenuated interpretation. In fact,

Table 7.5

Unreduplicated form		(i) Intensive, emphatic		(ii) Attenuated, X-like	
yala/yelo	'yellow'	yala-yala /yelo-yelo	'very yellow'	%yala-yala/ yelo-yelo	'yellowish, yellow-spotted'
difren	'various'	difren-difren	'very miscellaneous'	??difren-difren	??'somewhat various'
priti	'pretty'	priti-priti	'very pretty'	*priti-priti	*'prettyish'
brikl	'brittle'	brikl-brikl	'very brittle'	??brikl-brikl	??'brittle, crumbly'

several of our informants know only the intensified interpretation, whereas others accepted both the attenuated interpretation (such as in *having yellow spots*) and the intensified interpretation (as in 'very yellow'). The fact that judgements on the acceptability of the attenuated form were found to vary across different speakers is marked by the percent symbol (%).

The different interpretations of reduplicated *yala-yala*, while segmentally nondistinct, can be related to different prosodies: *yala-yala* 'very yellow' is associated with an emphatic prosody with the first reduplicant produced on a higher pitch than the second reduplicant.[2] Informants who accepted both the intensifying and the attenuated interpretations were clearly aware of this difference. Gooden's (2000) preliminary acoustic measurements confirm this observation.

Other bisyllabic adjectives appear to submit only to type (i) reduplication. For many reduplicated adjectives, such as *priti-priti*, there is no doubt that the intensifying reduplication is the only one available. In Table 7.5, an asterisk (*) marks the unacceptability of the attenuated interpretation. Similarly, for *brikl-brikl*, although quoted in Cassidy and Le Page (1980) as 'brittle, crumbly', suggesting a type (ii) interpretation, we found confirmation only for an intensifying interpretation. The difference between a type (i) and type (ii) interpretation of *difren-difren* is subtle, but here too we were unable to elicit a type (ii) interpretation. In Table 7.5, the double question mark (??) marks acceptability of the attenuated interpretation as marginal at best. The fact that *yala-yala* has both an interpretive and an attenuated interpretation for many, if not all, speakers is clearly unusual. Unfortunately, elicitation is made difficult by the fact that there are few bisyllabic adjectives in Jamaican, with *yala-yala* the only such colour adjective. It is, however, possible that other bisyllabic adjectives are to be found which, like *yala-yala*, clearly submit to both types of reduplication, distinguishable by their different prosodies.

Concluding Remarks

We have shown in the preceding that Jamaican *yala* submits to a reduplicative process which produces adjectives. This particular process effects a semantic change which we refer to as "X-like", resulting in the attribution of the entity (in the case of nouns), activity (in the case of verbs), or property (in the case of adjectives) denoted by the base as a characteristic attribute. The reduplicative process requires bisyllabic input. Where the input form is monosyllabic, a bisyllabic form is created by the addition of an /i/-augment. The categorial, semantic and phonological changes involved clearly mark this reduplicative process as derivational. In the case of *yala* 'yellow', the reduplicated form thus derived is *yala-yala* 'yellowish' 'yellow-spotted', with an attenuated interpretation. Despite the fact that the interpretation of *yala-yala* can now be considered perfectly predictable from the reduplicative process which creates this form, *yala* contrasts with other bisyllabic adjectives which submit to whole-word reduplication with an intensifying or emphatic interpretation (our type [i]), rather than "X-like" adjective forming reduplication (our type [ii]). The intensifying or emphatic type (i) interpretation can be compared to whole-word reduplications of nouns and verbs, with similar semantic effects. We characterize these jointly as involving increased quantity. We consider these reduplications, which fully preserve the semantic and the categorial properties of the input, inflectional. The evidence from several speakers who considered an intensifying interpretation of *yala-yala* 'very yellow' the only one available, and the marginal status of "X-like" reduplications of other bisyllabic adjectives, lend additional credence to the distinction between inflectional (type [i]) and derivational (type [ii]) reduplication. The varying judgements on the acceptability of attenuated *yala-yala* 'yellowish' suggest that regularization may be taking place in favour of the more productive inflectional reduplication.

Notes

1. Reduplication is taken to refer to a morphological relation which involves the affixation of a copy of part or all of the base. Forms such as *chaka-chaka* 'disorderly', *nyaka-nyaka* 'untidy' 'slovenly' do not constitute morphological reduplications, as there are no unreduplicated forms – **chaka*, **nyaka* – to which these relate.
2. Our sources are: Kouwenberg 1994 for Berbice Dutch Creole; Valdman 1978 and Carrington 1984 for French Creole; Cassidy and Le Page 1980 for Jamaican; Huttar and Huttar 1994 for Ndjuka; Bradford 1986 for Negerhollands; Dijkhoff 1993 for Papiamentu; Bakker 1987 for Saramaccan; and Sebba 1981 for Sranan. The Jamaican data are supplemented by native speaker intuitions. (See Kouwenberg and La Charité 1999 and n.d.)
3. But note that Carrington, *St Lucian Creole*, cites the St Lucian form *piti-ti* 'very small' < reduplication of *piti* 'small', and that some native speakers of St Lucian prefer *sa-salé* to the fully reduplicated form *salé-salé* cited by Carrington.
4. It is worth noting that all reduplications discussed here are produced under a single intonation contour; none of the forms considered is produced with an intonation break between the reduplicants.

References

Alleyne, M.C. 1980. *Comparative Afro-American*. Ann Arbor, MI: Karoma.
Bakker, P. 1987. Reduplications in Saramaccan. In *Studies in Saramaccan Language Structure*, edited by M.C. Alleyne. Caribbean Culture Studies 2. Amsterdam/Jamaica: University of Amsterdam/University of the West Indies.
Bradford, W.P. 1986. Virgin Islands Dutch Creole: A morphological description. *Amsterdam Creole Studies* 9.
Carrington, L.D. 1984. *St Lucian Creole: A Descriptive Analysis of Its Phonology and Morphosyntax*. Hamburg: Helmut Buske.
Cassidy, F.G. 1957. Iteration as a word forming device in Jamaican folk speech. *American Speech* 32.
———. 1971. *Jamaica Talk: Three Hundred Years of the English Language in Jamaica*. 2d ed. London: Macmillan Caribbean.
Cassidy, F.G., and R.B. Le Page. 1980. *Dictionary of Jamaican English*. 2d ed. Cambridge: Cambridge University Press.
DeCamp, D. 1974. Neutralizations, iteratives and ideophones: The locus of language in Jamaica. In *Pidgins and Creoles: Current Trends and Prospects*, edited by D. DeCamp and I.F. Hancock. Georgetown: Georgetown University Press.

Dijkhoff, M.B. 1993. Papiamentu word formation. PhD diss., University of Amsterdam.

Gooden, S. 2000. Reduplication in Jamaican Creole: Semantic functions and prosodic constraints. In *Twice as Meaningful: Morphological Reduplications in Contact Languages*, edited by S. Kouwenberg. London: Battlebridge Press.

Hancock, I.F. 1980. Lexical expansion in Creole languages. In *Theoretical Orientations in Creole Studies*, edited by A. Valdman and A. Highfield. New York: Academic Press.

Huttar, G.L., and M.L. Huttar. 1994. *Ndjuka*. London/New York: Routledge.

Kouwenberg, S. 1994. *A Grammar of Berbice Dutch Creole*. Mouton Grammar Library 12. Berlin: Walter de Gruyter.

Kouwenberg, S., and D. La Charité. 1997. Adjective reduplication in Jamaican Creole: Echoes of Africa? Paper presented at the Conference on West Africa and the Americas: Repercussions of the slave trade, University of the West Indies, Mona, February.

———. 1999. Iconicity in Caribbean Creole reduplication: Inflection versus derivation. *Proceedings of the 1998 Annual Meeting of the Canadian Linguistics Association*, edited by J. Jensen and G. van Herk. Ottawa: University of Ottawa Press.

———. 2000. The meanings of more of the same: Iconicity of reduplication and the evidence for substrate transfer in the genesis of Caribbean Creole languages. In *Twice as Meaningful: Morphological Reduplication in Contact Languages*, edited by S. Kouwenberg. London: Battlebridge.

———. N.d. *Echoes of Africa: Reduplication in Caribbean Creole and Niger Congo Languages*. MS.

Sebba, M. 1981. Derivational regularities in a Creole lexicon: The case of Sranan. *Linguistics* 19.

Valdman, A. 1978. *Le Créole: Structure, Statut et Origine*. Paris: Klincksieck.

Chapter 8

The Use of *Se* in Jamaican

Dhanis Jaganauth

The Jamaican sentences below illustrate a type of structure common among Afro-American languages (see Alleyne 1980: 94–95).[1]

1. *Mi tel im se im fi go-op a Mis Mak.*
    And I tell him *say* he for go up to Miss Mac.
    'And I told him that he should go up to Miss Mac.'

2. *Dem biliiv se dem mis da a skuul.*
    They believe *say* they miss that at school.
    'They believed that they [must have] missed that at school.'

3. *Mi hier se di kompini dem kom-iin.*
    I hear *say* the company PL come in.
    'I heard that the companies had come in.'

In all these languages, a word related to (if not identical with) a verb meaning 'speak/talk/say' is used after certain main verbs to introduce an "object clause" or "sentential complement". These main verbs are said to come from one of three categories:

- verbs involving communication or "speech act verbs", with such meanings as 'tell', 'promise', 'call', 'ask';
- cognition verbs, that is, verbs referring to mental activities such as 'think', 'know', 'believe', 'realize'; and
- perception verbs such as 'see' and 'hear' (Plag 1993: 40; Veenstra 1996: 155).

One of the debates surrounding these constructions is whether to classify the "verb of saying" that follows these main verbs (for example, Jamaican *se*) as a verb (in a serial verb construction), as a complementizer, or both (see, for example, Kihm 1990; Sebba 1987: 55, 78–79; Alleyne 1980: 94–95, 169–70). For Romaine (1988: 143–44), Plag (1993: 36–82) and Veenstra (1996: 154–57), it is a verb that has grammaticalized into becoming a complementizer, losing, in the process, some of the semantic and syntactic properties of verbhood. This, in their view, is a diachronic process that took place as a pidgin grew into a Creole.

The theory that Plag favours (155) suggests that Sranan would have taken from the substrate a "verb of saying" that had a more literal function and reanalysed it over time until it became more abstract. The description provided by Alleyne (1980: 94–95, 169–70) is just the opposite.

Alleyne points to the more abstract uses which this "verb of saying" had/has in the substrate (Kwa) languages, and suggests that in Jamaican (and some other Afro-American languages) this verb might be losing some of those functions, gradually becoming more restricted to appearing after "verbs of thinking, speaking, thinking and believing". For him, this construction is a type of verb serialization in which the "verb of saying" also functions as a general subordinating conjunction

My aim in this essay is to catalogue the various uses of Jamaican *se*. As in the case of Sranan, it would seem that all of Plag's and Romaine's diachronic stages are reflected in the synchronic data from Jamaican. However, the features identified seem to have explanations that are not peculiar to the constructions under study.

It is generally assumed that, outside of constructions such as those listed earlier, the main verb function of *se* is to introduce spoken discourse, whether as direct or indirect speech. It is on this assumption that much of the grammaticalization theory rests. However, as I hope to illustrate, *se* also introduces hypothetical situations, introspections, and ideas as presented in books and other written sources. This is in addition to its idiomatic use in *Mi se!*, used to express the speaker's opinion that some situation mentioned in the previous or following portion of the discourse (uttered by the speaker or someone else) is remarkable in some way. In the examples discussed, square brackets ([ ]) enclose the interviewer's interventions.

Idiomatic Use

4. *Mi se! It nais yu si!*
   I *say!* It nice you see!
   'It's really good!' (Or 'I say! It's really good!')

5. [*So yuu az a boi, nou . . . huu tiich yu?*] *Mi?! [ehe] Mi se!*
   So you as a boy now . . . who teach you? Me?! I *say!*
   'So when you were a boy, . . . who taught you? Me?! [Ehe] I *say!*

   Aal Bush, Mis Kie brada, [*ehe*] . . . *im se,* "*Granpa, hou yu manij*
   All Bush, Miss Kay brother, [ehe] he *say*, grandpa how you manage
   'Up to Bush, Miss Kay's brother, [ehe] he said, "Grandpa, how did you manage

   kantien dem ting fram yuut?" [*mhm*] *Mi se,* "*Bwai mi no nuo,*"
   contain DEM thing from youth? [mhm] I *say*, boy I NEG know.
   to remember those things from such a long time back?" [mhm] I said, "Boy! I don't know."'

In (4), the speaker wishes to emphasize how good the bun tastes, while in (5) the implied answer to the question is that the interviewee has a remarkable mind and therefore did not need to be taught.

Introducing Hypothetical Propositions

6. *Se yu a kuk rais, put likl bota . . .* (elicited)
   Say you ASP cook rice, put little butter
   'Let's say you're cooking rice, put a little butter . . .'

7. *Mi no ben - se a fait mi a fait im yu nuo.*
   I NEG TNS - *say* is fight I ASP fight him, you know.
   'I wasn't actually fighting him, you know.'

8. *Im no ben go bak-lef aaf, go bak, se im go bak agen.*
   She NEG TNS go back, leave off, go back, *say* she go back again.
   'She didn't stop going, so it isn't that she went back.'

9. *Di chorch duont se, rou yu nuo.*
   The church don't *say*, quarrel, you know.
   'The church doesn't chastise you, you know.'

10. *A no se im tiif, bot . . .* (elicited)
    Is NEG *say* he thieving, but . . .
    'It isn't that he is a thief, but . . .'

None of the above uses of *se* refers to speaking. As is clearly indicated by (6), *se* can have the meaning 'let's say'/'hypothesize that X is the situation'. This idea of "hypothetical" could, however, be extended to cover all the other examples in the group as well. In each of them, the informant considers a particular word or phrasing that comes closest to describing the particular situation under discussion, but indicates that the word/phrase in question does not adequately capture the nuances of the situation.

The word or phrase may come from the interlocutor's stated or implied conclusions about what the speaker meant (7), about what the norms are (8) and (9), or it may represent a conclusion that the speaker anticipates someone might draw (10). In the case of (7), for instance, the informant has just revealed that her father tried to, but could not, flog her for becoming pregnant. The interviewer asks why he could not and the response is that he could not "manage" her, so the interviewer (partly questioningly) concludes aloud that she fought with him. In her response (7), the informant is saying that what she did could not be considered fighting since, as she goes on to explain, all she did was hold on to the whip and thereby prevented him from flogging her. For (9), the interviewer's question suggested that she was assuming the norms of the previous generation or of other churches, whereby a women pregnant and unmarried would be ostracized by the church.

Examples (7) to (10) all involve the presence of a negator, but (10) is a cleft sentence. While the pattern found in that example is quite common in current Jamaican (in Kingston, at least), I have not found any instances of this type of cleft in the texts from older Jamaicans. This could mean that it is a syntactic innovation, replacing structures such as those in (7) to (9). Further, there is no affirmative counterpart of this type of cleft sentence, so that while *A no se . . .* ('It is not that . . .') is grammatical, **A se . . .* ('It is that . . .') is not. This could be because the hypothetical meaning of *se* would be in contradiction with the idea behind 'It is that . . .'

This hypothetical function of *se* is also seen in combinations such as *laik se, ivm se*. In some contexts, this *usage* would translate into English 'if', in others as English 'that', but the basic meaning remains 'hypothetical'. Notice the similarity between (6) and (11).

11. *Yes, wel, laik se nou, ai kom-in wid a gyal . . .*
    Yes, well, like *say* now, I come in with a girl . . .
    'Yes, well, say for instance that I come in with a girl . . .'

12. *Ivn (if) se yu wan di dres . . .* (Alleyne 1980: 169)
    Even if you *say* you want the dress . . .
    'Even if you want the dress . . .'

13. *Supuoz se yu fiil laik yu hav a kuol ar yu bilyos.*
    Suppose *say* you feel like you have a cold or you bilious.
    'Suppose you feel as if you have a cold or you are bilious.'

14. *An di man dem kom-iin laik se dem wies-op di moni.* (*Prime Time News*, Super Supreme TV, Jamaica)
    And the man PL come-in like *say* they waste-up the money.
    'And the men, seems that/as if they wasted the money.'

15. *Im a gwaan laik se a im ron tingz.* (elicited)
    He ASP go on like *say* is him run things.
    'He's behaving as if he's the one in charge of everything.'

In the case of *uonli se*, a hypothetical interpretation is not as obvious as in (11) to (15). In (16), a hypothetical situation is presented: the person speaking has to be dressed as if for church, and *uonli se* introduces a modification to this hypothetical situation.

16. *Mi ha-fi wel taidi laik mi a go a chorch!* [ehe] *Uonli se mi wudn*
    I have to well tidy like I ASP go to church! [Ehe] Only *say* I wouldn't
    'I have to be well-dressed as if I'm going to church! Only that I wouldn't

Due Respect

> *wier a kuot. Mi ha-fi hav aan mi tai!*
> wear a coat. I have to have on my tie!
> wear a coat. But I have to have on my tie!'

Talking to Self

17. *An iz wen a kudn waak fram ya tu Mongt Alivet, a stap a Mizpa.*
    And is when I couldn't walk from here to Mt Olivet, I stop at Mizpah.
    'And it's when I couldn't walk from here to Mt Olivet, I stopped at Mizpah.'

    A se wel, dis az chiip a jain Mizpa . . . An wen mi a go,
    I *say* well, just as cheap I join Mizpah . . . and when I ASP go,
    'I said, well, joining Mizpah or Mt Olivet — it's all the same. And when I was going,

    mi se tu miself, bot i luk foni. Di siem Gaad we giv di komyunian a
    I say to myself, but it look funny. The same God that give the communion at
    I said to myself, but this is silly. The same God who gives communion at

    Mongt Alivet, a'him giv it a Mizpa.
    Mt Olivet, is him give it at Mizpah.
    Mt Olivet, he gives it at Mizpah.'

In Plag's account (1993: 46–47) of the development of the complementizer *taki*, the use of it with cognition verbs is an important transition point between the more literal quotative function and the more abstract complementizer-like functions that follow. According to him (Plag 1993: 46–47), with verbs such as 'know', 'find', 'believe', *taki* has lost its quotative function since there is no discourse to mark. The construction is still transparent, however, "because in some figurative sense the thoughts of a person are quoted" (p. 47). This figurative use is, however, also part of the main verb function of *se* (the Jamaican counterpart of *taki*), as (17) illustrates. There the speaker is describing how she convinced herself to switch churches.

This talking to self is usually indicated by *se* alone, but can be reinforced, as in *se tu miself / imself* (see [17] above). For cognition verbs such as 'believe', 'know', 'feel', 'think', the same is true. This use is illustrated in (18). Communicating with self is so much a part of the meaning of these verbs that even in relatively formal speech, when 'that' is used instead of *se*, as in example (19), some speakers feel the need to insert 'to myself'/'himself', and so on.

18. *Bot mi fiil tu miself se im wi biit mi.*
    But I feel to myself *say* he will beat me
    'But I felt [certain] that he would beat me.'

19. *Atherton must be thinking to himself that . . .* (Cricket commentator, CBU)

The next stage in the grammaticalization process for Plag is the extension beyond the figuratively quotative function to one in which no quotative function can be detected, not even figuratively. At this point, *taki* spreads to perception verbs ('see', 'hear'). However, it is doubtful whether these verbs are truly perception verbs. Plag himself notes (1993: 48) that perception verbs are ambiguous between a perception–cognition interpretation. 'I see/hear' could also mean 'I understand/realize/learn'. In the case of Jamaican, while *si se* often involves both seeing and understanding, there are cases where it can mean only understanding, as in (20), but none where it means simply 'seeing'.

The woman referred to in (20) comes to her conclusion based on what she heard/did not hear: Everyone spoke in support of the other person's case, none in support of hers.

20. *When shi see now se she nah get no support . . .*
    When she see now *say* she NEG ASP get NEG support . . .
    'When she saw that she wasn't getting any support . . .'

21. *Him se [ehe] im sent se [ehe] man [ehe] man [ehe] sliip a di yaad.*
    She say [ehe] she scent *say* [ehe] man [ehe] man [ehe] sleep in the yard.
    'She said she smelled that a man had slept in her house.'

22. *Mi hier se mi granmada se* . . .
    I hear *say* my grandmother say . . .
    'I heard that my grandmother said . . .'

It seems to me that 'understanding' is always the primary focus of these constructions. Further, the true perception verb does not take *se*.[2] Thus, in (23), *se* is not used.

23. *Mi hier dem a taak bout Afrika Bonggo.*
    I hear them ASP talk about Africa Bongo.
    'I heard them talking about Africa Bongo.'

If we take *si se, hier se, sent se* as cognition verbs, then *se* would have the same figurative quotative function for these verbs as well.

Inanimate Subject

24. *Di buk se,* [ehe] *"Ef yu giv love yu wi get lov."*
    The book *say* [ehe] "if you give love, you will get love."
    'The Bible says, [ehe] "If you give love, you will receive love."'

This use of *se* raises the possibility that, in (25), the noun *invitieshan* could be the subject of *se*, as in [*Di*] *invitieshan se, "Wi havin a miitn"* (The direct object of the verb *gi* 'give' then becomes the subject of *se*.)

25. *Iz uonli wen di taim kom, yu nuo, yu go-gi dem invitieshan se, "Wi havin a miitn."*
    Is only when the time come, you know, you go-give them invitation *say*, "We having a meeting."
    'It's only when the time comes, you know, you invite them saying, "We're having a meeting."'

Quotative Function

26. *Mi se: "Tek mi wid yu, no. A want a uman fi stie wid."*
    I *say*: "Take me with you, no. I want a woman to stay with."
    'I said: "Take me with you, won't you? I want a woman to stay with."
    Si mi workin pans ya? Di uman se no, a no mi workin pans dat.
    See my working pants here?" The woman *say* no, is not my working pants.
    'Here are my work pants. The woman said no, those were not my work pants.'

In its quotative function, main verb *se* introduces both direct and indirect speech. The same is true when *se* follows other communication verbs, such as 'tell', 'sing', 'write'.

However, when *se* follows main verb *se* or *aks*, it seems to be restricted to introducing direct speech only.[3]

27. *An mi breda se tu mi se: "Miemie, mek wi go a Maakos Gyaavi miitn tinait."*
    And my brother *say* to me *say*: "May-May, make we go to Marcus Garvey meeting tonight."
    'And my brother said to me: "May-May, let's go to Marcus Garvey's meeting tonight."'

28. *An im se tu di yong fela se: "Yu apierans iz di paaspuot; . . ."*
    And he *say* to the young fellow *say*: "Your appearance is your passport; . . ."
    'And he said to the young fellow: "Your appearance is your passport; . . ."'

29. *Mi aks wan uman se: "Wat apn tu di Kuopi mek wi na-a hier im agien?"*
    I ask a woman *say*: "What happen to the Kopi make we NEG ASP hear him again?"
    'I asked a woman: "What happened to that Copi that we no longer hear him?"'

143

30. *Im aks mi se:* "*Wai?*"
    He ask me *say*: "Why?"
    'He asked me: "Why?"'

Indirect questions seem to allow *se*, as in (31):

31. ... *bot duon aks mi ef a chru!*
    ... but don't ask me if is true!
    '... but don't ask me if it's true!'

In their definition of Jamaican *se*, Cassidy and Le Page (1980: 396) cite Christaller's description of Twi *se*: "after a previous verb ... introducing the words spoken ... = *saying*, is often not to be translated and serves as a mere quotation mark". In the case of *se* ... *se* it would seem that *se* is just a quotation mark. Interestingly, the Saramaccan version of *se*, also behaves as a quotation mark in one particular structure (Veenstra 1996: 155).[4]

In the light of such similarity, the following Guyanese examples seem to be significant. Here the quotation is broken up, perhaps for dramatic effect, but each of the noninitial segments of the question is reintroduced by *se* alone.

32. *Den di daadi go tel am se,* "*Gaad bles yu mi son.*" *Se,* "*Tide*
    Then the father go tell him *say,* "God bless you my son *say* today
    'Then his father would tell him: "God bless you my son." Today

    aabi-mi get swiit fuud." (Guyanese)
    we-I get sweet food."
    we-I got sweet food."'

33. *So den ii go-in di kichin an ii aks shi, ii se,* "*Wa kain a fuud yo*
    So then he go in the kitchen and he ask she, he *say,* "What kind of food you
    'So he went into the kitchen and he asked her: "What kind of food are you

    a kuk?" *Se,* "*Waan ... yo a kuk waan-tuu badi fuud a salt*
    ASP cook?" *Say,* "one ... you ASP cook one-two person food ASP salt
    preparing? One ... you are cooking one-two persons' food is salty

an tuu badi fuud a swiit? Se, "Mii an yuu yo a kuk swiit
and two person food ASP sweet? *Say,* I and you food ASP cook sweet
and the other two is sweet? Yours and mine you prepare sweet

an mi moda an faada fuud yo a kuk salt?!" (Guyanese)
and my mother and father food you ASP cook salt?!
while my parents' you make salt?!"'

In the immediately preceding example, we find a structure described by Plag as "subject copying": *ii aaks shi, ii se . . .* Example (34) illustrates the same process:

34. *Gaad tel yu in-a im baibl [ehe] im se, "Chilren wil bi havin chilren."*
God tell you in his Bible, [ehe] he *say,* "Children will be having children."
'God tells you in his Bible. He says, "Children will be having children."'

Both Plag and Romaine see this structure as a preliminary step in the verb-to-complementizer process. The next step, they say, is the dropping of the copied subject to produce *aaks shi se . . ., tel yu se . . . .*

It is worth noting, however, that there is a subtle difference between these two types of structures. The "subject copying" structure is used for emphasis and dramatic effect rather than to present information about what was said. In both of the above cases the listener has that information already; it is the topic of the preceding discourse. The emphasis is on the fact of the asking or the telling, not on what was said. In the case of *aaks/tel yu se*, on the other hand, the following clause presents new information.[5]

Se in Other Contexts: Implied Speech Act?

The final stages in the development of the complementizer in Plag's account is when it spreads to "new domains of application", that is, to "final clauses", "consecutive clauses", and "noun complements" (1993: 49). He provides (35) from Sebba (1987: 79) and (36) as instances in which *taki* 'say' is used "as a conjunction of consecutive subordinate clauses" (Plag 1993: 49–50).

Due Respect

35. *Den de so don taki yu musu . . .*
    'They are so dumb that you have to . . .'

36. *Kofi gwe sondro taki/dati Amba si en.*
    'Kofi went away without Amba seeing him.'

Plag's "consecutive clauses" do not have Jamaican equivalents with *se* and, as he observes (n. 26), seem unique to Sranan. He suggests these may be recent superstrate-influenced creations as *taki* becomes merged with *dati* 'so that'.

The next example he gives, (37), from Herkovits and Herkovits (1936: 208–9), illustrates his category of "final subordinate clause" (which, he admits, can also be interpreted as a speech act).

37. *Ma Anansi go strei nanga Dagu, taki, eng sa si suma sa ta' moro langa nanga maskita.*
    'But Anansi went to contest with dog that they should see which of them would remain longer with the mosquitoes.'

The Jamaican examples in (38) to (43) would probably fit into this category of "final clauses".

38. *Yu nuo ou lang mi de op ya se mi a kom kom iit?* (Woman in cafeteria line)
    You know how long I LOC up here *say* I ASP come come eat!?
    'Do you know how much time has gone since I came up here to eat?'

39. *An mi have it dong se shi fi op de.*
    And I have it down *say* she to up there.
    'And I expected her to be up there.' (according to the record in my mind)

40. *Im no ben haid i se a no im*
    He NEG hide it *say* is NEG him.
    'He didn't deny that it was he.'

41. *Dem kyar im go a kuort se a fi-im hag. Valyu it an suu im se a fi-im hag.*
    They carry him go to court *say* is his hog. Value it and sue him *say* is his hog.

'They took him to court claiming it was his hog [that did the damage].'

42. *Dem en kaal i Tamsn Tong, se a tong.*
    They TNS call it Thompson Town, *say* is town.
    'They called it Thompson Town, saying it's a town.'

43. *Wich-paat im kyan flai? Se im a go flai.*
    Which part he can fly? *say* he ASP fly.
    'Where can he fly? Claiming he's going to fly!'

The next two examples, (44) and (45), would qualify as "noun complements".

44. *Iz uonli wen di taim kom, yu nuo, yu go-gi dem invitieshan se, "Wi havin a miitn."*
    Is only when the time come, you know, you go-give them invitation *say* we having a meeting.
    'All that you have to do is, when the time comes, you invite them saying, "We're having a meeting."'

45. *A da taim di ma gi di gyal aal dem linngo, se im . . . im sent man.*
    Is that time the mother give the girl all DEM fancy talk *say* . . . she scent man.
    'That is the time when the mother gave the girl the speech saying that she smelled a man.'

The next example, (46), could be either a noun complement or final clause.

46. *A wen mi go bak di gyal a gi mi juok [oo]. Se im-him di Ma.*
    Is when I go back the girl ASP give me joke [oo]. *Say* she-she the mother.
    'It was when I returned that the girl gave me the joke. That she-that is, the mother.' (The girl's mother said that as soon as she entered the yard she smelled a man.)

In all the above cases, *se* could be related to some of the uses discussed earlier. Both (38) and (39) would fit under figurative quotative; in (38), it introduces intention figuratively "declared" to herself, her workmates, or both; in (39) it introduces knowledge; and in (40) the use of *se* qualifies as hypothetical, in (41) as quotative (*se* introduces an accusation). In the case of the "noun complements" (44) and (45), the function of *se* is quotative.

In (42), (43) and (46), the quotative function is evident. In these cases, *se* introduces old information and appears as a reflective or ruminative echo in a separate sentence. However, as the following very common patterns demonstrate, there is nothing unique about the above cases other than that they contain *se*, and *se* often translates into English 'that'. In these examples, the second sentence has no expressed subject and the information it contains merely amplifies, in a nonessential way, what was stated in the first sentence.

47. *Di mada a gud smadi! Kier fi wi!*
    The mother is a good person! Care for we!
    'Our mother was a good person! (She) cared for us.'

48. *Wan man aawiez kom a yaad, niem Jiems Kyambl, [ehe] aawiez gi*
    A man always come at yard, name James Campbell; always give
    'A man by the name of James Campbell often comes here (to my home); and he always calls

    mi wan nikniem, kaal mi Magriga.
    me a nickname call me McGregor.
    me by the nickname he gave me: McGregor.'

The examples in (49) to (52) illustrate the use of *se* to seek clarification of a preceding question and its use in echo questions.

49. [*So hou kom yu muuv fram uova Alsaid?*] *Se hou lang?* [*Hou kom?*]
    [So how come you move from over Allside?] *Say* how long? [How come?]
    '[So how come you moved from Allsides?] How long? [How come?]'
    Se-hou mi kom fi muuv? [Ehe]
    say-how I come to move? [Yes]
    'How I came to move? [Yes].'

50. [*Yu wor marid in di Angglikan chorch?*] -*Se ef mi marid in-a*
    [You were married in the Anglican Church?] -*Say* if I married in
    '[Were you married in the Anglican Church?] Was I married in

    Hangglikyan chorch? [E-e]
    the Anglican church? [Yes].
    the Anglican church?' [Yes]'

51. [*Hou yu did nuo wen yu wor a big wuman?*] -*Se wa mi nuo?*
    [How you TNS know when you were a big woman?] -*Say* what I know?
    ['How did you know that you had become a woman?'] 'What did I know?'

52. [*Dee didn veks?*] *Se ef dem didn du wa?*
    [They didn't vex?] *Say* if they didn't do what?
    ['Didn't they get angry?'] 'Didn't they do what?'

One type of sentence involving *se* which seems to have escaped notice is the type of "echo question" illustrated in (49) to (52). These sentences probably derive from *Yu miin se* . . . as (53) suggests.

53. *Miin se if im nuo?*
    Mean *say* if he know?
    'Do you mean if he knows?'/'Do you mean to ask me whether he knows?'

In discussing *aks* . . . *se* 'ask . . . that', I noted that embedded questions are not allowed with *se* . . . (but see note 5). Example (53) would suggest that they are allowed with main verb *miin*, expressed or understood. Perhaps the explanation is that they are partial quotes.

In these examples, all or part of the questions asked is repeated. They either contain embedded Yes/No questions, in which case the Yes/No question (as understood) is introduced by *ef/if*, or embedded WH-questions in which case the WH-question appears with the appropriate understood WH-word. (The example in [52] combines both types.)

Due Respect

In a third type of "echo question", the question word (or WH-word), does not represent a questioned constituent or item of information within a question. Instead, it represents the entire question and requires that the entire question be repeated. In this case, *Se wa?* is used.[6] Note the difference between (51) and (52), in which *wa* represents a constituent within a sentence, and (54), where it represents a sentence.

54. [*Shi did oon it? Ar shi did rent it?*] *Se wa?* [*Shi oon it ar shi rent it?*]
    [She TNS own it? Or she TNS rent it?] *Say* what? [She own it or she rent it?]
    ['Did she own it? Or did she rent it?] What? [Did she own it or rent it?]'

The Clause to Which *Se* Belongs

In support of his claim as to how *taki* becomes a complementizer, Plag feels that prosodic information (a pause) indicates that, with speech act verbs, *taki* can be grouped with either the main clause or with the subordinate clause. In the case of cognition and perception verbs, however, such information always places *taki* with the subordinate clause.

The majority of my examples (as well as the echo questions in [49] to [54]) support this claim.

55. *Mi ha-fi kyari mi iej piepa go shuo im bifuo im wuda biliiv, yu nuo*
    I have to carry my age paper go show him before he would believe, you know,
    'I have to show him my birth certificate for him to accept

    se mi baan naintiin onjrid.
    say I born 1900.
    that I was born in 1900.'

However, the next two examples ([56] and [57]) suggest otherwise.

56. *No mosi nuo se wel, a tiif di man tiif im fi go sel im*
    No must be know *say*, well is thief the man thief him to go sell him.
    'Isn't it natural to conclude that (she) probably knew that, well, what the man had done was to steal her in order to sell her.'

57. *A sombadi, mi hier se, miit di madaop in-a Grienj an tel im se
"..."*

Is somebody, I hear *say*, meet the mother up in Grange and tell her say "..."

'It was someone, I hear, that met his mother in Grange and told her "...".'

In this last example, *mi hier se* is inserted parenthetically between the two clauses of a cleft sentence, or between the subject of the complement clause (which appears in the first clause of a cleft construction) and its predicate. In the next set of examples, (58) to (60), the entire complement clause represented by *wa*, is moved (WH-movement), leaving *se* with the main clause, a case of "complementizer stranding" perhaps.

This pattern occurs only with the WH-word *wa*. Based on the fact that *se* accepts only (finite) clausal complements and, based on the evidence from echo questions involving *wa*, we can conclude that this *wa*, too, represents clausal complements only.[7]

58. *Hou mi a go memba?! ... Wat mi a go memba se?*
How I ASP go remember?! What I ASP go remember *say*?
'How will I remember (that kind of information)? What will I remember?'

59. *Yu nuo wa mi fain se? Mi fain se ...* (Passenger on bus)
You know what I find *say*? I find *say* ...
'Do you know what I've discovered (to be the case)? I've found that ...'

60. *Mi no nuo wat tu tel yu se.*
I NEG know what to tell you *say*.
'I don't know what to tell you.'

Examples (57) to (60) indicate that *se* is functioning as a complementizer, therefore, unlike languages like English, Jamaican Creole does not bar the sequence of complementizer-trace. Jamaican allows extraction of the subject of a lower clause if there is an overt complementizer preceding that clause. Compare the following English examples with their Jamaican Creole equivalent:

61. *Who do you think that did it?

62. Who do you think did it?

63. *Huu yu tingk se dw-iit*

    This "that-trace filter", however, is not a defining characteristic of complementizers. As Haegeman (1991: 362–63) observes, it is not universal and there is much idiolectal variation even in those languages which manifest it.

    Both Plag (1993: 48) and Veenstra (1996: 154) raise the question of whether semantic bleaching precedes syntactic reanalysis in the process of grammaticalization. In their analysis of Sranan and Saramaccan data, they suggest that, contrary to previously held positions, the semantic shift seemed to occur contemporaneously with, or only after, the syntactic shift. The expectation is for the verb of saying to first lose its semantic content, become a function word and then eventually turn into a grammatical morpheme. Instead, Plag argues (pp. 48–49), the shift from verb to complementizer occurred even though the semantics remained more or less intact. The meaning is strongest in the use of the "complementizer" after verbs of saying, becoming weaker after cognition verbs, and weaker still in final clauses, consecutive clauses and noun complements.

    The Jamaican evidence suggests that *se*, in its main verb or "noncomplementizer" functions, is more than just a verb of saying. This raises questions as to whether there truly is a semantic shift that is peculiar to the development of a complementizer function, or at least whether it occurs in the stages proposed by Plag (1993) and by Romaine (1988), among others.

Notes

1. The analysis presented here was begun while I was a Junior Research Fellow with the Institute of Caribbean Studies, UWI, Mona. During the period 1989–1992, I received three such fellowships for periods totalling just under three years. The data used in the essay comes mainly from Brodber 1980. Additional sentences are taken from local TV programmes, from conversations heard, and, where I did not manage to record some structures that I heard, some sentences were elicited.

2. If *se* is inserted, this meaning changes. In the rare cases where it may be possible to distinguish nominative and accusative pronouns (Jamaican *ar* 'her', Guyanese *am* 'him/her/it'), the NP following the perception verb shows accusative behaviour. Further, the second clause in this sentence does not take a tense marker, which suggests that it is nonfinite. See Veenstra 1996: 57–62, also Bailey 1966: 115–16.
3. *Aks* needs more thorough investigation, but preliminary examination of the data and the judgement of one informant support the position stated here. See also Bailey 1966: 112–14. My intuition as a native speaker of Guyanese tells me that embedded questions can follow *aaks se*, but only if there is a pause after *se*. In other words, a partial quote midway between direct and indirect speech.
4. Saramaccan *taa*, according to Veenstra 1996: 154–55, when it appears as a main verb.
5. This speaker is a descendant of Indian indentured labourers. I cannot say whether the structure is widely used. One explanation would be that it comes from Bhojpuri (according to Mohan 1978, cited in Romaine 1988: 145–46.
6. With a change of intonation, the echo question *Se wa?* becomes the rhetorical exclamation *Se wa?!* with the same connotations as the African American *Say what?!*
7. We could use *se* as a tool for testing the clausal status of a variety of constructions.
    Im tel mi se fi tel mi mada fi get wait ail not
    Mi hier se a yong man nou
    Mi nuo se a wen mi an im marid
    Mi memba wen im biit mi
    Mi no memba a ou moch

References

Alleyne, M. 1980. *Comparative Afro-American*. Ann Arbor, MI: Karoma.

Bailey, B. 1966. *Jamaican Creole Syntax: A Transformational Approach*. Cambridge: Cambridge University Press.

Brodber, E. 1980. *Life in Jamaica in the early Twentieth Century. A Presentation of Ninety Oral Accounts*. Mona, Jamaica: Institute of Social and Economic Research.

Cassidy, F.G., and R. Le Page. 1980. *Dictionary of Jamaican English*. 2d. ed. Cambridge: Cambridge University Press.

Haegeman, L. 1991. *Introduction to Government and Binding Theory*. Cambridge, MA: Basil Blackwell.

Kihm, A. 1990. Complementizer, verb or both? Kriyol kuma. *Journal of Pidgin and Creole Languages* 5, no. 1.

Plag, I. 1993. *Sentential Complements in Sranan: On the Formation of an English-based Creole.* Tübingen: Niemeyer.

Romaine, S. 1988. *Pidgin and Creole Languages.* New York: Longman.

Sebba, M. 1987. *The Syntax of Serial Verbs.* Amsterdam and Philadelphia: John Benjamins.

Sistren. 1986. *Lionheart Gal: Life Stories of Jamaican Women.* London: Women's Press.

Veenstra, T. 1996. *Serial Verbs in Saramaccan: Predication and Creole Genesis.* Den Haag, Holland: Academic Graphics.

Chapter 9

A Comparison of Tense/Aspect Systems in Caribbean English Creoles

Donald Winford

This chapter is a contribution towards our understanding of the relationships among Caribbean English Creoles, an old question which is part of the more general issue of the typological and genetic relationships among Creoles in general.[1] Among the pioneers of research on these issues, as they relate to the Caribbean Creoles in particular, was Robert Le Page. His contribution in this area is sometimes overshadowed by his well-known pioneering work on the social motivations of language choice in Caribbean communities, and his *Acts of Identity* hypothesis, in particular as articulated in Le Page and Tabouret-Keller (1985), not to mention his impressive reconstruction of the sociohistorical background to the emergence of Jamaican Creole (Le Page 1960). But there were other important contributions as well. The *Dictionary of Jamaican English,* which he co-authored with Frederic Cassidy, contains priceless information on the lexicon of Jamaican Creole and on lexical similarities across the Caribbean (Cassidy and Le Page 1980). Le Page (1957) attempted perhaps the first comprehensive overview of these Creoles, providing an informative comparison of their verb complexes and other aspects of grammar. This chapter is dedicated to him for his important contribution to this and other areas of our knowledge about Caribbean English Creoles.

My main aim is to establish some groundwork for accurate and fuller comparisons across Creole tense/aspect systems as a basis for understanding their relationships and origins. I will compare the tense/aspect systems of four

Due Respect

Creoles (Sranan, rural Guyanese, Belizean and Jamaican) which I have been researching for several years. If we are to achieve accuracy in our comparison of these systems, we need an approach which builds on established practice among typologists and semanticists in the comparative study of Tense/Mood/Aspect (TMA) systems cross-linguistically. Such an approach is rendered necessary by the fact that scholars who have analysed Creole TMA systems employ different data collection methods, terminology, and theoretical assumptions, all of which makes the task of comparison across Creoles more difficult. The approach I use here has been described more fully in other studies (Winford 1993, 2000a). It is modelled on typological studies of TMA systems such as Dahl (1985), Comrie (1976, 1985) and Bybee and colleagues (1994). To summarize briefly, the framework is based on the following assumptions:

1. Comparison is based on actual TMA categories, rather than on the semantic features out of which such categories can be built. As Dahl explains:

    > I shall suggest that the most salient 'universals' or better, basic units of the general theory of TMA systems are rather atoms than elementary particles, ie categories rather than features. More concretely speaking, this means that I think of a language specific category like, say the English Perfect, as the realization of a crosslinguistic category or better, category type PERFECT, rather than as the realization of a set of features, say /+x, y, +z/. (1985: 33)

    In the following, I adopt Dahl's practice of using capitals to refer to category types (PAST), initial capitals to refer to language specific categories (the English Past), and lower case letters with single quotation marks to refer to notional semantic categories ('past').

2. TMA categories in every language typically have a range of meanings and uses, that is, they can be interpreted variously in discourse.

3. Every TMA category has a dominant meaning and often has other sec-

ondary meanings. In general, the dominant meaning of a category is represented in its primary or prototypical uses, while secondary meanings are interpretations that arise from contextual uses of the category. As Dahl explains:

> the main criterion for identifying TMA categories cross-linguistically is by their foci or prototypical uses, and . . . languages vary essentially in two respects: (i) which categories they choose out of the set of crosslinguistic categories and (ii) how they reduce the impreciseness that these categories have in choosing among the possible secondary or nonfocal uses they have. (Dahl 1985: 33)

4. It follows that the discourse context plays a vital role in the interpretation of TMA categories. Hence the methods used to collect data must be designed to include as much discourse context as possible for the use of each tense/aspect category. (This is discussed briefly below.)

5. The interaction between TMA categories and the inherent aspectual characteristics or *aktionsarten* of different predicates affects interpretation. As is well known, for instance, certain tense/aspect categories can have rather different interpretations with stative as opposed to nonstative predicates.

Data and Methodology

The present study employs data of two types: (1) elicitations from native speakers based on a modified version of Dahl's (1985) TMA questionnaire, and (2) tape recordings of conversations among native speakers of the Creoles. The questionnaire is somewhat different from traditional ones in that the sentences presented for translation by informants were placed in a discourse context which made the intended meaning as clear as possible. For example, to elicit sentences containing a verb with past time reference, one of the prompts used is illustrated in (1).

(1) [It is cold in the room. The window is closed.]
     Q: You OPEN the window (and closed it again)?

The sentences in square brackets provide a context for the utterance to be elicited (the English version of which is outside the brackets). The eliciter explains the context and asks the informant to translate the utterance, keeping that context in mind. Verbs are given in bare form (capitalized in the text) to minimize the possibility of interference from English when translating. As Dahl (1985: 45) notes, this approach meant that "the information necessary to choose the correct TMA category in the translation would have to be deduced from the sentence itself together with its context." This approach often involved discussions between the investigator and the informants to clarify the precise context and intended interpretation of the sentence to be translated. (See Dahl 1985: 44–50 for further discussion of the assumptions, methods and problems associated with the use of the TMA questionnaire.)

Most of the data for the present study, however, came from recordings of actual conversations made by fieldworkers who were themselves native speakers of the Creoles in question. The study focuses on tense and aspect categories only. The area of modality is rather complex, and space does not permit discussion of it here. I will present a brief summary of the similarities and differences in the categories employed in the four Creoles, with appropriate illustration. The findings reported here are based on studies I have done on these Creoles over the last decade.

The Unmarked Verb

The unmarked verb displays a remarkable similarity of uses and interpretations across all Caribbean English Creoles (CEC). I have argued elsewhere (Winford 1993) that the unmarked verb is unanalysed for any of the parameters of tense, mood or aspect. Hence it can lend itself to various interpretations, depending on the discourse context and the predicate involved.

It was once widely accepted that the unmarked verb expresses present time reference with statives and past time reference with nonstatives. But recent research (Jaganauth 1988; Winford 1993, 2000a) has shown that this is only part of the picture. In fact, unmarked verbs have a range of interpretations, most of which are shared across all CEC. We can summarize these as follows:

1. The default interpretation of an unmarked stative is present, while that of an unmarked nonstative is past, provided that speech time (S) is the point of reference. These represent prototypical uses of unmarked verbs. In examples (2) and (3), from Sranan and Belizean, respectively, the relevant predicates are differentiated. (Due to limitations of space, examples are not provided for all Creoles.)

Sranan

(2) a. *A pikin wani go sribi.*
'The child wants to go and sleep.'

b. *A kamra kowru bikaa me opo a fensre.*
'The room is cold because I opened the window.'

Belizean

(3) a. *Jan noo di ansa fu da problem.*
'John knows the answer for that problem.'

b. *I kyeri di sou, di red sou de an I kros ā wid i boo.*
'He took the sow, the red sow there and he crossed her with the boar.'

2. Unmarked verbs may convey quite different interpretations in other discourse contexts. For instance, once the discourse context establishes the reference point as past, unmarked statives can have past time reference. This is one of the secondary uses of unmarked verbs, illustrated in (4) and (5).

Sranan

(4) *A bigi suma kon dape dan a si mi. Dan a lobi mi. Omdat a so pikin mi de a e si mi e wroko.*
'The elderly lady came there and saw me. And she liked me. Because I was so little and she saw how I worked.'

Belizean

(5) *Bot dē mi veks wid ā bikaa dē noo da George mi rang wid mii.*
'But they were angry with him, because they knew it was George who was at fault with me.'

Due Respect

Similar uses of unmarked statives have been demonstrated for Guyanese Creole and Jamaican Creole (see Jaganauth 1988; Winford 1993).

3. Certain uses of unmarked verbs seem to correspond to a kind of perfect, as various researchers have pointed out (see Voorhoeve 1957; Seuren 1981). This secondary use occurs in (6) and (7).

    Sranan

    (6) A: *Ma unu no si a man dya a Coronie?*
    'But you haven't seen the guy here in Coronie?'

    B: *Persoonly noyti mi no si en dya a Coronie.*
    'Personally I've never seen him here in Coronie.'

    Belizean

    (7) *A no noo if i sel it yet, inoo, bot mm, i get it kot aredi.*
    'I don't know if he's sold it yet, you know, but mm, he's got it cut already.'

The sense of a "perfect" in these examples is conveyed partly by the discourse context and partly by adverbials like *noyti, yet* and *aredii* rather than by the unmarked verb *per se*.

4. Unmarked verbs are used freely in the protasis (*if*-clause) of open conditionals to express future possibility.

    Sranan

    (8) *En efu a man dati wini en, a kondre e kon bun zeker.*
    'And if that man wins it [the election], the country will surely improve.'

    Guyanese

    (9) *If yu weet ten minit, di waata go hat.*
    'If you wait ten minutes, the water will get hot.'

Again, these uses have parallels in all the other Caribbean Creoles (and indeed in Creoles of other lexical affiliations). Table 9.1 sums up the various uses of the unmarked verb in all CEC.

Table 9.1: Summary of the meanings of the unmarked verb

Perfective (Zero-marked)

Basic meaning	Unanalysed event or state, viewed as a single whole
Primary uses	Simple (absolute) past; present habitual (Western Caribbean only)
Secondary uses	Past states; present perfect
Discourse function	To refer to situations which have current relevance, or are currently in focus. Default choice once the temporal reference is established by the context

Cross-Creole Similarities

The range of uses of unmarked verbs shown here is identical in all four Creoles surveyed, and no doubt in other Caribbean English Creoles as well. Holm (2000) shows that the similarities extend to a wide variety of Creoles of different lexical affiliations. However, apart from these similarities, there is an interesting contrast between Eastern and Western Caribbean English Creoles in their use of unmarked verbs. In the latter, which include Jamaican Creole (JC), Belizean (BelC) and Providence Island Creole (PIC), unmarked verbs are used in all the functions just outlined, but are also used to convey habitual and generic meanings. By contrast, habitual/generic meaning is subsumed under the Imperfective category in Sranan (SN) and conservative Guyanese Creole (GC), and grammaticized as a distinct category (instantiated by *doz*) in other Eastern Caribbean English Creoles (see discussion below). These differences suggest that there is no fixed "prototype" associated with zero-marked verbs across all these Creoles, even though they share a common core of meanings and uses.

Tense Categories

As is well known, there is a broad distinction across languages between tense systems in which the reference point or tense locus is S (absolute tense systems), and those in which it may (also) be some other point in time (relative tense systems). All varieties of CEC discussed here have a relative tense system. In addition, they all have in common three tense categories, Relative

Past and Future and a Prospective Future. None of them has a present tense category; rather, present time reference is conveyed by categories that are primarily aspectual in character, such as Imperfective, as in SN and GC, or Progressive and Present Habitual in other Creoles. Let us consider the tense categories in turn.

Relative Past Tense

The Relative Past auxiliary in all these Creoles derives from English *ben/been*, though its phonetic form varies from Creole to Creole (*ben* in SN, *bin* in GC, *mi* < *min*, *bin* in BelC, and [*b*]*en/wen* in JC). There is now wide agreement among creolists that the primary function of the Relative Past is to locate a situation in the past in relation to either the moment of speech or some reference point in the past. For instance, Bickerton (1975) observed that the meaning of GC *bin* shifts between 'simple past', 'remote past' and 'past before past'. As Jaganauth (1988) points out, if we bear in mind that it is the reference point which moves, then there is no need to view the various uses of *bin* as distinct. Similar conclusions have been shown to apply to JC *ben* (Pollard 1989; Winford 1993), SN (Wilner 1992, 2000a), and BelC (Winford 1994). The prototypical use of *ben* is to locate some situation as occurring prior to the reference point under focus in the discourse. The effect of this is to distance the situation from the reference point, and "background" it in some way, illustrated in (10) and (11).

> *Sranan*
> (10) [Q: Did you open the window (and close it again)? The window is now closed.]
> *Aay, na mi ben opo a fensre.*
> 'Yes, it was me that opened the window.'
>
> *Belizean*
> (11) *Dē mi hav wā man da landin we dē mi juuztu kaal ool dik arnal.*
> 'There was a man at (Bermudian) Landing whom they used to call old Dick Arnold.'

As Pollard (1989) and Wilner (1992) have shown, however, the uses of *ben* are best illustrated from natural discourse. Narratives in particular provide good examples of the prototypical uses of *ben*. Example (12) is from Sranan:

(12) a. *Ma wan vyftien yari, wan twintig yari pasa tu, wan man K. ben dede a Coppename. Leti so wan sortu fasi, tog.*
b. *A ø gwe ina busi, an no ø kon noyti moro a dorosei.*
c. *Ma a man dati, sani ben musu fu miti a man dati. Omdat a man dati ben abi tapu na en skin. A man, dus, a man ben kin kapoewa, ala meti san kon a ben kiri.*
d. *Dus a ten ø kon now taki a san ø drai onderste boven gi en. A ø go wan leisi a busi, noyti moro a ø kon a syoro. Dati kan de so wan twintig, kande wan tertig yari tori.*

a. 'But some fifteen to twenty years ago, a man by the name of K. died at Coppename. In a similar fashion, right?
b. He went into the woods and never came out again.
c. But things were bound to happen to that man. Because he had obeah on his body. The man had killed kapoewa, all kinds of animals.
d. So now the time came when the tables were turned on him. He went into the woods and never returned. That might have been some twenty, perhaps thirty years ago.'

Note how the use of *ben* in the opening sentence distances the situation from S, while unmarked verbs in the following sentence (b) introduce the narrative. The following three sentences (c) provide background information to explain the cause of these events, and *ben* is used once more to establish this background. The final sentences return to the main story line, which calls once more for the use of unmarked verbs. It is clear that Pollard's explanation of the uses of *ben* versus unmarked verbs in JC narratives applies equally well to Sranan, and indeed to GC and Belizean. Information that is more highly relevant as a response to a given question, that is salient or in focus when compared with other information, is foreground information and is expressed by the unmarked form of the verb. Information which is perhaps necessary but less highly relevant, less salient, less in immediate focus . . . is background information and is expressed by the verb plus particle *en* (Pollard 1989: 63).

Due Respect

Another function of the Relative Past marker, which all these Creoles share, is its use in conditional clauses. In all of them, Relative Past is used in the protasis of conditions to convey counterfactuality, and is also used in combination with future markers in the consequent (apodosis) to convey past or present counterfactuality or a hypothetical future. The only exception to this is JC, which uses *wuda (ben)* in the latter cases. (Note that Belizean also uses *wuda (mi)* in addition to *mi wā*.) The following examples illustrate. (Note that SN has a choice of two different futures, discussed further below.)

Sranan

(13) *Efu mi ben de datra, mi ben sa/bo abi furu moni.*
'If I were a doctor, I might/would have a lot of money.'

Guyanese

(14) *If mi bin gat taim, mi ben go/sa kom sii yu*
'If I had time, I would have come to see you.'

Belizean

(15) *Oo laad if a mi noo somoch a dem mi wā de de, a mi wā gaan, a wuda mi gaan man.*
'Lord, if I'd known so many of them would have been there, I would have gone, I would have gone.'

Table 9.2 presents a summary of the meanings and uses associated with similarity in the meaning and use of the Relative Past category in Caribbean English Creoles.

Table 9.2 : Summary of meanings of Relative Past

Basic meaning	Absolute/relative past temporal reference
Primary use	To locate situation in past (before S or another point in the past)
Secondary (modal) uses	To express counter-factuality in conditionals; to mitigate requests, advice, etc.
Discourse function	To distance situation from the reference point; to provide background for situation in focus

Based on the available studies (Bickerton 1975, 1979; Jaganauth 1988; Pollard 1989; Wilner 1992; Winford 1993), there is a remarkable similarity in the meaning and use of the Relative Past category in Caribbean Creoles as well as others, like Haitian Creole as described by Spears (1993). The similarities extend across the Atlantic to varieties like Nigerian Pidgin, as described by Agheyisi (1971: 133-34) as well as other English-lexicon Creoles of West Africa (Bickerton 1979: 313). Indeed, this is one TMA category that we can safely say is practically identical across all these Creoles. It is therefore a strong candidate for inclusion in the inventory of the "core" or, if you prefer, "prototypical" Atlantic Creole TMA categories.

Future Tense

The use of two futures – one predictive future and the other prospective, one conveyed by a combination of a progressive or imperfective marker plus *go* – is found in all varieties of CEC, although there are some differences in the form of the predictive future. In the Eastern Caribbean, it is some form of *go* (SN *o*, GC *go*), but in the Western Caribbean, JC and Belizean employ *wi* and *wã* (< *want*), respectively. However, all these Creoles have the usual prospective future expressed by *go* in the progressive aspect (*e go* in SN, *a go* in GC, *a/de+go* in JC, *gwain* in BelC). According to Boretzky (1983), this distinction is also found in other Creoles of various lexical affiliations, though full accounts of future marking are not available for all. At any rate, the near universality of the distinction between predictive and prospective futures, at least among Caribbean Creoles, suggests that this is part of the core TMA system they all share. However, the Surinamese Creoles and GC have an uncertain future category, expressed by *sa*, which is not found in other varieties of CEC. The uses of the predictive future are quite similar across all these Creoles surveyed. Its basic meaning is "later time reference" and its prototypical use is to make predictions about the future, as in (16) and (17).

Sranan

(16) *Pas te unu kaba nanga skoro dan wi o meki pikin nanga den sani dati.*
'Only when we finish with school, then we'll have kids and all those things.'

Belizean

(17) *Junie see I wã kom luk fi yu wan a diiz deez.*
'Junie says she'll come and look you up one of these days.'

Due Respect

In all these Creoles, the predictive Future can refer to future in relation not to S, but to some point in the past, as in (18) and (19).

Sranan

(18) *Traesde mi miti en even. A ben taigi mi a o kon na fesisey baka.*
'I saw him briefly the day before yesterday. He told me he would come to the front again.'

Belizean

(19) *I se I wã stee rait ya, I see I nat gwain outside.*
'He said he would stay right here, he said he wasn't going outside.'

This suggests that *o* marks relative future, just as *ben* marks relative past, and that the tense system of SN in general is a relative tense system. In this respect, SN and BelC are similar to GC, JC and other varieties of CEC, which also employ their future markers in this way (Winford 1993: 60). There are also certain secondary uses of the predictive future which all these Creoles share. For instance, it can be used to express predictability or characteristic behaviour in both present and past contexts.

Sranan

(20) *Yu o wasi a krosi, wan heri tobo krosi nanga wasi planga. Omeni a suma o gi yu? Vyftig cent. Ma yu ben det evreden.*
'You'd wash clothes, a whole tub of clothes. How much would the lady give you? Fifty cents? But you were satisfied.'

Belizean

(21) *Yu wã fain de no wã kum ya da dee, tiicha, bot de kum da nait.*
'You'll find they won't come here by day, teacher, but they come at night.'

Table 9.3 summarizes the various uses and interpretations of the predicative Future.

Table 9.3: Summary of meanings of Future

Basic meaning	Relatively certain future time reference (R=S or some point in past)
Primary uses	Future time reference Prediction Intention
Secondary uses	Future in the past Predictability or characteristic behaviour (present or past)

Prospective Future

As I noted earlier, all of these Creoles employ *go* in the progressive to convey the sense of an immediate or prospective future. This category appears to be more fully grammaticized in the other Creoles than in SN, but the sense of futurity is often clearly in evidence.

> *Sranan*
> (22) *Ma yu melde yu mama dati wi e go pley bal?*
> 'But have you told your mom that we're going to play basketball?'
>
> *Belizean*
> (23) *I see if yu no pee mi fu ā a gwain shuut yu nou.*
> 'He said if you don't pay me for it, I'm going to shoot you now.'

Similar uses are quite frequent in JC, GC and other varieties of CEC.

Aspect in CEC

As Comrie (1976: 4) has pointed out, aspect characterizes the internal structure of a situation. In other words, situations may be characterized in terms of notions such as dynamicity (progressive/nonprogressive), closure (perfective/imperfective), iterativity and habituality, durativity, and so on. The distinction between perfective and imperfective is most relevant to the aspectual systems of Caribbean Creoles. Another relevant category is the so-called Completive, a subtype of PERFECT.

"Imperfective" Notions in CEC

The semantic space occupied by the label "imperfective" represents one of the areas that are grammaticized quite differently across Caribbean Creoles. The two primary notions subsumed under imperfectivity, "progressive" and "habitual", are subsumed under a single Imperfective category in Sranan and (apparently) the other Surinamese Creoles, as well as in conservative rural GC.[2] The same also seems to apply to non-English-lexicon Creoles such as the Caribbean French Creoles and Papiamentu (Andersen 1990). I discuss GC and SN first.

In these two Creoles, both stative and nonstative predicates can be marked by Imperfective, though the interaction between *aktionsart* and the category leads to somewhat different interpretations in each case. In combination with dynamic predicates, Imperfective conveys the sense of an activity or event in progress, a "progressive" meaning, illustrated in (24) and (25).

Sranan

(24) *Nownow yu e teki en kba nownow?*
'Are you already taping right now?'

Guyanese

(25) *Jan a iit rait nou.*
'John is eating right now.'

Imperfective is also used with both statives and nonstatives in SN and GC to express repeated or habitual situations.

Sranan

(26) *En te yu si wan moi film a tv, yu e wan go luku. Yu e prakseri a schrift, yu e bonk a schrift go na wan sey. Yu no e abi ten.*
'And when you see a nice movie on TV, you want to go watch it. You consider the notebook, you throw the notebook aside. You don't have time.'

Guyanese

(27) *Jan a iit seem taim evridee.*
'John eats at the same time every day.'

Finally, Imperfective is quite neutral with respect to time reference, which it picks up from the discourse context. When the reference point is S, as in the above examples, Imperfective is interpreted as having present time reference. But when the time reference has been established as past, it can have past reference.

Sranan

(28) *Faya no ben de. No wan gado faya. Kronto bon ben furu a strati. Faya no de. A so te neti yu e waka. Efu yu no abi flashlait efu munkenki, yu no es si. Yu e dyam srefi nanga suma.*
'There were no lights. Not a single light. There were lots of coconut trees along the street. There were no lights. That's how it was when you walked at night. If you didn't have a flashlight or moonlight, you couldn't see. You'd even bump into people.'

Guyanese

(29) *Dis ting hapn tu mii tuu, chrii taim, dat enitaim mi waan di de de, mi a heer somting faal, an wen mi go, mi na a sii notn.*
'This thing happened to me two or three times, that whenever I was there by myself, I would hear something falling and when I went, I would see nothing.'

Table 9.4 summarizes the meanings and uses of the Imperfective in Sranan and Guyanese.

Table 9.4: Summary of meanings of Imperfective *e*

Basic meaning	Unbounded situation
Primary uses	Activities or events in progress at R (progressive)
	(R=S or some other point in time established by the context); habitual or generic situations (all predicates)
Secondary uses	Immediate future

None of the other Caribbean English Creoles surveyed here has an Imperfective category. Rather, Progressive and Past Habitual are grammaticized as distinct categories, while present habituality is conveyed by various means. In JC, for instance, Progressive is conveyed by *a*, alternating with *de* in some dialects, while in Belizean Progressive is conveyed by *di* (Winford 1994).[3]

Jamaican

(30)　*Jan a nyam i dina.*
　　　'John's eating the dinner.'

Belizean

(31)　*Bikaaz a tel mi waif, a tel ā a di get ool nou.*
　　　'Because I told my wife, I told her I'm getting old now.'

In both JC and BelC, Past Habitual is conveyed by *juuztu* (alternating with *doz* in some varieties of Belizean).[4]

Jamaican

(32)　*Im (ben) juuztuwaak ga a skuul evridee laas yier.*
　　　'She (or he) used to walk to school every day last year.'

Belizean

(33)　*Bikaaz di ool man neva juuztu iit bikaaz i doz trobl wid presha.*
　　　'Because the old man never used to eat, because he used to suffer with [high blood] pressure.'

In both JC and BelC (as well as other Western Caribbean Creoles, such as PIC), present habitual meaning is conveyed by the unmarked verb.

Jamaican

(34)　*Im waak gaa skuul evridee.*
　　　'He (or she) walks to school every day.'

Belizean

(35)　*Percy hi no kil dē ataal sa, no kil dē ataal. An hi no wees kyaatrij fu dat.*
　　　'Percy doesn't kill them [snakes] at all, sir, doesn't kill them at all. And he doesn't waste cartridges for that.'

It has been argued (Christie 1986) that the JC Progressive is increasingly being used to convey habituality as well, and may be evolving into an Imperfective marker. But, as I have argued elsewhere (1993: 43), Progressive

Winford – *A Comparison of Tense/Aspect Systems*

categories often develop secondary uses to describe activities that are customary, especially when used with temporal adverbs indicating habituality, as in *He's working on his paper every day*. As Bybee and Dahl (1989: 82) point out, "such usage represents a generalization of the earlier progressive meaning". However, there is no evidence to suggest that the JC Progressive has evolved completely into an Imperfective marker, displacing the unmarked verb in conveying habitual meaning. Table 9.5 presents a comparison of the way imperfective notions are grammaticized and expressed in the four Caribbean English Creoles which are the focus of this study.

Table 9.5: "Imperfective" in four Caribbean English Creoles

Semantic Notion		SN	GC	JC	BelC
'progressive'	Cat.	Impfv.	Impfv.	Prog.	Prog.
	Form	e	a	a/de	di
'present habitual'	Cat.	Impfv.	Impfv.	Unmarked	Unmarked
	Form	e	a	ø	ø
'past habitual'	Cat.	(Past) Impfv.	(Past) Impfv.	Past Hab.	Past Hab.
	Form	(ben)e	(bin) a	juuztu	juuztu

It is clear that only a certain group of (Eastern) Caribbean Creoles have an Imperfective category that matches the "Nonpunctual" aspectual category that Bickerton claimed to be part of the Creole prototype. These include the Surinamese Creoles (Huttar and Huttar 1994: 497; Winford 2000a), Guyanese Creole (Winford 1993: 38), Tobagonian Creole (James 1974, 1996), St Kitts Creole (Cooper 1978), and possibly others. It is interesting that this category is not found in the Western Creoles like JC and BelC, which are regarded as somewhat radical. It is equally interesting that Creoles of quite different lexical affiliations, Iberian, French and English, share this Imperfective category, and apparently use it in very similar ways. This sharing obviously calls for some explanation. At the same time, the differences across Creoles once more raise questions about the validity of a Creole "prototype".

Completive/Perfect Aspect

All varieties of CEC have a Completive/Perfect marker which is formally similar to a main verb that means 'finish'. Sranan and the other Surinamese Creoles have *kaba*, which they appear to have adopted from Portuguese *acabar* 'finish' or from either a Portuguese pidgin or from Saramaccan, in whose formation Portuguese lexical input played a significant role. In varieties of CEC, the Completive/Perfect marker and the main verb meaning 'finish' are expressed by *don* (< English *done*). The aspectual category generally conveys the sense of 'already', with exceptions as noted below.

There are some differences in the use of the Completive/Perfect across the four Creoles surveyed here. First, in SN, preverbal *kaba* functions only as a main verb meaning 'finish', and shows little evidence of having been grammaticized into an aspectual marker. In the other three Creoles, however, preverbal *don* functions as both a main verb meaning 'finish' and as a marker of Completive/Perfect aspect. Second, while SN, GC and JC use Completive/Perfect *don* in VP-final position, Belize Creole never does. Third, while the Completive/Perfect marker is compatible with all kinds of predicates in GC, SN and BelC, it occurs only with nonstative predicates in JC, where it preserves a strong 'terminative' sense. Finally, GC not only has both preverbal and VP-final *don*, one with high pitch, which is generalized to all predicates and conveys the (Completive/Perfect) sense of 'already', and another with low pitch, which is used primarily with nonstatives and conveys the sense of 'finish' ('terminative'). VP-final *don* in GC also appears to be used in both a terminative and Completive/Perfect sense (Winford 1993: 55–56).[5]

The following examples illustrate the use of SN *kaba* and Belizean *don* as main verbs with a terminative meaning.

(36) a. *Pikinso fosi mi doro na oso mi brada ben kaba a brifi.*
'A little before I arrived home, my brother had finished writing the letter.'

b. *A tel ã a di iit, man, weet til a don iit no sa.*
'I told him I'm eating, man, wait till I finish eating please sir.'

As already noted, preverbal *kaba* in SN is always main-verbal, with the sense of 'finish'. By contrast, preverbal *don* in CEC may be either main-verbal ('finish') or an auxiliary marking Completive/Perfect aspect, expressing the sense of 'already' and functioning in ways quite similar to a type of PERFECT. The latter type of meaning can be conveyed in SN only by VP-final *kaba*, which is compatible with predicates of all types.

Sranan

(37) a. *Mi miti nanga en wan leisi kaba, so mi sabi en.*
'I've met him once already, so I know him.'

b. *Mi no abi fanowdu fu yu leri mi rei wagi, bikaa mi sabi en.*
'I don't need to learn to drive a car, because I know how to already.'

Similar uses of VP-final *don* are quite common in GC, as the examples in (38) show:

(38) a. *Di pikni iit di fuud don.*
'The child has eaten the food already/finished eating the food.'

b. *Da leedi gat chrii pikni don.*
'That lady has three children already.'

However, in JC, VP-final *don*, like its preverbal counterpart, still retains a strong terminative sense and is compatible only with nonstatives and change-of-state predicates (Winford 1993: 48). This suggests that JC *don* is in an early stage of grammaticalization when compared with its counterparts in other varieties of CEC.

The various meanings and uses of Completive/Perfect are summarized in Table 9.6.

Table 9.6: Summary of meanings of Completive/Perfect in CEC

Completive Perfect

Basic meaning	'already' – Situations originating in the past with current relevance (both present and past contexts)
Primary uses	Past actions leading to current result (perfect of result) States already in existence with current implications (resultative) (except JC)
Secondary use	Adverbial modifying temporal phrases (SN)
Discourse function	To signal situations that have implications or consequences for the present situation

Cross-Creole Comparison

There are two important differences in the range of meanings and uses associated with Completive/Perfect markers across Caribbean (and other) Creoles. One has to do with the degree of generalization of their use with predicates of different semantic types. The other has to do with their integration into the AUX system. With regard to the former, we have already seen that, within CEC, JC is exceptional in limiting its Completive/Perfect marker *don* to non-stative predicates, while other varieties allow use of Completive/Perfect with predicates of all types. Also of interest is the fact that GC not only has both preverbal and VP-final *don*, but, unlike SN, distinguishes two preverbal forms *don*, one with low pitch ('terminative') and the other with high pitch ('already'). The differences in the range of uses of Completive/Perfect markers across Creoles may be explained in terms of differences in the processes of Creole formation, or in terms of internal developments within each Creole. It is not clear, for instance, whether all varieties of CEC originally restricted their Completive/Perfect markers to activity verbs (like JC), with differences emerging later as a result of internal change, or whether such differences date back to the earliest stages of Creole formation. Even if the latter were the case, we would still have to allow for continuing processes of grammaticization to explain, for instance, the further development of *kaba* into a kind of adverbial in SN, and the distinction in GC between Completive (high pitch) and Terminative (low pitch) auxiliary *don,* and, perhaps, also the development of VP-final *don* from serial verb to Completive marker, paralleling the evolution of VP-final *kaba* in SN.

The differences in the ways Creoles integrate their Completive/Perfect markers into AUX also calls for explanation. Bickerton (1981: 80) argued that Completive markers are integrated into the AUX category only in certain Creoles, but that in most they have a rather marginal status. He accounts for this by postulating three successive stages of development, as follows:

Stage 1: Completive markers remain marginal particles, occurring optionally in clause-final position.

Stage 2: They are incorporated into AUX without combining with other AUX constituents.

Stage 3: They are incorporated into AUX where they combine freely with other TMA auxiliaries.

There are at least two aspects of this scenario which are questionable. In the first place, it implies that the differences in placement and behaviour of

Completive/Perfect markers across Creoles can be explained in terms of some kind of developmental sequence, with all Creoles starting at more or less the same stage. We have no evidence that this was in fact the case. It seems more likely that different Creoles opted for different kinds of installation of their Completive/Perfect markers into the verb complex from the very beginning. The second problem with Bickerton's scenario is that it assumes that nonincorporation of a Completive/Perfect marker into AUX is synonymous with marginality. This is not borne out by the evidence from SN, where VP-final *kaba* is just as integral a part of the aspectual system as any of the preverbal TMA markers. In a similar vein, Stolz (1987: 302) notes that Future *lo* in Papiamentu is regarded as part of the TMA system despite the fact that it occurs clause-initially rather than preverbally. Rather than speak of marginality, we should refer to the different ways in which Completive/Perfect markers have been installed in the verb complexes of different Creoles. What we find are differences both in the positioning and combinatory potential of such markers. From this perspective, while Bickerton's historical scenario may be questionable, his grouping of Creoles according to the two criteria just mentioned provides a good basis for a more accurate classification. Building on his and Stolz's insights, we can identify the following categories of Creoles according to the way they employ their Completive/Perfect markers. (This classification is based on the available literature and is subject to revision as our knowledge increases.)

Category 1
Creoles which have a lexical verb meaning 'finish' and a VP-final Completive/Perfect with the same phonological form: These Creoles restrict the former to a purely main-verbal function and a terminative meaning. They employ the VP-final Completive/Perfect as an aspectual marker with the sense of 'already', for example, Sranan and Papiamentu (Andersen 1990: 67).

Category 2
Creoles which have a main verb meaning 'finish' as well as both preverbal and VP-final Completives with the same phonological shape: These Creoles have grammaticized preverbal 'finish' into an auxiliary marking completive aspect, while also employing the same form as a serial verb in VP-final position. Examples include GC and JC. According to Stolz (1987: 300), Portuguese-lexicon

Due Respect

Creoles like Tugu, Papia Kristang and Annobom appear to belong in this category.

Within this category, there may be differences in the degree to which different Creoles generalize the use of the completive markers to different types of predicate, or allow them to combine with other TMA markers. For example, JC limits both of its Completives to nonstative predicates, while GC imposes no such limits.[6] In addition, JC *don* can only be preceded by other auxiliaries (particularly tense markers), and never precedes them. By contrast, auxiliary *don* in GC and other varieties of CEC can both precede and follow other TMA auxiliaries, including aspect markers and modals (Winford 1993: 52). It appears fully integrated into the AUX system.

Category 3
Creoles which have only a main verb meaning 'finish' and a preverbal Completive/Perfect marker of the same form: This category includes basilectal varieties of CEC like Belizean, as well as intermediate varieties like Barbadian, Trinidadian, urban GC, and so forth.[7] Creoles in this category tend to generalize the use of the Completive/Perfect auxiliary to predicates of different semantic types. As far as different combinatory possibilities are concerned, preverbal *don* in Belize Creole and intermediate categories of CEC can both precede and follow other TMA auxiliaries, just like GC auxiliary *don*. It is a fully grammaticized Completive/Perfect auxiliary. The near universal use of Completive/Perfect markers in Creoles across the world is a strong argument that this category should be considered just as important as Bickerton's other three "prototypical" TMA categories, as various scholars, including Boretzky (1983: 4) and Stolz (1987: 294) have pointed out. The rough classification offered here indicates that different Creoles adopted different strategies in installing and further grammaticizing markers of completion. Hence it is difficult to speak of a "prototypical" Creole model in this case. However, all Creoles appear to have at least a preverbal Completive, so this may constitute the "common core". Creoles of Category 3 have only the common core. There appears to be a large group of Creoles (Categories 1 and 2) that have both preverbal and VP-final Completives. Explanations for these broad differences must no doubt be sought in the types of substrate influence as well as internal developments that affect each Creole.

Creole Tense/Aspect: The Common Core

As the cross-Creole comparisons above have shown, the differences among the New World Creoles can be found particularly in the area of aspect.[8] We have seen, for instance, that only the Surinamese Creoles, rural GC, Tobagonian Creole and St Kitts Creole (and perhaps others) have an Imperfective category. Other varieties of CEC treat this area of semantic space quite differently. Thus, Progressive and Past Habitual are grammaticized as distinct categories in JC, BelC and other Western Caribbean Creoles – like Miskito Coast English-lexicon Creole (Holm 1988: 150) – while "present habitual" is just one of the several meanings conveyed by the unmarked verb (ø marking). Other CEC varieties grammaticize the latter as a separate category. These and other differences suggest that the notion of a Creole "prototype" is just an abstract ideal that no Creole matches exactly. If so, it may be of rather limited usefulness.[9]

At the same time, we have seen that Sranan, and by all accounts the other Surinamese Creoles, share the same "common core" of Tense/Aspect categories as other Caribbean English Creoles and other Creoles of various lexical affiliations. The resulting common core includes the categories shown in Table 9.7.

Table 9.7: Tense/Aspect in New World Creoles: The common core

Tense categories
Relative past	(*bin* and variants)
Predictive future	(*go* in most cases, *wã* and *wi* in BelC and JC)
Progressive future	(Progressive + *go*)

Aspect categories
Perfective ø	(The unmarked verb, with differences in range of uses as noted)
Completive	(*don* or *kaba*, with differences in range and uses as noted)

What is even more striking is the fact that these categories, with some relatively minor exceptions, display practically the same range of primary and secondary uses in discourse across all these Creoles. In addition, there are several other respects in which these Creole tense/aspect systems resemble one another. For instance, they all have only a past and future tense, but no present tense category. Present time reference is conveyed by aspectual categories such as Imperfective, Progressive or Perfective ø. In all these Creoles, both tense categories are relative tense categories. They also employ a system of dependent time reference in secondary or subordinate events. Aspectual categories like Imperfective and Progressive are neutral with respect to time reference, which they pick up from the discourse context. Finally, in all these Creoles, the stative/nonstative distinction is crucial to the interpretation of temporal and aspectual meaning. The facts outlined above raise three important research questions that creolists continue to pursue:

1. Is this common core to be found in all Creoles, or only a subset of them?
2. What is the explanation for the common core?
3. How do we explain the departures from the common core?

With regard to the degree of similarity across Creoles, only exhaustive empirical research will shed further light on this question. For present purposes, it is sufficient to note that most New World Creoles of all lexical affiliations seem to share the common core described earlier.

The second question has occupied creolists' attention since the field emerged in the nineteenth century. It seems obvious that explanations must be sought both in the processes of Creole formation and in patterns of diffusion of earlier Creole varieties throughout the Caribbean (and elsewhere). Alleyne (1980) has suggested that the overall design of Caribbean Creole TMA and other systems can be explained in terms of a common West African "base". Perhaps this accounts for the "common core" described earlier. Recent research on substrate influence on Creole formation (Lefebvre 1996; Migge 1998; Bruyn 1994; Winford 2000a) is gradually producing evidence of similar West African influences on various Creoles. But this research is still in its infancy. In addition, of course, many of the similarities among Caribbean Creoles appear to be due to simple diffusion of varieties from one colony to another. The connections among Jamaican, Belizean, Providence Island and other Western Caribbean Creoles are a well-known example. Further historical research is needed to trace those patterns of diffusion. Finally, the differences among Creoles have to be explained. The relevant factors here include:

1. Differences in the "mix" of ingredients that provided the input to each Creole's formation.
2. Internal developments, for example, varying types and degrees of grammaticization.
3. The role of contact-induced change in the later development of the Creole.

There is clearly a great deal to be done if we are to achieve a clearer understanding of the historical connections and contemporary relationships among Caribbean and other Creoles.

Notes

1. The research on which this chapter is based was supported by NSF Grant #SBR930635, for which I wish to express my gratitude. I am also very grateful to the many informants who gave so freely of their time, to my fieldworkers, without whom it would have been impossible to collect the data, and to all the many other people who gave so freely of their time to assist me in my research.
2. The available data do not allow me to say whether this is also true of other conservative Eastern Caribbean Creoles such as Tobago Creole, St Kitts Creole, and so on. However, Winford James (1974) tells us that Tobago Creole *a* expresses both progressive and habitual functions, which suggests that it may be an imperfective marker.
3. In the Eastern Caribbean, Progressive is conveyed by *a* in all conservative Creoles, including rural GC, as well as Tobago Creole and St Kitts Creole. The available evidence from James (1974) and Vincent Cooper (1978) suggests that *a* also conveys present and past habitual meanings in Tobago and St Kitts (in which case it may be considered a true Imperfective like GC *a* and SN *e*), but the use of *juuztu* for past habitual and *doz* for present habitual is also common in these Creoles. It is not clear whether this variation has always been inherent in these Creoles or arose via contact with the intermediate varieties which employ these markers.
4. My thanks to Shelome Gooden for providing me with JC examples.
5. Across the Atlantic, Nigerian Pidgin uses preverbal *don*, in ways quite similar to CEC. Charles C. Mann (1996) informs us that it marks "perfect" and provides examples of its use with activity verbs like *bil* 'build' and adjectivals like *taya* 'tired'. It's not clear whether it can also precede statives like 'have', 'know' and so forth. In addition, Nigerian Pidgin uses *finish* as a VP-

Due Respect

      final marker of completion. This suggests that the functions of preverbal and VP-final markers of completion are distinct, and subject to different processes of grammaticization, as we have seen for SN.

6. Isle de France Creole allows use of Completive *fin* with both activity verbs and 'processive' predicates like *fatige* 'become tired', according to Corne (1983: 68). Corne erroneously claims that this use "does not exist in any other Creole language at all" (p. 70), apparently unaware that it is common in CEC and the Surinamese Creoles.

7. It seems that Isle de France Creole and perhaps other French-lexicon Creoles can be included in this category (Corne 1983). Also included here, apparently, are Portuguese-lexicon Creoles like Kriol, Cape Verdean, Sri Lankan and Principense. According to Thomas Stolz (1987: 300), these Creoles employ *kaba* in preverbal position only. He notes that Kriol and Cape Verdean, like Tugu, also employ *kaba* as a sentence-initial conjunction meaning 'then, after that'. If he is right that this had its source in sentence-final *kaba*, it would suggest that Kriol and Cape Verdean originally belonged in Category 2.

8. There are, of course, significant differences in the systems of modality, as well as the inventory of TMA categories, auxiliary combinations and ordering and so on, which cannot be discussed fully here. See Winford 1993 and Winford 2000b for further discussion.

9. An anonymous reviewer questions whether the contemporary differences across CECs in their treatment of "imperfective" notions includes all historical changes of these Creoles. In other words, did some which do not have an Imperfective category now have such a category in the past? The answer to this, of course, cannot be absolutely certain, but, as I argued earlier in the case of Completive/Perfect, it seems likely that, in general, contemporary TMA categories are close reflections of what they were in earlier stages of Creole development. With regard to Imperfective in particular, evidence from studies of grammaticization (Bybee and Dahl, 1989: 82; Bybee et al. 1994: 140ff.) suggest that Imperfective categories are never reanalysed as Progressives, though the reverse often happens (see discussion of this development in JC earlier). The latter development may well have taken place in the Surinamese Creoles, but historical (textual) evidence is required to test the claim. The reviewer cites L. Winer (1984, 1993) for examples of Imperfective *(d)a* in nineteenth-century varieties of Creole used in Trinidad (a category no longer found in contemporary Trinidadian Creole), implying that it has been lost in this Creole's evolution. But the change in question is not a case of internally motivated development, since contemporary Trinidadian Creole is not a later descendant of the basilectal varieties spoken in the nineteenth

century (which simply died), but rather the result of language shift towards an urban intermediate variety, the model for which was very probably Bajan. (See Winford 1997.) Obviously then, we must be careful to distinguish between "normal transmission" versus shift, and between internally versus externally motivated change in the evolution of Creoles before we draw conclusions about how far their contemporary structure preserves or excludes earlier features.

References

Agheyisi, R.N. 1971. *West African Pidgin English*. Stanford, CA: PhD diss., Stanford University.

Alleyne, M. 1980. *Comparative Afro-American*. Ann Arbor, MI: Karoma.

Andersen, R.W. 1990. Papiamentu Tense-Aspect, with special reference to discourse. In *Pidgin and Creole Tense-Mood-Aspect Systems*, edited by J.V. Singler. Amsterdam: John Benjamins.

Bickerton, D. 1975. *Dynamics of a Creole System*. Cambridge: Cambridge University Press.

———. 1979. The status of *bin* in the Atlantic Creoles. In *Readings in Creole Studies*, edited by I.F. Hancock et al. Ghent: E. Story-Scientia.

———. 1981. *Roots of Language*. Ann Arbor, MI: Karoma.

Boretzky, N. 1983. On Creole verb categories. *Amsterdam Creole Studies* 5.

Bruyn, A. Some remarkable facts in Sranan. Paper presented at the conference of the Society for Caribbean Linguistics, Guyana, 1994.

Bybee, Joan, and O. Dahl. 1989. The creation of tense and aspect systems in the languages of the world. *Studies in Language* 13, no. 1.

Bybee, J.L., et al. 1994. *The Evolution of Grammar: Tense, Aspect and Modality in the Languages of the World*. Chicago: University of Chicago Press.

Cassidy, F.G. 1980. The place of Gullah. *American Speech* 55.

———. 1986. Barbadian Creole: possibility and probability. *American Speech* 61.

Cassidy, F.G., and R.B. Le Page. 1980. *Dictionary of Jamaican English*. 2d ed. Cambridge: Cambridge University Press.

Christie, P. 1986. Evidence for an unsuspected habitual marker in Jamaican. In *Focus on the Caribbean: Varieties of English around the World*, G8, edited by M. Görlach and J. Holm. Amsterdam: Benjamins.

Comrie, B. 1976. *Aspect: An Introduction to the Study of Verbal Aspect and Related Problems*. Cambridge: Cambridge University Press.

———. 1985. *Tense*. Cambridge: Cambridge University Press.

Cooper, V. 1978. Basilectal Creole: Decreolization and autonomous language change in St Kitts-Nevis. PhD diss., Princeton University.

Corne, C. 1983. Substratal reflections: The completive aspect and the distributive numerals in Isle de France Creole. *Te Reo* 26.

Dahl, Ö. 1985. *Tense and Aspect Systems*. Oxford: Basil Blackwell.

Hancock, I.F., E. Polomé, M. Goodman, and B. Heiné, eds. 1979. *Readings in Creole Studies*. Ghent: E. Story-Scientia.

Harris, Martin, and Paolo Ramat, eds. 1987. *Historical Development of Auxiliaries*. Berlin: Mouton de Gruyter.

Huttar, G., and M. Huttar. 1994. *Ndjuka*. London: Routledge.

Holm, J. 1988. *Pidgins and Creoles*, Vol. 1. Cambridge: Cambridge University Press.

———. The Creole verb: A comparative study of stativity and tense reference. Paper presented at the conference of the Society for Pidgin and Creole Linguistics, San Diego, January 5–7, 1996.

———. 2000. The Creole verb: A comparative study of stativity and tense reference. In *Language Change and Language Contact in Pidgins and Creoles*, edited by John McWhorter. Amsterdam: John Benjamins.

Jaganauth, D. Relative time reference in Guyanese Creole: Some problems for sentence-level analysis. Paper presented at the seventh biennial conference of the Society for Caribbean Linguistics, Nassau, College of the Bahamas, 1988.

James, W. 1974. Some similarities between Jamaican Creole and the dialect of Tobago. Caribbean Studies undergraduate research paper. University of the West Indies, Trinidad.

———. 1996. Students' TAM errors in the context of the speech of Tobago. PhD diss., University of the West Indies, St Augustine.

Lefebvre, C. 1996. The tense, mood and aspect system of Haitian Creole and the problem of transmission of grammar in Creole genesis. *Journal of Pidgin and Creole Languages* 11, no. 2.

Le Page, R.B. 1957–58. General outlines of Creole English dialects in the British Caribbean. *Orbis* 6 and 7.

———. 1960. Jamaican Creole: An historical introduction. *Creole Language Studies* 1, edited by R.B. Le Page. London: Macmillan.

Le Page, R.B., and Tabouret-Keller. 1985. *Acts of Identity*. Cambridge: Cambridge University Press.

Mann, C.C. The tempo-aspectual system of Anglo-Nigerian Pidgin. Paper presented at the conference of the Society for Pidgin and Creole Linguistics, San Diego, 1996.

Migge, B. 1998. Substrate influence in Creole formation: The origin of give-type serial verb constructions in Ndjuka. *Journal of Pidgin and Creole Languages* 13.

Pollard, V. 1989. The particle *en* in Jamaican Creole: A discourse-related account. *English World-Wide* 10, no. 1.

Rickford, John. 1984. *Dimensions of a Creole Continuum*. Stanford: Stanford University Press.

Seuren, P. 1981. Tense and aspect in Sranan. *Linguistics* 19.

Spears, A. 1993. Stem and so-called anterior verb forms in Haitian Creole. In *Atlantic Meets Pacific: A Global View of Pidginization and Creolization*, edited by F. Byrne and J. Holm. Amsterdam: John Benjamins.

Stolz, T. 1987. The development of the AUX category in Pidgins and Creoles: The case of the resultative–perfective and its relation to anteriority. In *Historical Development of Auxiliaries*, edited by M. Harris and P. Ramat. Berlin: Mouton de Gruyter.

Voorhoeve, J. 1957. The verbal system of Sranan. *Lingua* 6.

Wilner, J. The use of *ben* in narrative texts in Sranan Tongo. Paper presented at the conference of the Society for Caribbean Linguistics, Barbados, 1992.

Winer, L. 1984. Early Trinidadian Creole: The *Spectator* texts. *English World-Wide* 5, no. 2.

———. 1993. *Trinidad and Tobago. Varieties of English around the World* 6. Amsterdam: John Benjamins.

Winford, D. 1993. *Predication in Caribbean English Creoles*. Amsterdam: John Benjamins.

———. Tense and aspect in Belize Creole. Paper presented at the conference of the Society for Pidgin and Creole Linguistics, Boston, 1994.

———. 1997. Re-examining Caribbean English Creole continua. *World Englishes* 16, no. 2.

———. 2000a. Tense and aspect in Sranan and the Creole prototype. In *Language Change and Language Contact in Pidgins and Creoles*, edited by J. McWhorter. Amsterdam: John Benjamins.

———. 2000b. Irrealis in Sranan: Mood and modality in a radical creole. *Journal of Pidgin and Creole Languages* 15, no. 1.

———. n.d. Substrate influence on the tense/aspect system of Sranan. Working paper, Linguistics Dept, Ohio State University.

Chapter 10

On the Sierra Leone–Caribbean Connection: Hot on the Trail of "Tone-Shifted" Items in Anglo-West African

Hubert Devonish

For some time now there has been a raging debate about the source of the similarities between the varieties of Anglo-West African. Some scholars, for example, Alleyne (1980), have argued for a common West African substratum explanation of them. Others, like Bickerton (1983), support the idea of a bio-programme which produces common linguistic structures in newly created native languages that emerge from situations in which a pidgin is spoken. Bickerton, however, explicitly states (Bickerton 1983: 121–22) that his bio-programme claim relates to syntax. He also concedes substratum influence on "Caribbean Creoles" in the areas of phonology and the lexicon. The label "Caribbean Creole", like any other which may be used (including Alleyne's "Afro-American"), is loaded with presuppositions about the origins of and relationships among the language varieties in question.

This essay focuses on phonology and more specifically on suprasegmentals. There is no doubt that the suprasegmental systems of the "Atlantic English-lexicon Creoles" resulted from the interaction between West African tonal systems and the stress accent system of English. The general tendency is for English stress accent to appear in Creole cognates as High tone (Alleyne 1980: 72). This is a straight case of substrate influence since, as indicated in

Carter (1987: 233, 239), the same pattern is followed when African tone languages, such as Twi and Yoruba, adapt loanwords from English. The label "Afro-West African" is therefore appropriate here in view of the stated focus of this discussion.

There is a whole class of exceptions to the above-mentioned tendency. These occur in all the Anglo-West African varieties, except those spoken in Suriname, namely Saramaccan, Djuka and Sranan, which are considered the most conservative and in many respects the most African-like of them all. The varieties in which the exceptions tend to occur, those of the Caribbean and Guyana and also those of West Africa, co-exist with English and have undergone continuing corrective pressures from that language. The exceptions cannot, however, be due to the influence of English, since they represent a deviation from the systematic correspondence with English which has been observed in the most conservative Anglo-West African varieties, those spoken in Suriname. The only plausible explanation is that they represent an innovation in the other varieties.

The next task is to ascertain whether the innovation, if it occurred only once, started among the varieties spoken in West Africa and spread to the non-Suriname American varieties, or vice versa. To examine this, a presentation is made in this essay of the tonal realizations of the exceptions in Guyanese Creole, as typical of the non-Suriname American varieties. A comparison is then made with the tonal realization of the exceptions in Krio, chosen to represent the West African varieties. The other possibility is that there was parallel development amongst the non-Suriname American varieties, on the one hand, and the varieties used in West Africa, on the other. A comparison between the exceptional items in the two sets, however, shows that there is a nonrandom relationship between them. The exceptional items in the West African varieties tend to be also exceptional in the non-Suriname American varieties. However, there is a much larger number of them in the non-Suriname American varieties than in the West African ones, and many exceptional items in the former set are treated as regular in the latter.

The linguistic evidence is used in this essay to evaluate historical claims that Sierra Leone Krio influenced the non-Suriname American varieties versus claims that the influence was in the opposite direction – that the latter varieties influenced Sierra Leone Krio.

Due Respect

Tone Shift in the Caribbean/Guyana varieties

From the perspective of their phonologies, Anglo-West African varieties may be divided, following Alleyne's analysis (Alleyne 1980), into two groups. The first would consist of the Suriname varieties, Saramaccan, Djuka, Sranan, which tend to retain, for the most part, syllables with the structure: C(onsonant) V(owel) or C(onsonant) V(owel) N(asal). The second group would include the other Anglo-West African varieties. These, as a result of English influence, generally permit syllables with the structure CVC, in which the final C may be a nonnasal consonant.

The tendency for words borrowed from English into Anglo-West African varieties to have the location of the first High tone (H-tone) corresponding to the location of word stress in the English cognate, is the norm. It is significant that it is the most conservative varieties, those spoken in Suriname, which almost invariably conform to this pattern. The sole exception is a small group of items on which a historical rule has operated, resulting in the shift of underlying items from the antepenultimate to the penultimate vowel.

In this essay I shall refer to the very large class of exceptions to the norm, which occur in the phonologically less conservative varieties spoken in the Caribbean and Guyana, as having been "tone-shifted". The literature on such items has been quite extensive, and the phenomenon has been remarked upon by Cassidy (1961) and Lawton (1963) for Jamaican, Allsopp (1972), Berry (1976) and Devonish (1989) for Guyanese Creole (GC), Collymore (1970) for Bajan or Barbadian Creole, and Spears (1972) for Caymanian, among others.

Devonish (1989: 92–110) gives a very detailed discussion of the GC words in which the first surface H(igh) tone, as distinct from a surface F(alling) tone (F-tone), does not occur in the syllable equivalent to the stressed one in English. Applying a more up-to-date analysis to the underlying representations in the examples in Table 10.1 , however, one sees

1. that a H(igh) L(ow) tone melody (HL) is assigned by rule to the first, as in (i) or, in cases lexically specified as exceptional, as in, for example, (ii), to the second syllable of the lexical item;[1]
2. that one subsequent syllable may be marked to bear a lexically assigned HL tone melody, as in (iii), (iv) and (v).

The operation of (ii) is subject to the proviso that, if the word receives a rule-assigned HL tone melody on the second syllable rather than the first, any lexically assigned HL must be on a nonadjacent syllable.

The phonetic implementation of tone in GC and other non-Suriname American varieties is as follows for all but a small class of exceptions: If the HL melody is the last such in the item, as a result of being the only melody or the second melody in the word, the syllable is realized with a level or maintained surface H-tone which will spread to the following syllables in the word. This spread takes place since the following syllables are not themselves specified for tone and the L-tone in the melody cannot associate word-internally. This L-tone, although not realized on the surface, causes the surface H-tone of the HL melody in a following word to be downstepped, that is, to be lower in pitch than it would otherwise be. If the HL melody is not the last melody in the word, both the H- and L-tones in the melody are realized on the syllable. This produces on the surface an F-tone.

Table 10.1

i.	ánimal	[ánímál]##L	'animal'
ii.	riisíiva	[rìisíivá]##L	'(kitchen) sink'
iii.	wáatá	[wáàtá]##L	'water'
iv.	rékamendéeshan	[rêkàmèndéeshán]##L	'recommendation'
v.	asóoshiiyéeshan	[àsóòshìiyéeshán]##L	'association'

The conventions for representing the segmental features of GC in Table 10.1 follow those developed by Cassidy (1961) for Jamaican Creole and subsequently adapted and used by Bickerton (1975), among others, for representing GC. A full discussion of this system is presented in Devonish (1989: 73–82).

The tone data is first presented phonemically. In the phonemic presentation, an HL melody assigned to a syllable is represented by aigu (′). Syllables without such a tone melody are left unmarked. Alongside this, in square brackets, is the phonetic representation. In this, L-tone appearing on a syllable is represented by grave (`) over the first vowel of the syllable, H-tone by aigu (′). F-tone over a single vowel is represented by circumflex (^), over that vowel, and F-tone over a double vowel sequence by a sequence of aigu and

Due Respect

grave (` `). L-tones which do not appear on a syllable within a word are represented by an L occurring after the word boundary, ##.

There is one set of cases most often discussed in the literature. These are the ones for which there are the most numerous examples in the non-Suriname American varieties and which, as I have argued (Devonish 1989: 91–94), represent the core group among the tone-shifted items. These involve items of two syllables in English which have stress on the initial syllable in that language, but which turn up in the restructured Anglo-West African varieties with first surface H-tone on the second syllable.

Three possible tone patterns for bisyllabic items exist in GC. In the first, an H(L) tone melody is assigned by rule to the first syllable and no HL melody is assigned lexically to the following syllable. Examples of this tone pattern, "Tone Pattern 1", appear in the first column of Table 10. 2(a). The items which undergo tone-shifting were originally of this type, as shown in the first column of Table 10.2(b).

There is a second pattern, "Tone Pattern 2", in which, as a result of lexical specification, the first syllable is treated as invisible to the rule which assigns an HL tone melody to the first syllable in a word. As a consequence, this rule assigned HL appears on the second syllable instead. In these items, no lexical assignment of HL can occur, since no additional syllables remain. Examples of this pattern are presented in the second column of Table 10. 2(a).

The third pattern, "Tone Pattern 3", operates in the following fashion. The first syllable receives an HL melody assigned by rule. In addition, however, a lexical HL melody is assigned to the second syllable. The tone-shifted items presented in the second column of Table 10.2(b) illustrate cases of this pattern. The items which belong to it in GC are almost entirely tone-shifted items.

Table 10.2 (a)

Non-Tone-Shifted Items with HL on 1st Syllable			**Non-Tone-Shifted Items with HL on 2nd Syllable**	
(Tone Pattern 1)			*(Tone Pattern 2)*	
i.	jóngl [jóŋgĺ]	'jungle'	bifóor [bifóór]	'before'
ii.	kálik [kálík]	'colic'	anóngs [ànóŋgs]	'announce'
iii.	bóta [bótá]	'butter'	konfór [kònfór]	'confer'
iv.	áshiz [áshíz]	'ashes'	biháin [bìháin]	'behind'
v.	lépod [lépód]	'leopard'	fogét [fògét]	'forget'

Table 10.2 (b)

	Historical Input Forms with HL on 1st Syllable only		"Tone-Shifted" Items with HL on 1st and 2nd Syllables
	(Tone Pattern 3)		*(Tone Pattern 3)*
i.	*bélii	'belly'	bélíi [bêlíí]
ii.	*mónii	'money'	móníi [môníí]
iii.	*páatii	'patty'	páatíi [páàtíí]
iv.	*báaskit	'basket'	báaskít [báàskít]
v.	*árinj	'orange'	árínj [ârínj]

GC Tone Shift

Let us apply the phonetic implementation rules already discussed to these tonal patterns. In Tone Pattern 1, the H-tone of the HL melody is spread by rule onto the following syllable, with the L-tone remaining unassociated. In Tone Pattern 2, the H-tone of the melody is assigned to the second syllable, with the L-tone remaining unassociated. The initial, unmarked syllable is assigned a default surface L-tone.

In Tone Pattern 3, both tones of the underlying HL melody assigned to the first syllable appear on the surface. This syllable is pronounced with an F-tone, the result of both the H-tone and the L-tone being realized over a single syllable. H-tone occupies only a portion of the syllable and is preceded by word-initial position. It is a general characteristic of word boundaries that they have a lowering effect on an immediately contiguous H-tone. The H-tone in the F-tone is therefore slightly lowered. In addition, it is followed within the same syllable by an L-tone, which also has a lowering effect. Both these environmental factors lead to the H-toned portion of the syllable being realized at a lower peak pitch than surface H-tones in other environments.

By contrast, the syllable which bears the second HL melody in the word, the lexically assigned melody, is realized on the surface with H-tone alone. As already noted, the L-tone of such a melody does not surface. The syllable is therefore pronounced on a relatively consistent high pitch over its entire duration. This makes it more salient than the preceding syllable, pronounced with a lowish H-tone at the beginning, this dropping to L-tone over the duration of the syllable. It is the salience of the second syllable relative to this one which is perceived as representing "tone shift" in these varieties. According to this perception, the phonetically salient syllable – the first syllable with a maintained H-tone – is not the first syllable, the one which is stressed in the English cognate, but the second, the one which is not.

Tone Shift in the West African Varieties

Like the restructured varieties of Anglo-West African spoken in the Americas outside of Suriname, the varieties spoken in West Africa also have a significant number of words in which the syllable bearing the first H-tone is not the one which is equivalent to the stressed syllable. This has been observed by Carter (1987) for Cameroon Pidgin English (CPE), by Worokwo and Faraclas (1983) and Faraclas (1984) for Nigerian Pidgin English (NPE), and by Berry (1961: 14–15), Hancock (1977: 1–66), and Jones (1983: 17–56) for Sierra Leone Krio.

As in my consideration of tone shift in the non-Suriname American varieties, I will here also focus on the behaviour of bisyllabic items. It should be noted that Krio, unlike GC, allows for only one HL tone melody per item in words of English origin. As a consequence, therefore, when the historical tone shift was applied in Krio to such items, it simply shifted them from membership of a class with the lexical HL on the first syllable to the class of items which had the HL melody on the second syllable. Let us look at some of the examples presented by Jones (1983: 177, 180).

Krio Tone Shift

The sentence medial implementation of the phonemic tone assignment in Krio is what is shown phonetically in square brackets. According to it, as in items ending in obstruents, such as items (ii), (iv) and (v) of Column 1 in Table 10.3(a), the H-tone of the HL melody spreads to the second syllable of the word. The L-tone remains unassociated. By contrast, in words ending in a sonorant, such as items (i) and (iii) in Table 10.3(a), the L-tone of the melody associates with the word-final vowel, producing a surface sequence of H-tone followed by L-tone over the two syllables.

The effect of tone shift in Krio has simply been to cause an item like *ɔrinch to behave tonally like items in the class to which *bifó* and *fogɛ́t* belong. In GC and the other non-Suriname American varieties of Anglo-West African,

Table 10.3(a)

Non-Tone-Shifted Items with HL on 1st Syllable			**Non-Tone-Shifted Items with HL on 2nd Syllable**		
i.	jɔngul [jɔ́ngùl]	'jungle'	bifó [bìfó]		'before'
ii.	kɔlik [kɔ́lìk]	'colic'	anáwns [ànáwns]		'announce'
iii.	bɔta [bɔ́tà]	'butter'	kɔnfá [kɔ̀nfá]		'confer'
iv.	áshis [áshís]	'ashes'	biɛn [bìɛ́n]		'behind'
v.	lɛpɛtɛ [lɛ́pɛ́t]	'leopard'	fɔgɛt [fɔ̀gɛ́t]		'forget'

Table 10.3(b)
Krio Tone Shift

Historical Input Forms with HL on 1st Syllable			**Tone-Shifted Items with HL on Second Syllable**	
i.	*bɛlɛ	'belly'	bɛlɛ	[bɛ̀ɛ́lɛ́]
ii.	*mɔni	'money'	mɔní	[mɔ̀ní]
iii.	*pati	'party'	patí	[pàtí]
iv	*baskit	'basket'	baskít	[bàskít]
v.	*ɔrinch	'orange'	ɔrínch	[ɔ̀rínch]

on the other hand, the change results in *arínj* and so on becoming a class with surface F-tone on the first syllable and surface H-tone on the second. This is distinguished from the class of item to which *bifóor* and *fogét* belong. These latter on the surface carry L-tone on the first syllable and H-tone on the second.

As indicated earlier, the tone-shifted items in the West African varieties have different phonetic realizations from those in the non-Suriname American varieties such as GC. The major difference involves the treatment of the first syllable. In the West African varieties such as Krio, this syllable simply takes a surface L-tone. Thus, a first syllable which bore stress in the English original but has undergone tone shift is simply L-toned. By contrast, in the non-Suriname American varieties, such a syllable is marked by a Falling surface tone.

The phonetic LH in the West African varieties represents the surface realization of an underlying LHL pattern. In the non-Suriname American varieties, the phonetic FH is a surface realization of an underlying HL HL pattern. The major surface difference is the Fall versus the Low on the first syllable of the word.

Due Respect

The prosodic systems of the two sets of Anglo-West African diverge in an important respect at the underlying level. The non-Suriname American varieties permit up to two HL melodies to be assigned in words of English origin. The West African varieties allow for only one such melody. It is this underlying difference that produces the divergence in the surface phonetic realization of tone-shifted bisyllabic items. In both sets of varieties, however, the first H-tone maintained over the duration of a syllable occurs on a syllable later than the one corresponding to that which bore word stress in English.

The Vocative: A Possible Source

Let us at this point dismiss any suggestion that any of this could be explained by an early proto-Krio as is proposed by Hancock (1986) as the source of all the Anglo-West African varieties. The fact is, as was observed earlier, that the most conservative of these varieties, the Suriname Creoles, have no tone-shifted items comparable to those being investigated here. Unless these varieties are somehow excluded from having the same origin as the other Anglo-West African varieties, any notion that the tone-shifted items are the result of a common origin can be dismissed.

There are three remaining possible explanations as to the parallel development of tone shift in the non-Suriname Anglo-West African varieties. One is that, under influence from speakers of Krio, the restructured American varieties re-interpreted Krio items such as *àrínch* with an LH surface tone sequence as having a surface FH sequence, an F-tone on the first and H-tone on the second, to produce GC *àrínj*. This seems hardly plausible since GC and related varieties already had items such as *fogét* with an LH surface tone sequence. There would have been no linguistic motivation to create an entirely new type of tone pattern to copy a Krio-type LH pronunciation.

The second explanation could be that the items such as *àrínj*, with F-tone on the first and H-tone on the second, was a non-Suriname American innovation. Then, through language contact, Krio speakers, who had no FH surface tone pattern in their language, came under the influence of Anglo-West African. This caused Krio speakers to reinterpret the FH pattern in terms of their closest equivalent, the LH surface pattern. This second proposal is easily the more plausible of the two.

I will now examine the evidence indicating that the innovation which introduced these tone-shifted items occurred once in one of the non-Suriname varieties and subsequently spread to other varieties in the area and eventually to West Africa. We hypothesize that there are some specific communicative factors which could actually have triggered this. It is these triggering communicative factors that I am about to explore.

The vocative is, in its most basic function, used to get and hold the attention of the intended recipient of a particular language communication. Perhaps the main means by which the vocative is expressed is through the use of personal names. When employed to perform the vocative calling and attracting functions, these names have to be pronounced in a manner which is especially salient or noticeable to the addressee.

It is precisely this which is achieved in the non-Suriname American varieties by having personal names acquire a lexically assigned HL melody, in addition to the HL melody assigned by rule to the first syllable. In bisyllabic items, this produced prominence on immediately adjacent syllables. This was an innovation. The new tonal/prominence pattern, having been established among vocatives, then spread to include other items.

It may be argued that this did not represent an innovation at all but had been introduced into these varieties. One source would be some metropolitan variety of English. This would have to be a variety which was not influential in the formation of Anglo-West African, since it is the most conservative varieties, those spoken in Suriname, which show a regular correspondence between H-tone and the stressed syllable in English cognates.

One cannot discount the possibility of some hitherto undiscovered and undescribed variety of metropolitan English showing features similar to those which appear in the non-Suriname Anglo-West African varieties. However, the phenomenon of tone shift in the non-Suriname American varieties has been noted and described in such literature for at least half-a-century, notably by scholars such as Cassidy (1961) and Wells (1982, 1987), whose major area of expertise is English dialectology. In fact, the Wells (1982) work, in which the phenomenon is referred to, is on the comparative phonology of varieties of English around the world. The fact that Wells makes no reference to any non-Anglo-West African variety exhibiting similar behaviour is at least suggestive. Further, Wells (1987) not only does not propose a possible English origin but instead attempts to seek a West African explanation. This further reinforces my view that, in the light of current knowledge, there is no plausible explanation that suggests an origin in a dialect of metropolitan English.

The problem, of course, is: which such West African languages? Vocative tone alternation does not seem to be a feature which has been reported for the major West African languages. Wells (1987: 65) does note the existence of the form *brɔdá* in Yoruba with an LH tone pattern. The form is used in the vocative as a form of address to an older male not old enough to be one's father. This, of course, is used with the identical meaning in Krio (Jones 1983: 181). Wells attempts to use the Yoruba form as a basis for explaining the vocative tonal forms which are so common in Anglo-West African varieties. In fact, of course, this form is in all likelihood a borrowing from Nigerian Pidgin English (NPE) which has the same form, *brɔdá,* bearing the same LH tone melody and signalling the identical meaning. NPE, we would argue, had this item along with vocative LH tone pattern transferred to it from Krio. Krio speakers, it has been well established, played a central role in the development and spread of NPE.

The absence of any credible West African or metropolitan English source for vocative tone alternation suggests that it represents an innovation in the non-Suriname Anglo-West African varieties. Let us at this point examine how it developed.

First names as well as some last names which, in English, are stressed on the initial syllable, have the first maintained H-tone on the final syllable in restructured Anglo-West African varieties. This is currently true, whether the names are used in the vocative or not. As is stated in Devonish (1989: 97) for Guyanese and Jones (1983: 179) for Krio, this pattern is often also employed

Table 10.4

	Krio	Guyanese	Jamaican	English
a.	Jenɛt [jènɛt]	Jánít [jânît]	Jànét [jânét]	'Janet'
b.	Dɛnís [dènís]	Dénís [dénís]	Dènís [dênís]	'Denis'
c.	Será [sèrá]	Séerá [séèrá]	Sìerá [sìèrá]	'Sarah'
d.	Tɔmós [tòmós]	Táamás [táàmás]	Tàmás [tâmás]	'Thomas'
e.	Frɛdí [frèdí]	Frédíi [frédîi]	Frèdí [frêdí]	'Freddie'

Note: The Krio data comes from Jones (1983: 176, 179).

in nicknames. Tone-shifting seems to have applied to a variety of polysyllabic items, for example, GC *ántaníi* [ântàníi] 'Anthony (first name)', *Kyârintón* [kyârìntón] 'Carrington' (surname), and so on. However, my focus here will be on two-syllable items, shown in Table 10.4.

Historical Vocative First-Name Tone Patterns in Anglo-West African

In all of these varieties of Anglo-West African, the shifted tone pattern is not restricted to a name used in actually addressing someone. It is also used as a means of referring to someone in the third person. The tone-shifted forms have become part of the underlying lexical representation of first names. This, I would suggest, probably represented the first stage in the transference of the originally vocative tone pattern to items not used as vocatives.

Related to this is the case of nouns which are used in their most basic sense to signal a family relationship, for example, 'mother', 'brother', 'sister' and so on. Often, when used in the vocative, these terms are employed to address a much wider class of persons, as in the use of the term 'Father' to address a priest, 'Sister' for a senior nurse, and so forth. In the Anglo-West African varieties, as well as in English, these forms of address, along with their extended meanings, are converted to ordinary nonvocative use.

When this occurs in non-Suriname Anglo-West African, the tonal pattern of the item in its extended meaning retains the vocative tone pattern. It then has to be lexically marked as receiving that pattern. This creates a tonal contrast with the segmentally identical form which signals the basic meaning. In Guyanese, this produces the contrast between *bróda* 'brother' (relative) and *bròdá* 'member of a church'. The same occurs in Krio with the distinction between *fáda* 'father' (parent) and *fadá* 'monk' (Jones 1983: 181). Faraclas (1984: 72) similarly reports on the distinction made in the Rivers Pidgin English variety of Nigerian Pidgin English between *sísta* 'sister' (relative) and *sistá* 'nurse'.

What was originally a vocative tone pattern in the restructured varieties had now become a part of the lexical representation of certain items, for example, *brɔdá/bròdá* 'member of a church', *fadá/fàadá* 'monk', and *sistá/sìstá* 'nurse'.

The moment this became necessary, the gate was open for a range of other items not ever used in the vocative to shift also to the vocative tone pattern. It is possible that this process could have occurred separately in several different communities in which Anglo-West African varieties were used.

The idea of some kind of parallel development on the two sides of the Atlantic is, in fact, suggested by Jones (1983: 17–56). He notes that both the Caribbean/Guyana and West African varieties have a tendency to have accentuation, tonal prominence, on a syllable later than the one stressed in other varieties of English. Using two bisyllabic items cited for Caribbean varieties of Anglo-West African, from Wells (1982: 572), and comparing them with the tonal shape of their cognates in Krio, Jones (1983: 176) concludes that "although the trend is common to both Krio and West Indian dialects, it seems to affect actual words in the two cases randomly". According to this hypothesis, speakers of each group of languages would have carried out tone changes to affect the lexical specification of a randomly selected portion of items within its own lexicon. Evidence of such randomness when the restructured non-Suriname American and West African varieties are compared would support the notion of parallel development. Where cognates across the two groups of languages are similarly affected, these would represent straight cases of coincidence.

I will test the notion of a random relationship between the tone-shifted items in the two sets of language varieties, and analyse the results of a comparison between the tonal forms in one non-Suriname American variety, GC, and those of a restructured West African one, Krio. The Krio data consists of bisyllabic items in Krio which originate in English forms with stress on the first syllable and which have cognates in GC. The GC data consists of cognates of the Krio items selected. Items which are personal names or compounds are excluded.

In order to collect an appropriate sample of such Krio items, we selected from the Fyle and Jones (1980) dictionary of Krio, one hundred such items at random. The results indicate that in 91 percent of the Krio items, the syllable with the lexically assigned HL melody is the first syllable, the syllable which corresponds to the one bearing stress in English. In the case of Guyanese, only 81 percent of the items have word-initial prominence, coupled with no lexically assigned HL on the second syllable.

Devonish – *"Tone-Shifted" Items in Anglo-West African*

Clearly, GC has a higher number of words which deviate from the expected reflex of English word-initial stress. What is interesting is that in all of the nine cases where Krio deviates from English, so too does Guyanese. In addition, however, there are another ten cases which deviate where the Krio and English forms agree. In Table 10.5(a), nine items are presented for which there is deviation from English in both the Guyanese and Krio forms. Table 10.5(b) shows cases in which the Guyanese form is deviant but the Krio form conforms with the original English item.

Table 10.5(a)

	Guyanese Deviation		Krio Deviation		English Form
i.	blángkít	[blǎŋgkít]	ŋblankít	[blàŋgkít]	'blanket'
ii.	brándíi	[brândíi]	brandí	[bràndí]	'brandy'
iii.	chéríi	[chêríi]	chɛrí	[chɛ̀rí]	'cherry'
iv.	gwáavá	[gwáàvá]	gwɛvá	[gwɛ̀vá]	'guava'
v.	íivnín	[îvnín]	ivnín	[ìvnín]	'evening'
vi.	láríi	[lâríi]	lɔrí	[lɔ̀rí]	'lorry'
vii.	shéríi	[shêríi]	shɛríi	[shɛ̀ríi]	'sherry'
viii.	yélá	[yêlá]	yalá	[yàlá]	'yellow'
ix.	ményúu	[mênyúu]	mɛnyú	[mɛ̀nyú]	'menu'

Table 10.5(b)

	Guyanese Deviation		Krio Conformity		English Form
i.	béesń	[béèsń]	bésin	[bésìn]	'basin'
ii.	chíkín	[chîkín]	chíkin	[chíkìn]	'chicken'
iii.	dískyánt	[dîskyánt]	dɛskyant	[dɛ́skyànt]	'descant'
iv.	góblít	[gôblít]	gɔblɛt	[gɔ́blɛ̀t]	'goblet'
v.	kyábíj	[kyâbíj]	kábej	[kábèj]	'cabbage'
vi.	páadń	[páàdń]	pádin	[pádìn]	'pardon'
vii.	píkník	[pîkník]	píknik	[píknìk]	'picnic'
viii.	kyárát	[kyârát]	kárat	[káràt]	'carrot'
ix.	gínís	[gînís]	gínɛs	[gínɛ̀s]	'Guinness'
x.	fínggá	[fîŋggá]	fíŋgaz	[fíngàz]	'fingers'

Due Respect

Guyanese and Krio Deviation from Expected Tone Pattern

The results of this sampling suggest that wherever there is a Krio deviation, a GC one is predicted also, but not vice versa. In general, this is indeed so. However, there do exist some cases in which Krio is deviant and Guyanese not, for example, Krio *chalénj* versus Guyanese *chálinj*. What the results of the analysis therefore point to is a very high probability, not certainty, that whenever there is a deviation in Krio relative to English, GC will deviate also.

The items which deviate in GC are generally the same for the entire group of restructured Anglo-West African varieties spoken in the Americas outside of Suriname, with a very restricted amount of variation across language varieties. The relationship between the deviant items in Krio, on one hand, and those in Guyanese and by extension the other restructured varieties of the Americas, is not a random one. The notion of parallel independent development cannot explain this nonrandom relationship. Either West African varieties introduced specific deviations in the suprasegmental shape of items into non-Suriname American varieties, or vice versa. The non-Suriname American varieties, as represented by GC, are likely to show a deviation from the expected reflex of English word stress in about 19 percent of the relevant items, as compared with the 9 percent for Krio. This represents another important piece of evidence for this effort at historical reconstruction. The deviation has affected a much larger proportion of the vocabulary of the non-Suriname American varieties than it has Krio, and, by extension, the other West African varieties. It is, therefore, the former group whose speakers are more likely to have initiated the deviation. Subsequent to tone shift having taken place in the non-Suriname American varieties, speakers of the two language groups came into contact. In this contact situation, Krio speakers only adopted the altered shapes of some, roughly half, of the items to which the non-Suriname American innovation had applied.

One question arising in all this concerns which of the speech communities might have been the source of this innovation. A potential candidate would be a community in which (1) a phonetic FH pitch pattern occurs, (2) vocative and related items are at the core of the system involving tonal alternation, and (3) speakers are likely to have had an influence on the rest of the Anglo-West African-speaking world without themselves being subject to much outside influence from this source. Barbados seems the best candidate by far.

The Case for Barbados

Barbados does have the phonetic FH. It is interesting that, of all the Caribbean/Guyana Anglo-West African varieties, it is for Barbados Creole (Bajan) that we have the most detailed nonlinguist's description of the tonal and the segmental prominence features of a tone-shifted bisyllabic item. Collymore (1970), a subsequent edition of a work first published in 1955 on *Barbadian Dialect*, with reference to the accented initial syllables of phonetic FH bisyllabic items, describes speakers of Bajan as "overemphasizing this accent, holding on to it, as it were, making the slightest of pauses thereafter, and then allowing the voice to rise ever so slightly for the second syllable" (p. 84). This overemphasizing of the prominence on the initial syllable is his way of analysing the HL pitch fall on this syllable combined with its relative length, its VV nucleus. He refers to a pause at the end of the syllable and gives examples of syllabification in the affected words, for example, *work*-er (a milliner), *cop*-y (*copy*, the noun), *Rock*-ley (Rockley, place name).

Collymore further suggests that the effect of what he calls "over accentuation" is to make speech in Bajan slow when compared to metropolitan varieties of English (p. 84). I suggest that this represents a recognition that such words have two prominences when compared to their English equivalents, which have only one. At the end of the preceding section, I proposed that the first criterion which any potential source of the tone shift innovation should fulfil is that of having a FH pattern on bisyllabic words. It can be seen that Bajan, like GC and the other Caribbean/Guyana Anglo-West African varieties, fulfils this first criterion.

Let us now examine Bajan in relation to the second criterion, regarding tonal alternation and vocatives. Collymore (1970: 84) cites for Bajan FH examples such as *Pet*-er (Peter, first name) and *Tay*-lor (Taylor, family name). Also interesting are some items for which tone alternation is the feature which distinguishes between members of minimal pairs. There is *brother* and *sister*, with normal accentuation on the first syllable to signal a member of the same family, and *sis*-ter and *bro*-ther with special accentuation to signal members of the same religious organization. This makes Bajan like GC and the other non-Suriname American varieties, as well as similar to the West African varieties such as Krio. Bajan, by using the innovated tone pattern to signal vocative type meanings, fulfils the requirements of the second criterion.

Let us now look at Barbados in relation to the third criterion, that speakers should have had an influence on the rest of the Anglo-West African-speaking world without themselves being subject to much outside influence. Barbados was one of the first two permanent British settlements in the Caribbean. The other early colonies in the Americas, which the British subsequently established in Jamaica, Suriname and even the distant South Carolina, were initially settled by white Barbadian settlers and their slaves. Subsequent British settlement of other territories was either carried out from Barbados or from some territory which had itself been colonized from Barbados. Barbados was historically in an ideal position to influence the language behaviours of other territories in the Americas where Anglo-West African varieties developed.

Barbados, from early in its settlement by the British, was an island with limited land resources and a relatively high population density. Consequently, it possessed a labour surplus when compared to other colonies in the British-controlled Caribbean. This means that, throughout its history, Barbados has been a quite sizeable exporter of labour to other territories in the Americas and, at the same time, has not received any significant numbers of immigrants from these sources. The detailed comment on this question in Rickford and Handler (1994: n. 18) speaks of this in relation to the period before the British abolished slavery in 1834. This situation continued in the post-emancipation period, until at least the 1970s.

Given the labour surplus in Barbados, it is not surprising that indentured servants were not imported during the post-emancipation period, at least not in any significant number. Indentured servants from India, China and Sierra Leone were imported in considerable numbers to labour-short territories such as Guyana, Trinidad and Jamaica. In relation to immigrants from Sierra Leone, who are particularly pertinent to this discussion, Rickford and Handler (1993: 18) point to the fact that there is no evidence that any numbers of migrants from this source were ever brought to Barbados after the abolition of slavery in 1834. They also state that there is no evidence that any of the Africans liberated from slave ships bound for Brazil and Cuba between 1834 and 1867 were ever sent to Barbados. Such Africans were sent to the territories with a labour shortage, notably Guyana, Trinidad and Jamaica.

The only other potential source of language influence from Anglo-West

African varieties outside of Barbados would be Barbadian migrants returning home. The factors of land shortage and labour shortage never really changed throughout Barbadian colonial and postcolonial history. There would have been no factors which would have encouraged significant numbers of Barbadian migrants abroad to return and settle in their homeland. With reference to the first burst of migration after emancipation, when by 1842 some three to four thousand Barbadians had migrated to Guyana and in smaller numbers to Trinidad, Rickford and Handler (1994: 18) cite a contemporary source as stating that no more than between three and four hundred returned. These returnees were few in number. In addition, they had, in the main, migrated as adults at a point when their own language behaviour had already been formed. The likelihood that they would be able to introduce into Barbados the kind of phonological innovation under discussion is slight. Bajan was, therefore, we would argue, isolated from both the influence of other non-Suriname American Anglo-West African varieties and from the imported influence of Krio.

By comparison, Krio did have exposure to Bajan-influenced non-Suriname Anglo-West African varieties. Two versions of the relationship between American varieties and Krio exist. The first of these, presented by Hancock (1981: 247–49), Hancock (1986) and Jones (1983), argues that the existence of an Anglo-West African variety spoken in Sierra Leone predated the arrival of Anglo-West African influence from the Americas. According to this version, potential language influence from the Americas did come in the form of eleven hundred ex-slaves from the British colonies in the Americas arriving in Free Town, Sierra Leone, via Nova Scotia, in 1792. Hancock argues that two years later this settlement was destroyed by the French. This fact he uses to claim that they would have had minimal influence on Krio.

However, though the settlement may have been destroyed, what about the people who inhabited the settlement? Presumably many, if not most of them, would have survived and joined or been absorbed into existing Krio-speaking communities on the Sierra Leone coast. The destruction of their distinct community may have, in fact, produced conditions favourable to a spread in the linguistic influence of these new settlers. Hancock (1981: 248) also refers to 550 Jamaican Maroons who arrived in 1800, but of whom "by 1810 over half of these had died, and the remainder were beginning to leave for other parts of the coast, or to return to the West Indies". If one accepts this version of events, one should note that the weight of numbers does not always determine the degree of influence which a group of speakers may have on the language of a community. In many situations, the determining factors involve the status and the functions which the group performs in the community. An obvious example of this is the tiny minority of economically, politically and militarily dominant Europeans in plantation slave societies in the Americas in which Creole languages emerged. In every case, the bulk of the vocabulary of such languages is derived from the language of the European group.

There is another, more traditional version of events according to which varieties from the Americas played a dominant role in the formation of Krio in Sierra Leone (Alleyne 1980). This is the position taken up with renewed vigour by McWhorter (1997: 19–20). He argues, citing Fyfe (1962: 114), that, contrary to the Hancock (1991: 248) statement about the number of Jamaican Maroons in Sierra Leone in 1810, no fewer than 807 out of a total population of 1,917 persons in Freetown, Sierra Leone, in 1811 were Jamaican Maroons. In addition, another 982 were liberated slaves from North America. Together, the two groups from the Americas constituted, in 1811, a total of 1,789 out of a total population if 1,917 (McWhorter 1997: 20). This would suggest that the varieties of Anglo-West African from the Americas would have had a significant influence on Krio. It does not matter which interpretation of the historical evidence one wishes to make. From the point of view of the linguistic evidence available on the tonal correspondences, it is clear that the likelihood of a strong American Anglo-West African language influence on Sierra Leone is much greater than that of Krio influence on Bajan.

In Table 10.6, I present a synopsis of this discussion. It shows the three criteria set up and then indicates, by means of "+" or "–", whether a particular Anglo-West African variety fulfils each one. The language varieties thus dealt with are Djuka, Krio, Guyanese and Bajan.

Table 10.6: Likely sources of tonal innovation

	Influences other varieties/Receives no influence	Fall High Melody	Vocative Tone Alteration
Djuka	–	–	–
Krio	–	–	+
Guyana, and others	–	+	+

Likely Source of Tonal Innovation

Of the potential candidates, Bajan is clearly the only likely source of the innovation. The linguistic evidence presented in this discussion provides a basis for historians to reanalyse the impact of the Caribbean presence in Sierra Leone. The influence of Caribbean varieties of Anglo-West African on the tonal forms of Krio must have far exceeded what one would expect relying purely on the Hancock (1981, 1986) version of the historical facts.

The relationship between history as a discipline and linguistics is a two-way one. Historical records give linguists clues with which to pursue reconstruction of language origins. In turn, linguistics provides historians with clues about hitherto unnoticed linguistic influences which beg for historical explanation. We suggest that the tonal analysis of West African and Caribbean/Guyanese varieties of Anglo-West African point to the powerful influence of the latter on the former. It is for the historians to take this piece of information and to use it to analyse and evaluate the nature of the historical evidence on the history of the contact between the peoples of the two regions

Note

1. A tone melody is any tone or sequence of tones which is assigned, either underlyingly or on the surface, to a phonological unit, be it a phrase, a word or a morpheme.

References

Alleyne, M. 1980. *Comparative Afro-American*. Ann Arbor, MI: Karoma Press.
Allsopp, R. Some suprasegmental features of Caribbean English. Paper presented at the Conference on Creole Languages and Educational Development, University of the West Indies,Trinidad, 1980.
Beckles, H. 1989. *A History of Barbados*. Cambridge: Cambridge University Press.
Berry, J. 1961. English loanwords and adaptations in Sierra Leone Krio. In *Creole Language Studies* II, edited by R.B. Le Page. London: Macmillan.
Berry, J. 1976. Tone and intonation in Guyanese English. In *Festschrift for Joseph H. Greenberg*, edited by A. Juilland. Stanford: Stanford University Press.

Bickerton, D. 1975. *Dynamics of a Creole System*. Cambridge: Cambridge University Press.

———. 1981. *The Roots of Language*. Ann Arbor, MI: Karoma Press.

———. 1983. Creole Languages. *Scientific American* 249, no. 1

Carter, H. 1983. How to be a tone language: Theoretical considerations in the classification of the Caribbean Creoles as tonal or otherwise. In *Studies in Caribbean Language*, edited by L. Carrington et al. Port of Spain, Trinidad: Society for Caribbean Linguistics.

———. 1987. Suprasegmentals in Guyanese: Some African comparisons. In *Pidgin and Creole Languages: Essays in Memory of J. Reinecke*, edited by G. Gilbert. Honolulu, HI: University of Hawaii Press.

Cassidy, F. [1961] 1971. *Jamaica Talk: Three Hundred Years of the English Language in Jamaica*. London: Macmillan.

Collymore, F. [1955] 1970. *Barbadian Dialect*. Barbados: The Barbados National Trust.

Cruickshank, J. 1916. How the later negro learned his English. Reproduced in *A Festival of Guyanese Words*, edited by J. Rickford. Georgetown: University of Guyana, 1976.

Devonish, H. 1989. *Talking in Tones: A Study of Tone in Afro-European Creole Languages*. London: Karia Press.

Faraclas, N. 1984. Rivers Pidgin English: Tone, stress, or pitch-accent? *Studies in the Linguistic Sciences* 14, no 1.

———. 1985. Rivers Pidgin (Creole) English: Tone, stress, or pitch-accent? *Studies in African Linguistics*, Supplement 9.

———. 1989. A grammar of Nigerian Pidgin English. PhD diss., University of California–Berkeley.

Fyfe, C. 1962. *A History of Sierra Leone*. London: Oxford University Press.

Fyle, C., and E. Jones 1980. *A Krio-English Dictionary*. Oxford: Oxford University Press.

Hancock, I. 1977. Lexical expansion within a closed system. *Sociocultural Dimensions of Language Change*, edited by B. Blount and M. Sanches. New York: Academic Press.

———. 1981. Review of *A Krio-English Dictionary* by C. Fyle and E. Jones. *English World-Wide* 2, no. 2.

———. 1986. The domestic hypothesis, diffusion and componentiality: An account of Atlantic-Anglophone Creole origins. In *Substrata versus Universals in Creole Genesis*, edited by P. Muysken and N. Smith. Amsterdam: John Benjamins.

———. 1987. A preliminary classification of the Anglophone Atlantic Creoles with syntactic data from thirty-three representative dialects. In *Pidgin and Creole*

Languages: Essays in Memory of John E. Reinecke, edited by G. Gilbert. Honolulu: University of Hawaii Press.

Holm, J. 1989. *Pidgins and Creoles*, Volume 2: Reference Survey. Cambridge: Cambridge University Press.

Jones, F. 1983. English-derived words in Sierra Leone Krio. PhD diss., University of Leeds.

Lawton, D. 1963. Suprasegmental phenomena in Jamaican Creole. PhD diss., Michigan State University.

McWhorter, J. 1997. It happened in Cormantin: Locating the origin of the Atlantic English-based Creoles. *Journal of Pidgin and Creole Languages* 12, no. 1.

Obilade, A. 1976. The nominal phrase in West African Pidgin English (Nigeria). PhD diss., Northwestern University.

Rickford, J., and J. Handler. 1994. Textual evidence of early Barbadian speech. *Journal of Pidgin and Creole Languages* 9, no. 2.

Smith, N. 1987. The genesis of the Creole languages of Surinam. PhD diss., University of Amsterdam.

———. Gbe words in the creole languages of Surinam. Paper presented at the Workshop on Creoles, University of Amsterdam, 1987.

Spears, R. 1972. Pitch and intonation in Cayman English. Paper presented at Conference on Creole Languages and Educational Development, University of the West Indies.

Wells, J.C. 1982. *Accents of English*. Vol. 3. Cambridge: Cambridge University Press.

———. 1987. Phonological relationships in Caribbean and West African English. *English World-Wide* 8, no. 1.

Worokwo, G., and N. Faraclas. 1983. The sound system of Rivers Pidgin English II. In *A Language Synopsis of Rivers Pidgin English, Language Synopsis No. 1*, edited by N. Faraclas et al. Nigeria: Dept. of Linguistics and African Languages, Faculty of Humanities, University of Port Harcourt.

Section Three

Analysis of Conversational Interaction

Introduction

The everyday use of language very often involves at least two persons in conversation with each other. Nevertheless, it is only within the past two or three decades that scholars have begun to seriously observe the behaviour of individual participants as they interact in this way. Important areas of investigation so far have included efforts to discover what, if any, are the rules governing conversation and the roles of variables such as topic, gender and personality in its manifestation. The traditional neglect is mirrored in the Caribbean where, too, research on language in use has lagged behind investigation of other aspects of language. This is illustrated by the paucity of papers focusing on conversational interaction among those presented at the biennial conferences of the Society for Caribbean Linguistics since 1976. The first of these was Anita Herzfeld's "Exploring Conversational Involvement", which was read at Mona in 1984. Worthy of mention in this context, too, are Peter Patrick's "Aspects of Doctor–Patient Interaction in Jamaica: A Doctor's Questioning Strategy", presented at the St Maarten conference in 1996, and Kathryn Brodber's "Discourse Analysis in Caribbean Contexts: A Missing Link in Caribbean Language Research".

The disproportion is reflected, too, in the fact that this section of the volume consists of only two essayss. In these, Kathryn Brodber and Valerie Youssef explore different characteristics of conversational data. Brodber illustrates the tendency of many Caribbean participants to occupy the floor simultaneously and in competition with each other, contrary to the sequential ordering of exchanges that has generally been promoted as the norm. The

Section Three – *Analysis of Conversational Interaction*

pattern of "performance" interaction evokes for her the image of musical counterpoint, an analogy which she illustrates from Jamaican examples. Youssef's essay is more wide-ranging. Her immediate concern is the role of different types of questions in the internal dynamic of discourse. However, she investigates this through the medium of discussions of selected topical issues by small single-sex and mixed-sex groups of Trinidadian university students. Her conclusions suggest how gender, personality, role relationships and topic interact to determine conversational behaviours.

Le Page would no doubt welcome even these preliminary investigations into the dynamics of conversation since, like his "acts of identity" theory, they reflect an interest in the psychological and social bases of individual performance.

Chapter 11

Contrapuntal Conversation and the Performance Floor

Kathryn Shields-Brodber

Conversation in a "Performance" Mode

"Repetition of theme characteristic of argument, the lack of strong norms against interruption, the acceptance of two or more voices talking at the same time, the pattern of entry into a conversation by knocking several times . . .": thusly did Reisman (1974: 124) describe what he considered remarkable in informal village conversation in Antigua. Exchanges exhibiting such features appeared unusual to him, because, as far as the structure of prototypical polite conversation is concerned, exchanges which admit only one person at a time to the floor (Sacks et al. 1974) were then – and still are – promoted as the norm.[1]

The one-at-a-time floor is organized so that speakers enter sequentially, at an appropriate transition relevance place (TRP), either upon being identified by the current speaker or on self-identification at a pause, and favours the completion of a conversational turn by individual voices in single file sharing a single space (Edelsky 1981). Speakers who ignore the procedures are marked, not only as violating a current speaker's right to complete a turn, but also as contributing to the silencing of that speaker (Zimmerman and West 1975; West and Zimmerman 1983). Interrupters, stereotypically male (Fishman 1983; O'Barr and Atkins 1980; Sattel 1983; Tannen 1990, 1993), are regarded, in a one-at-a-time structure, as having captured the floor illegally, while those who succumb to interruption are characterized as submitting to servitude.[2] In this model, there is general agreement that interruption is anathema as far as balanced conversation is concerned.

The other kind of conversational floor – a collaborative one – which has stimulated some interest in the literature, where it has been generally presented as marking female rather than male conversation (Coates 1996), promotes cooperation between those conversing. The resultant speaker collaboration in "multilayered development of topics" (Coates 1995: 23) allows for early clarification of ambiguous or complicated points and interaction between participants. In this organization, which focuses on the voice of the group in a shared space, overlapping and concurrent speech, rather than indicating a malfunctioning floor, are represented as a vehicle for the bonding of speakers who simultaneously create mutually reinforcing utterances.

It is interesting to note that the disadvantages of the one-at-a-time hierarchical floor constitute the advantages of collaborative organization. Participants on a collaborative floor do not experience inordinate delays in the clarification of ambiguities created by self-indulgent speakers. On the other hand, those speaking one at a time are not usually able to benefit from the immediate and sometimes crucial input of interlocutors. Despite their obvious differences, however, there is something common to both kinds of organization: Verbal competition for space on the floor, especially on public/formal occasions, is neither intended nor encouraged. Collaborative exchanges are similar to one-at-a-time sequences, inasmuch as, in either case, the model presents its speakers as concurring towards a common end, whether it be to allow one person at a time dominance of the floor or to enable joint collaboration between them.

The major difference between floors referred to above and the Antiguan conversational floor which Reisman described, is the absence, with regard to the latter, of a similar kind of concurrence among speakers. In fact, on a floor on which there is participation, not in a single space with individual voices, or in a shared space with collaborating voices, but in a shared space in which competitive voices vie for prominence, several sets of voices sing their individual melodies simultaneously – the one not necessarily harmonizing with the other – though each contributes to the general development of the theme.

Floors of this kind, which I have named "performance floors", are the subject of this essay. They provide, especially in communities where the focus is on oral rather than written communication, a platform for both formal and informal conversation, in which floor space, which is at a premium because competition for it is so great, is actively negotiated and contested verbally. Performance floors are an integral component of verbal interaction in many primarily oral societies such as those of the Caribbean, especially on those occasions when what is at issue is not the substance of speakers' inputs, but performers' acumen with words. In Jamaica, for instance, "performance" episodes permeate conversation, not only in informal but also in public/informal domains.

The Structure of "Performance" Conversations

> *Engineering a footing: 'the pattern of entry into a conversation by knocking several times'* (Reisman 1974: 124).

In performance floors, as in those organized around one-at-a-time and collaborative principles, a usually short initial exchange of pleasantries precedes a first speaker's presentation. Next speakers may wait to be identified by the current speaker, or may self-select sequentially; however, more usually, they self-select at any point at which they feel inclined to do so, regardless of the state of readiness of the current speaker, or the level of completion of his or her presentation. Such attempts at entry may occur even as the current speaker continues to develop his or her points simultaneously, without being subject to any constraint to fall silent.

Example 1

A: *Accounting is an expensive operation* (.)
accounting for it (.)
So what the farmers' organizations do when they are strapped for funds, they turn the funds over to other sources

B: *Mr [X*
[and therefore that's why all of them
is not my organization alone

B: *But [Mr X (.)*

A: *[(inaudible) cane farmers (.) banana (.) coffee aal a dem (.)*
all the other coffee cooperatives are all
is not my or[ganization alone (.) and the reason

B: *[no, but you are the Secretary Manager*

A: *[why the accounts are behind is because of lack of funds (.) now we have*

B: *[you Mr X it is on your head for Co-op A. Mr X (.) would you*

A: *[been concentrating]*

B: *[agree or not agree]*³

Thus, very early in a presentation, a current speaker may have to contend with competing voices which test his or her ability to survive the challenge. Intellectual rigour may well be relegated to the wings, as displays of verbal dexterity and stamina, and the stimulation of participation from other interlocutors, take centre stage.

A speaker aspiring to participate in the fray will often have to "knock" over and over, until she or he can engineer a footing, in defiance of current speakers' exhibited or expressed dissatisfaction with their timing, or their attempts at postponing the entry of newcomers; it is, nevertheless, incumbent on a current speaker to accommodate competitors. Further, there is no limit to the number of concurrent voices which may participate in a similar manner.

> *Sustaining competition: 'the lack of strong norms against interruption*
> *[and] the acceptance of two or more voices talking at the same time'.*
> (Reisman 1974: 124)

Because the primary function of a performance floor is to provide speakers with an equal or even certain chance of being heard only in the face of formidable challenge from others, interruption is a central, cultivated feature. There is a variety of contexts in which interruption may occur: An interrupter may wish to concur on the facts as presented by a current speaker, or to engineer a shift in the focus of a particular conversation. Competition may equally be provided by speakers offering support or dissent to a current speaker, since it is the issuing of the challenge itself, rather than the grounds which prompt it, which is important. Being allowed to speak, uninterrupted, is usually regarded as an indicator of one's failure to engage the interest of others, and therefore to stimulate their active involvement.

Interruption functions as a catalyst for spirited exchanges, in which combatants display their verbal and aural abilities. Aural abilities are important because speakers are expected not only to engage in verbal sparring, but also to concurrently react to their responses. They may actively listen to others, hearing, processing and responding intelligently and even seemingly independently, without overt reference, to contributions made simultaneously with theirs, as in Example 2 below:

Example 2

A: [*yu jos se it a wail ago*
B: [*lisn ai hier Mr S. se im no ina notn wid Jongl so wat* [*kaina piis*
A: [*yu iz a layad*
B: [*yu kyan tel mi se im ina*
A: [*yu iz a layad I was* [*in*
B: [*You you can' tell me I am a layad*[4]

The art, therefore, is in developing a capacity to process other points of view while, at the same time, not being impeded by the articulation of one's own. Making a sound logical point is often peripheral in this exercise, since scoring points in terms of verbal dexterity and tenacity is the major focus.

Simultaneous speech is the predictable, desired outcome of interruption in a performance context. Once having interrupted a current speaker, a new entrant is expected to proceed simultaneously, and even independently – without reference to the current speaker or his or her perspective. Interestingly, while the wider audience may not be able to decipher all the strains of simultaneous interaction, this is not a luxury generally afforded to an interlocutor who is directly affected by the proceedings.

The above should not be interpreted to mean that silence does not occur in performance conversations. A speaker with overt power – for example, a programme moderator, an expert or a more articulate speaker who finds himself or herself outclassed – may resort to silence as a means of (re-)gaining control. This is especially effective when the volume, quantity or speed of words spoken by an antagonist militates against another speaker's chance of being heard, or when it is clear that she or he is intent on ignoring the contribution of others, rather than processing it and incorporating a response to it within the conversation. Silence, therefore, is a means by which to isolate a speaker, thereby suspending the normal, desirable levels of interaction. It disturbs the equilibrium of a performance floor, where, instead of encouraging another to continue speaking, it creates a halt in the proceedings, and often also leads to an enquiry of some sort into its interpretation.

Anyone may also demand silence from another so as to facilitate contributions from those who might seem to require assistance in getting in a word edgewise. However, such an intervention is interpreted as signalling the inability of the speaker on whose behalf it has been made to manipulate the discussion to his or her own advantage, or to effectively sustain animated conversation.

In performance structure, then, the greater the degree of simultaneous speech, the greater the possibility of interlocutors displaying their capabilities at conversation and of their receiving positive evaluation from their audience. In conversations of this genre, it is the faint-hearted or slow-tongued participant who is deemed to be a failure, with uninterrupted speech and the silence of others being generally negatively evaluated as indicating a speaker's inability to sustain a spirited contest.

Performance Conversations in Counterpoint

There are various musical analogies which have been made with conversation. Reisman (1974) describes Antiguan village conversation as contrapuntal, an analogy which Chafe (1997) applies to topic development in discourse; Falk (1980) discusses conversational duets; and Coates (1996) compares collaborative exchanges with a jam session. Performance conversations are, in essence,

Due Respect

comparable neither to a set of unharmonized solos in linear sequence (one-person-at-a-time) nor to a series of simple duets, trios, and so on within the same harmonic and rhythmic pattern (cooperative). They are also unlike a jam session, inasmuch as there is no assumption of all participants being entitled to the accompaniment of others while they feature in an exposition on the theme. In fact, it is indeed the analogy to musical counterpoint which is most appropriate, and which I will expand on here.

In performance conversations, as in, for example, seventeenth-century madrigals or the fugues of the famous composer, J.S. Bach, there is a focus on statements and restatements of a subject and closely allied counter-subjects. In Example 3, for example, for the exposition, the theme is first stated alone (A) and then restated/developed by different voices (B and C) which continue while the earlier voice (A) continues and others enter.

Example 3

A: *I remember quarrelling with Michael Manley when he proposed to increase the price of a house in Garveymeade from eleven thousand to thirteen thousand dollars (.) That cannot even buy a toilet [at this moment right*

B: [*eleven thousand was the price of the houses?*=

A: =*yep*

C: [*If I bought a house in Bridgeport for thirteen thousand*

A: [*so we're* [*talking about we're talking about*

B: [*you can't buy a fridge for that now*

In the development of the theme of a performance conversation, as in a fugue, individual voices, employing individual phrasal structure, combine with a great deal of complexity and diversity, so that the subject may reappear in its original form, or in a state of inversion, augmentation or diminution. In addition, tension may be further created by overlapping of various entries of the subject. Episodes which follow the exposition may be based on material derived from the subject, or may be entirely new; thus, in performance conversations, as in Bach fugues, a theme which is undergoing elaboration and development experiences a series of metamorphoses which may make it unrecognizable once conversation has been in progress for some time.

At any point in a conversation, there may be several patterns of simultaneity; Example 4 below illustrates, for instance, duets (A and C [lines 2–3], C and B [lines 4–5], B and A [lines 7–8]), followed by a trio (A and B andD)[lines 11–13]), and culminating in a quartet (A and B and D and E [lines 14–17]):

Example 4

1. A: But Sir, you are not listening to me
2.   [*I say we have two arms*
3. C: [*What other agency would you require besides the*
4.   [*Public Complaints Authority*
5. B: [*I am simply saying to you I am simply saying to you*
6.   *that if you are talking about the internal investigations by the police*
7.   *I don't really treat them with any degree* [*of credence I don't*
8. A: [*no I object to that*
9.   *You know sir because there are they are officers with impeccable records=*
10. B: =*I don't know that*
11. A: [*They are I am telling you that sir I am telling you as somebody*
12. B: [*I don't know that Ms* [*Ramsay I don't know that I don't know that*
13. D: [*No sah you know that there are people.*
14. A: [*can you look at the number of police officers who've may I*
15. B: [*But hol' on what I am trying to say (.) I don't know that*
16. D: [*come on come on sir no no*
17. E: [*records are there you know*
18. A: *finish making the point please (.) jus' look at the amount of police officers*
19.   *Who have been put before the court who have been charged disciplined*
20.   *And convicted as a result of these officers*

Sometimes the meaning of the interaction may be obscured by the volubility of interlocutors, at other times it may be made tangential. In such cases, it is the stamina of participants and the competition between the voices which is the hallmark of the arrangement. Each voice is expected to hold its own, however complicated the task may eventually become.

There are two points of divergence between counterpoint and performance conversations, however, which underscore the contemporary nature of the latter. Participants in contrapuntal conversations do not subscribe to tacit agreement that a new voice has prominence, while the current voices play a supporting role. Thus, speakers already engaged in performing may not necessarily reduce their volume in deference to an aspirant who attempts to introduce or elaborate on the theme. Further, unlike a fugue, which is predicated on the notion of tunes blending to particular harmonic combinations, the voices in this conversational structure are free to participate in any "key" of their choice.

Example 5

A: [*We who are workin' we work an we*
B: [*Because you don' work there because*
A: [*protec' our wages an' don' want anybody to*
B: [*you do not work there*
A: [*come in an' cause us not to be workin'*
B: [*hello (.) wan' to tell you*

The effect of the competing, simultaneous voices is a quality reminiscent of twentieth-century musical compositions: a kind of confused dissonance, at least to the uninitiated ear.

Conclusion

I do not mean, by this discussion of contrapuntal conversations with reference to Jamaica, to imply that all conversation in such a community can be categorized in this way. What I am asserting is that there is an important "performance" element responsible for generating simultaneous speech which is not confined to informal village interaction, but characterizes conversation in both English and Creole and at all levels of formality in Jamaica and in many other territories of the Caribbean. As I noted in an earlier paper (Shields-Brodber 1992b), this must be incorporated into any model that attempts to account for conversation in comparable contexts. The analogy to counterpoint not only captures the essence of "performance" interaction, it also brings into focus, for the primarily oral communities of the Caribbean, a disguised cultural link to a European part-heritage which, though considerably transformed, nevertheless remains pervasive.

Notes

1. An earlier version of this essay, entitled "When Are Interruption and Simultaneous Speech not Anathema?" was presented at the eleventh biennial conference of the Society for Caribbean Linguistics, St Maarten, 1996.
2. However, see Stanback 1985 and Shields-Brodber 1992a and n.d. for an alternative perspective.
3. All examples were recorded from Jamaican radio conversation.
4. A free translation into SE:
   A: You just said it.
   B: Listen I heard Mr S. say that he has no concern for the residents of Jungle; so how do you expect me to believe that he is interested in peace?
   A. You are a liar.

References

Abrahams, R. 1983. *The Man of Words in the West Indies.* Baltimore: Johns Hopkins.
Chafe, W. 1997. Polyphonic topic development. In *Conversation: Cognitive, Communicative and Social Perspectives,* edited by T. Givón. Philadelphia and Amsterdam: John Benjamins.
Coates, J. 1995. Language, gender and career. In *Language and Gender: Interdisciplinary Perspectives,* edited by S. Mills. London: Longman.
———. 1996. *Women Talk.* Oxford: Basil Blackwell.
Edelsky, C. 1981. Who's got the floor? *Language in Society* 10.
Falk, J. 1980. The conversational duet. *Proceedings of the Sixth Annual Meeting of the Berkeley Linguistic Society.*
Fishman, P. 1983. Interaction: The work women do. In *Language, Gender and Society,* edited by B. Thorne et al. Rowley, MA: Newbury House.

O'Barr, W., and B. Atkins. 1980. Women's language or powerless language? In *Women and Language in Literature and Society*, edited by S. McConnell-Ginet et al. New York: Praeger.

Philips, S., et al. 1992. *Language, Gender and Sex in Comparative Perspective*. Cambridge: Cambridge University Press.

Reisman, K. 1974. Contrapuntal conversations in an Antiguan village. In *Explorations in the Ethnography of Speaking*, edited by R. Bauman and J. Scherzer. Cambridge: Cambridge University Press.

Sachs, H. et al. 1974. A simplest systematics for the organization of turn-taking in conversation. *Language* 50.

Sattel, J. 1983. Men, inexpressiveness and power. In *Language, Gender and Society*, edited by B. Thorne et al. Rowley, MA: Newbury House.

Shields-Brodber, K. 1992a. Dynamism and assertiveness in the public voice: Codeswitching and turn taking in radio talk shows in Jamaica. *Pragmatics* 2, no. 4.

———. 1992b. Hens can crow too: the female voice of authority on Air in Jamaica. Paper prepared for the 9th Biennial Conference of the Society for Caribbean Linguistics, Barbados, 1992.

———. Are interruptions and simultaneous speech always anathema? Paper presented at the 11th Biennial Conference of the Society for Caribbean Linguistics, St Maarten, 1996.

———. n.d. When crowing hens are not aberrant: Gender, culture and conversation: A Jamaican perspective. In *Gendered Realities*, edited by P. Mohammed et al. Barbados, Jamaica and Trinidad and Tobago: The Press UWI.

Stanback, M. 1985. Language and Black woman's place. In *For Alma Mater: Theory and Practice in Feminist Scholarship*, edited by P. Treichler and C. Kramarae. Urbana and Chicago: University of Illinois Press.

Tannen, D. 1990. *You Just Don't Understand: Women and Men in Conversation*. New York: Ballentine.

———. 1993. *Gender and Conversational Interaction*. Oxford: Oxford University Press.

Thorne, B., C. Kramarae, and N. Henley, eds. 1983. *Language, Gender and Society*. Rowley, MA: Newbury House.

West, C., and D. Zimmerman. 1983. Small insults: A study of interruptions in cross-sex conversations between unacquainted persons. In *Language, Gender and Society*, edited by B. Thorne and N. Henley. Rowley, MA: Newbury House.

Zimmerman, D., and C. West. 1975. Sex roles, interruptions and silences in conversation. In *Language and Sex: Difference and Dominance. Gender and Society*, edited by B. Thorne and N. Henley. Rowley, MA: Newbury House.

Chapter 12

Working out Conversational Roles through Questioning Strategies

Valerie Youssef

This study arose out of an examination of conversational features used by students in group discussions in a variety of areas of topical interest on the University of the West Indies campus, St Augustine, Trinidad in late 1995/early 1996. The discussions were recorded for purposes of examining intra-sex and inter-sex discourse, but did not assume gender-based differences. The study was motivated by the following:

1. A concern to investigate conversation further in the Caribbean context.[1]
2. A concern to investigate genderrelated linguistic behaviour in the Caribbean.[2]
3. A concern to elucidate the complex of social and stylistic factors that may motivate and determine conversational behaviour. The tendency within sociolinguistics and gender studies has been to look for exclusive explanations for particular conversational behaviours, when the reality entails a complex of sometimes conflicting factors.

As these particular interactions were analysed, it was observed that each conversation had an internal dynamic which was supported by interaction-sustaining devices, in particular, questions. It was possible to perceive the conversations as negotiations of reality which sought to resolve both the topic under discussion and the relationship among the participants to the interaction.

A focus on questions, in the contexts in which they were framed, made it possible to chart the dynamics of each interaction, as well as the roles which individuals within those interactions played out. This allowed assessment of the range of functions that questions performed, while simultaneously giving insight into speaker roles and their relative consistency across the interactions. These two foci provided further specific research directions.

4. A concern for the role and functions of questions in sustaining interactions.
5. A concern for the working out of speaker roles within and among interactions.

It emerged that conversational control or dominance was negotiated according to topic, role relations and goals. Questions were key devices not only for sustaining interaction but for establishing the roles of individuals in the context of specific conversations.

Explanatory Models

It has become increasingly apparent in the course of the last twenty-three years, since Lakoff's (1975) major publication in the gender arena, that social variables such as gender, age and ethnicity cannot be analysed in isolation, since each interacts with the other social features which make up an individual's identity and operates differently, dependent on the interactional dynamics of any given situation. Social network ties, as well as market forces, have proven the most critical elements determining broad linguistic choices for women (see James 1996) in the context of gender research and, within conversation, strategies have shown themselves to be determined by speaker role and relative empoweredness (O'Barr and Atkins 1980) rather than gender *per se*.

It has also become clear that models of gender-based language variation which claim male dominance (for example, Fishman 1978; Uchida 1992) as well as models of cultural difference governing gender-based variation (for example, Maltz and Borker 1982; Tannen 1990) are both inadequate to the extent that they seek exclusive explanations for gender-based variation and focus on gender as a static variable as well as one which functions exclusive of other social-variables. Meyerhoff has recently set up a model of speaker identities which considers the way in which speakers assume roles according to group and personal identities and potential network ties. It is not that the assumed roles are not genuine but that they represent aspects of the individual's identity played out differently according to the dynamics of particular interactional situations: "speaker identity is seen as a network of interconnected identifications operating together as if they were part of a moveable sphere" (Meyerhoff 1996: 216).

Just as for Le Page and Tabouret-Keller (1985), each encounter would involve more or less movement towards a particular addressee, dependent on how far the speaker wished to identify with the addressee, so Meyerhoff's model takes into account the fact that an individual enters into a number of group and personal identities; no single identity is independent of the others or exists in isolation from them. In each theory of speaker identity, there is an adjustment in the language use of the speaker dependent on the relationship he or she wishes to establish with the addressee. For Meyerhoff, the interactional networks into which the individual enters are seen as one of the more stable bases by which to assess a speaker's production in any given situation. Her model further sharpens the network model and emphasizes the complex of social and stylistic variables which militate against any generalized gender identity. Like Le Page before her, she sees how a network model may serve to support and develop an identity theory.

Meyerhoff's model is derived specifically from a consideration of the need to understand better the relationship between the individual and the group, which is a main concern of social psychology. Within social identity theory (Hogg and Abrams 1988), individuals are recognized as having both social and personal identities, the former relating them to social groups and the latter to individuals. "The multiplicity of identities that speakers possess" (Meyerhoff 1966: 205) must be taken into consideration in meaningful studies of language variation. With this background, Meyerhoff notes a number of studies of linguistic variation which reveal different linguistic variants dominating for individuals in different situations according, apparently, to their salience as markers of different aspects of a speaker's identity. She refers to Trabelsi's (1991) study of Arabic-speaking Tunis women, for example, which shows older women categorically using variables /uː/ and /iː/, which are variable for middle-aged women and do not occur for young women, who use forms associated with men in the society. The complex variation is explained by the author as emanating from the middle-aged women's entrapment between a desire for modernity, on the one hand, and for tradition, on the other, and consequently of their using the variables differentially according to the addressee. Similarly complex is the young women's behaviour since they differ from men in their pronunciation of the (r) variable, favouring a French uvular /R/ more than the men, apparently because of its association with French values of education and freedom for women. Depending on which identity is dominant in a particular situation, the Tunis woman's linguistic choices will vary, and this could occur within a single situation, as well as among situations.

Meyerhoff also shows that gender identity specifically may vary in salience for individuals of different backgrounds according to situation (see Meyerhoff 1996: 207–11 for detailed discussion). This sort of information affects concepts like that of the speech community which depends on a notion of shared norms; such notions may need to be tightened to allow salient group and personal identities within the community, while acknowledging individual differences in the importance of particular identities, which in turn allows sharp differentiation in the use of specific linguistic variables.

To summarize then, speakers' personal and group identities will vary in salience according to situation and, within this, according to factors such as topic, addressee and goals. These changes may be represented by means of specific features of linguistic performance. In the context of this study, conversational dominance proved to be relative and to be mitigated according to the features identified above, with the result that the same speaker could assume different roles in different interactions.

The Study of Questions

Why focus on a discourse feature like questions? Certainly it is very different in kind from phonological variation of the type which Meyerhoff calls on for exemplification of her theory. The point has been made by Edelski (1981, 1993: 190), however, that early research on gender viewed "women and men as mechanical entities and used variables that were designated a priori", when, in fact, power imbalances generally are constructed through the structuring of discourse strategies and cannot be determined by isolated words or even syntax.

We will be able to see clearly through this study, the ways in which different question types are highlighted at times of salience of particular identities and diminished at times of identity negotiation and change. The range of functions that questions perform can be assessed, while simultaneously giving insight into speaker roles and their relative consistency across interactions.

It should be noted at this point that it is impossible to treat questions and their functions, any more than gender-based variation, under a single unifying umbrella. While questions generally were early associated with the powerless speech of women (Lakoff 1975; Fishman 1978) and subsequently with other powerless groups in society (O'Barr and Atkins 1980), research on professional interviews has shown questions to be a means of controlling discourse by the empowered (Ten Have 1991; Perakyla and Silverman 1991). Clearly the function that questions perform goes far beyond mere information-seeking. For the empowered there emerges a controlling/manipulating function, for the disempowered a strategy for sustaining involvement and commitment on the part of the empowered.

The tendency today is to analyse questions carefully according to their type and function (for example, Holmes 1995). Most recently, Freed and Greenwood (1996) have subdivided questions according to their form and content. Not only did they distinguish Yes/No questions from WH questions (three categories) from tag questions and full declaratives with a final rise but, in interaction with three discrete segments, they distinguished *external*, *talk*, *relational* and *expressive* questions according to "functional use within the conversation" (Freed and Greenwood 1996: 14). External questions focused on information outside the circumstances of the conversation; talk questions clarified or reaffirmed the content of the current conversation; relational questions sustained the conversational flow; and expressive questions actually conveyed information to the hearer via humour, rhetorical questions, and so on. By analysing them in these ways, Freed and Greenwood were able to find a preponderance of a particular question type in particular segments of the conversation and thereby to gain a fuller grasp of the pragmatic value of specific subtypes in specific interchanges. This approach coincides with that suggested by Edelsky, since each subtype defines its own functional parameters. It has turned gender research on its tail by showing that, in similar interactional circumstances, both males and females are likely to perform synonymously (Freed 1996), but this does not conflict with the notion of flexible and negotiated identities mediated through a variety of situational factors (Meyerhoff 1996).

The present essay then surveys a series of student discussions with a main focus on questions, examining their pragmatic value and their effect on the development of the speaker's role identity. It acknowledges and supports Freed and Greenwood's approach, as well as Meyerhoff's theoretical base, and supports and develops both.

The Study

Background

The class within which the recordings were made comprised twenty-five second- and third-year undergraduates in the then Faculty of Arts and General Studies, UWI, St Augustine, Trinidad and Tobago.

There is some competition between males and females for places at the University, with women having overtaken men in all Faculties except Engineering and Medicine. The Faculty of Humanities and Education remains predominantly female, to the extent that males in classes are often singled out for special treatment inadvertently: They are easier to remember and identify than the females, so that their numerical minority gives them an advantage in terms of relative attention. As regards this particular class and study, only three males constituted part of the class, so they had to play roles in both single-sex and mixed-sex groups.

Though the university is a regional one, the majority of students on campus and in this study are Trinidadian. A single female in Conversation 4 was from St Vincent. Although Trinidad is divided evenly between an Afro-Trinidadian and an Indo-Trinidadian population, the majority of students were Afro-Trinidadian; single females in Conversations 2 and 4 were Indo-Trinidadian. Such national and racial differences as existed within the groups, although they would affect phonology, lexicon and even grammar occasionally, were not expected to make a difference to the conversational norms employed by the subgroups, who were part of a UWI speech community where shared interactional norms have been informally established out of a common identity and commonality of sociocultural development and experience. In the context of the wider Trinidad speech community, it is important for us to acknowledge the importance of *picong*, a verbal bantering sometimes entailing word play, which is a peculiar feature of Trinidadian interactional culture, particularly among males. It allows for a humorous jostling for positions within interactions which was found to characterize Conversations 1 and 3 in particular. In inter-sex interaction this speech event type occurs much less frequently, since the jostling for dominance which it entails is mitigated for males by their concern for appropriate relations to females in the group.

Informants and Procedures

The conversations discussed below involve four subgroups of undergraduate students (median age twenty), each group numbering three or four, who were asked to discuss a controversial subject current in Trinidadian society at the time of the recording, over a half-hour period. Only one phase of the interaction, embodying discourse on the given topic, was recorded. The researcher set up the tape recorder and then left the group alone to conduct the conversation. Following the recording session, the researcher transcribed each conversation, endeavouring to achieve an equal body of data for analysis in each case.

Among the conversational groups, one was single-sex male, one single-sex female and two were mixed sex. Three males took part in two interactions and one in three. The first conversation involved all three males in a single-sex interaction, while the following two involved two of them with two separate pairs of female students. The fourth involved three females. The accident of having three males have to take part in three of the conversations led to the possibility of comparing their roles and their use of questions in different interaction types. This allowed the researcher to assess how consistently they were performing throughout the interactions and to tie this specifically to questioning techniques in each interaction.

Due Respect

Questions either sought information on the given topic (IS questions), sought clarification of it (talk questions), sustained the conversational flow (relational questions) or queried or commented on information for rhetorical effect (expressive questions). As the first subset involved genuine information-seeking questions as well as those which sought to maintain the interaction for its own sake, it is clear that there was some overlap among these subtypes.

Data

Conversation 1: The Trinidad elections

This conversation was recorded among three Afro-Trinidadian male students the week after a controversial change of government in Trinidad and Tobago. Issues of race were prevalent, as the country had just elected its first Indian prime minister. The young men were good friends, "limin" partners according to the local Creole, who apparently took delight in teasing and heckling one another; there was much overlap within the conversation, intense involvement and competition to speak, as well as much shared laughter. The interaction was typical of the "picong" mentioned previously, during which individual parties to an interaction, most typically male, compete with one another verbally, often through word play, for conversational dominance.

One member of the group, let us call him Alan (A), started the conversation by asking a leading IS-question, then turned to a less demanding Yes/No type, and finally reverted to the WH-question, which was repeated.

The transcription of the beginning of the conversation between the three male students follows.

A:	*Yeh, well. Who you vote for? You eh vote?*[3]	1
B:	*I vote. I vote.*	
A:	*Who you vote for? Who you vote for?*	3
B:	*Well, that's a personal thing.*	
A:	*Yeh. Sorry. Sorry.*	
B:	(to A) *You vote? You only askin questions!*	6
A:	*No. I eh vote. It didn make sense. I eh votin for no losin party. I eh votin for J.B. I eh agree with you. I know why I didn vote. I eh vote because I find I didn have a sensible option.*	8

As soon as Brian (B) formed a coherent statement (line 8) he was challenged by Alan's demand for clarification which Brian then repeated back to him.

A:	(Mocking tone) *What that mean?*	9
B:	*What that mean?*	10
A:	*What you mean?*	11

Brian responded by repeating the challenging question back to Alan, and Chris attempted to divert the conversation to policies. Brian quickly came back with:

| B: | *What policies? All them talk in the same thing.* | 12 |

Already a number of roles and strategies have emerged:

- Alan opened the discourse with a series of leading IS-questions on the topic at hand. His questions put their recipient in the position of having to self-reveal and justify his own position, while freeing the speaker from both.

- Brian has already twice (lines 6 and 10) fended off Alan's questions by returning them to him, apparently stalling for time and letting him "taste" his own approach; he has apparently perceived a strategy at work, declaring, "You only askin questions!"

- In line 12, however, Brian apparently took up the same attacking questioning technique he had attempted to counter in Ian against Chris (C).

Following from this, the conversation turned to racial issues and there was some concern on Chris's part that this was inappropriate for a recording situation. The support of Alan and Brian for one another, with Alan as leader and Brian as support, was reinforced here (lines 13 and 14). Once again, in line 18, Alan asked a leading IS-question.

B:	*Doh panic.*	13
A:	*Tell him.*	14
B:	*Doh worry about that. Leh we get the thing done.*	
	(Group laughter)	

> *You make me forget what I was going to say, nah.*

C: *Nah, I eh do that.*

A: *Without gettin into racism. All yuh happy with the result?* 18

From this point on, the conversation took on a self-sustaining dynamic, during which comment and counter-comment went back and forth and questions were rare. Alan and Brian vied with one another in knowledgeability on the election issue, but Alan only sustained a lengthy utterance once, at the beginning, apparently to establish his position as a nonvoter. At the end of this statement (line 24), Brian supported by a question explicating Alan's stance.

A: *It go have to. There will be another election momentarily because nothing will be able to get passed. The same reason M. called the election in the first place. P. wudn get nothing passed so he go have to call a nex one. It jus be wastin taxpayers' money payin parliament for everythin. They eh servin no purpose. Jus arguin back an forth, back and forth. So they really have to call a nex election and that time I will dip mih finger in the ink!*[4] 23

B: *An then you go vote?* 24

A: *Yeh.*

Beyond this Brian offered commentary and Alan commented on it, gaining supportive laughter from Chris, who occasionally got in a knowledgeable statement. The remaining questions in the extract are of two kinds, incredulous, mocking, semi-rhetorical from Alan and information-seeking from Brian. They are included below:

B: *I figure he destroy party X by doin that.* 26

A: *What? You know he break up with them. Now he goin back with them. That eh makin no sense. Jus to further your own cause?* 28

A: *I see a woman get Attorney General.*

B: *Who?* 30

C: *Um Y.*

A: *Attorney who? So the results of these ministries out already?* 32

C: *No no.*

B: *They not official the ministry positions?* 34

C: *Nah, nah, nah. They can't be official at this point in time. Because J. say he still waitin for K. to contact him.*

In the entire extract Chris only asked one question, which was partly overlapped by a comment of Brian's and entirely overlapped by a statement from Alan. Alan's statement won out and continued after both Chris and Brian had stopped speaking.

C: *But what what [what's that truth?* 37
B: *[They want to . . .*
A: *But J. wasn in parliament then. J. wasn there. L. shoulda stand by he own.*

It is very clear that each speaker had a very particular role in the interactional dynamic of the group and that the dynamic was sustained by the type of question and statements offered by each speaker.

- Alan set up the interaction and his own externality to it by provoking aggressive and repeated questions. Nevertheless, it established him as leader.

- Brian defended himself by retaliating with the same strategy but then supported and sustained Alan's position against Chris. As the interaction was worked out, Brian sustained the interaction by asking information-seeking questions himself. Ultimately, Alan left the interaction-sustaining questions to Brian and retreated into the mocking semi-rhetorical question type.

- By attempting to display knowledgeability about the elections, Chris attempted to maintain a control that his role as passive respondent negated.

- All three speakers were using conversational devices to jostle for relative positioning within the group, while maintaining jocularity throughout.

Due Respect

Conversation 2: De winer girl ting

This conversation recorded a discussion of a controversial newspaper article questioning the motivation of women who dance obscenely as a standard backdrop to the singing of calypsos at Carnival time. The researcher had commented on the article in an earlier lecture and had suggested it as a possible conversation topic. Unlike the first, it was a mixed-sex interaction between two young women and Alan and Chris (of Conversation 1). The conversation took on an interview dynamic with Alan assigning Chris to interview Sally (S), a female who had witnessed the incident out of which the newspaper article had been written. In this way he avoided taking on the role of aggressor, which he had been comfortable with in single-sex interaction. The conversation began as follows:

A: *Well C., you're on the air.* 1

(Stifled laughter)

C: *Well S., you were telling us something about er?*

(Coughs)

S: *Basically this is a book. I was at the Soca Monarch Finals when this woman came on stage in this black in this short black jumpsuit that she starts off this article talking about, but the impression I got – well it did have holes on the bottom and I don't know if it was to give you an illusion that she was wearing underwear but some people said she might have been wearing tights but she was incredibly obese.*

C: *Uh-uh?*

S: *She was huge.*

A: *So what they're saying here is an understatement?* 9

As the conversation progressed, the other female participant, Karen (K), volunteered a question, but she could not get an answer because of a different question produced immediately by Alan as if she had not spoken:

K: *So what was the reaction of the crowd around you?*

A: *What was your reaction? It bothered you?* 11

Sally apparently tried to deal within the first question. Superficially this might appear to be supportive (lines 14 and 15). Actually it was critical and verged on the antagonistic.

S: *Obviously the men went wild. The men went crazy. Actually people were I'm not too sure if they went wild – well, she had wining skills I suppose. But I'm not too sure if they were* [13
C: [*What are wining skills if you doh mind me askin?*
S: *No, what I mean is, I'm no too sure if they were not laughing at her but if they were mm turned on, I suppose.*
C: *More amused than turned on?* 18

At this point (line 18, *More amused than turned on?*), Chris offered clarification, assisting Sally in an apparent difficulty of expression. At the same time, his assistance potentially underlined the difficulty as a flaw and did not apparently help Sally!

S: *Yeh, I wasn too sure.* 19

Sally was continuing to try to frame a response, when Alan came in again (line 22):

S: *Actually I wondered I find these things don't really serve much purpose to have winer girls on stage it doesn't really* [21
A: [*What about the winer men? It doz have winer men too* 22
S: *That's a different thing!*

While Chris continued in his assigned role of interviewer, Alan made comments and questions at points where they could be most rhetorically effective. The interaction became heated as the group discussed the relative exploitation of males and females in society. Sally asked one question in the midst of this that was drowned out by a comment from Alan (line 25). Subsequently she framed another and managed to supercede Chris (lines 27 and 28).

S: *So C. [so what you see ( )?* 24
A: [*Aside from all that*

Due Respect

C: As far as I'm concerned if she chooses to allow herself to be exploited by the almighty dollar. [

S: [*But who is to say that she was actively exploited; suppose it's something that she enjoys doing?*

K: *I'm saying if it's her choice.*

Once again here we see Sally's question being superceded by a semi-rhetorical one from Alan (line 30), but this time he and Sally agreed on the fact that the woman was not embarrassed and the questioning ceased in their agreement and mutual support. Alan did not desist from interruption altogether, but he was now agreeing with Sally and Karen (line 32):

S: *Carnival time people seem to latch*   31

A: [*I know people who like fat women like that so she probably* [*find she was looking good*

S: [*She's probably the hottest thing out*

Further on, Chris took up the interrogation, as the interaction seemed to have become hostile again (lines 34 and 35).

C: *But you doh sound as if you have a problem with that at all? The one on the stage. You didn have a problem with that?*   35

S: *What! Let me see. I doh really, you see. I doh really have a problem with people wearin what they want to wear. It's your life. You have to live it . . .*   37

C: *If you had a sister? I think we have to personalize it a little more if you had a sister or a mother . . . ?*

S: *I would disown her!*   39

C: *Uh-huh. Then you not true to what you say then . . .*

As the conversation continued and the issue at hand took precedence, the second female speaker (K) began to question, addressing the issue at hand rather than an individual.

K: *I think it's a real fear that they're being exploited I mean are they doing it for free? How much money are they being paid to do that?*   42

A: ˋ*I feel* [

K: ˋ[*What kind of money are they getting? Or is it just that they're getting* [*free entrance to the Soca monarch*?   45

B: [*that too you know* . . .

A number of features of this interaction are worth noting:

- The male speakers conducted an interview initiated by Alan with Chris as interviewer, which allowed Alan to remain sufficiently external to the interaction to interject questions and comments as and when he saw fit. The role of conversational controller which he played out in the first interaction was again taken up here, but he distanced himself from the interviewer role in this case.

- Chris largely sustained the interaction with information-seeking questions which became increasingly aggressive the more Sally expressed uncertainty, while Alan came in only for rhetorical effectiveness. Chris reached a stage of actually baiting the "defendant": *Uh-huh. Then you not true to what you say then*? (line 40).

- At the point at which Alan and the interviewee reached agreement he ceased to ask her questions. This belies the overall adversarial quality in the questioning which he no longer wished to sustain and, perhaps, explains his eschewing the interviewer role. Here a subtle gender dynamic may be observed, motivating Alan not to attack the females but to cast Chris in that role. Chris's role, as assigned by Alan, was quite different from his role in the first interaction, in which he was disempowered as respondent and much closer to Brian's role (Brian was now absent). He assumed this role under Alan's direct instruction, however, unlike Brian, who had voluntarily taken up this role in the first conversation.

- Overall, the interaction had the style associated with a professional interview in which the professional, the doctor, dominates and controls the course of the interview by his questions. In this case, the males were the empowered and the females the disempowered, each

Due Respect

gender taking up the roles traditionally associated with them and alluded to here in my earlier consideration of the literature. Consistent with the argument that such roles cannot be absolutely defined, the dynamic of the next interaction is different again.

Conversation 3: The Resurrection
Set at Easter time against the backdrop of a newspaper article disputing the validity of the Resurrection, this conversation occurred among male speakers, Alan and Brian of Conversation 1, and two new female speakers, Jenny and Gillian. The dynamic of this discourse looked as if it might develop in the same way as the previous interaction, in that Alan started off by voluntarily putting Brian in the role of controller. Brian became the chief protagonist, apparently because he was more "religious".

A: *Well you is the church man. I mean, I go to church too, but is on Sundays* (Young women laugh) *talk yuh talk boy.*   2

Following this, Brian made a statement of belief complete in itself. Jenny, apparently uncertain, followed up with a question. Gillian was an articulate and committed Catholic, Jenny an unsure agnostic Presbyterian.

J: *What do you think?*   3
G: *What do I think? Well I suppose it starts from whether or not you believe Christ is the son of God. If he is that means he did rise from the dead. I am a Christian so I believe . . .*   5

Jenny's question (line 3) was the first in a series of that type of information-seeking question which actively sustained the conversation. At the same time, it relieved her from having to frame an opinion which subsequently proved to be difficult for her to answer. Gillian repeated the question, apparently gaining processing time. Jenny followed up Gillian's statement of belief by one concerning her own confusion, finishing thus:

J: *It's jus I'm not sure I believe in Christianity an religion.*
    (B. laughs incredulously)

At this point Brian took up the interviewer role again, apparently gaining confidence from Jenny's uncertainty:

B:	Well, what religion are you?	7
J:	I'm not quite sure. I'm a Presbyterian by birth but I'm not really a practising Presbyterian.	
B:	Mmhm. Mmhm. Do you think that may have might be one of the factors for the doubt?	
J:	It's not that I doubt I more or less believe that he did, you know, just like any other supernatural occurrence in any other religion but um Christianity on the whole, I'm not sure if I'm – I can't call myself a Christian, kind of thing.	12

Brian then asked a direct question of Alan and, for the first time in any of the three interviews, Alan (line 14) expressed uncertainty himself. As soon as he did so, Gillian took up an antagonistic position (line 15), deliberately emphasizing the contradictions in Alan's stance and entering into the bantering "picong" style more usually associated with males. She followed up with an IS question which directly challenged his knowledge base (line 20).

B:	Mmhm-mmhm. So A, what are your views on this issue?	
A:	Well I agree with everything you all were saying. (Laughter) I mean (Coughs).	
G:	OK. That means you believe an you doh believe?	15
A:	No, I believe. Well from what I see on TV an stuff an what you hear in Church, you got to believe.	
B:	That's so profound, A!	
A:	Yes.	19
G:	What part do you believe?	
A:	(Coughs)	
G:	I doh understand sign language.	
A:	Well, I believe that he rose again an almost everything. I mean it's not up to me to believe I jus have to have faith in what the Bible says, right? Cos half of it's unbelievable anyway. But it's not up to me to-to-to judge that, right? So it's just up to me to have faith in what is said. Nah, jus give me a	

Due Respect

chance (Laughter) *right? So it's up to me to have faith in what is written. An jus need to* [

Alan's repetition of *It's not up to me* (lines 23 and 25), *I jus have to have faith* (lines 24 and 25), and *It's just up to me to have faith,* as well as his three repetitions of tag-question *right?*, here underlined his own uncertainty and lack of confidence. He does not repeat himself elsewhere in the discourse or use the tag.

Right (spoken with a rising intonation) is a commonly used tag question in the Trinidadian context and seeks confirmation of the speaker's statement from the addressee. Its distribution, from my own counts of individual speakers in AIDS counselling sessions (see Youssef 1993), varies greatly from speaker to speaker, there being some speakers who use it only occasionally to confirm agreement and others who use it to confirm up to 50 percent of their statements. Clearly it can be equated with that feature which Lakoff originally associated with women, of ending statements with a questioning intonation, as though unsure of their validity.

A discomfort with the topic and the presence of a confident female speaker had apparently discomfited Alan as he had lost his controlling pose. Brian seized the opportunity to take issue with him at this point, and the interaction turned on word play and pseudo-jocular jostling for position via the difference between unbelievable and incomprehensible (lines 28–33).

B: *No, but the whole issue of faith is to believe in what may be incomprehensible.*

A: *What incomprehensible about the Bible?*

B: *You said that half of the Bible is incomprehensible.*   30

J: *Unbelievable.*

B: *So what is unbelievable for you?*

It was at this point that Alan seized the opportunity to throw a question back at Brian (line 33), employing the same retaliatory strategy which Brian had used in the first encounter to attempt to even the conversational balance.

A: *So nothing unbelievable in it for you?*   33

B: (Low) *No, not really.*

A: *Everything believable?*

G: *You have to take it from the top. It's about God's plan for man. You have to take it from the top. You have to know what God is about and where Jesus fits in. It's not just a question of the Bible, it's something more (.) it's more philosophical than that . . .*   38

Seconds later Alan suggested that they go on to another topic and also commented on how much "better" the previous interaction (Conversation 2) had been! This interaction had a dynamic which put him at a disadvantage as the "set upon", the disempowered, and overturned the whole conversational dynamic and his own role. A number of points are worth mentioning:

- The uncertainty of both Alan and Jenny on this topic rendered them both powerless, while to some extent it empowered Brian, who became more confident in the face of Jenny's uncertainty, just as Chris had in the face of Sally's uncertainty in the previous interaction.

- Gillian took control in strong statements of conviction and challenging semi-antagonistic information-seeking questions which put the questioned on the spot. Her personality and certainty on the subject rendered her the empowered in the entire sequence.

- Alan was forced back on uncertain statements, which he rounded off with the uncertainty tag, *right?* It was only at the end, when he caught Brian at an uncertain moment, that he was able to challenge a question with a question and gain a little ascendancy. It was unsurprising that he favoured previous interactions!

It becomes clear that, although Alan had a preferred role as controller and moderator of interactions, relative to which the two other males played out supporting roles assigned to them, this role might itself have been the product of an insecurity which was unveiled in the final interaction. Certainly the role was not consistently maintained but broke down under the pressure of a difficult relational dynamic vis-à-vis other group members.

Overall, Alan took the role of interviewer and controller of the discourse, preferring, however, in the single-sex discourse, to distance himself from the

Due Respect

interaction by designating an interviewer, and coming in himself with rhetorically effective questions and statements at appropriate moments. His comments often appeared designed to provoke laughter. The other males took their cue as to their own roles from his lead and their relative positions in the interaction varied according to the other participants as well as the topic. Brian was Alan's chief supporter when the three males were together, taking up his style from Alan against Chris. Without Brian present, and with two female participants, Chris adopted the role earlier assigned to Brian and interrogated Sally, apparently unaware of the fact that Alan had set him to perform a role which he encouraged but distanced himself from to maintain his own good relations with the females.

If we had left the interaction series at this point, we might have been tempted to assume a consistent dynamic among three male personalities of different strengths in Conversation 1, with the weakest male gaining sufficient strength, once females were involved in an inter-sex interaction (Conversation 2), to become empowered in Conversation 3. In Conversation 3, however, Brian gained ascendancy over Alan as well as Jenny through the greater comfort with the given topic, and Gillian gained ascendancy through conviction and knowledge on the topic, as well as personality.

Conversation 4: Lack of security on campus
This conversation took place among three female students, Liz, Naomi and Holly, shortly after an incident of rape on the university campus. Holly was living in a hall of residence as a nonlocal student, and Liz and Naomi were living at home. Each situation presented its own problems for moving around on campus, particularly after dark. The researcher was present in the room during this discourse, but had minimal input and the atmosphere was very comfortable. The girls were united in their concern for the problem and the conversation sustained itself with a minimum of questions. As one person stopped speaking, another readily took up the topic. There was considerable minimal response via *mm, OK, yeh* and more emphatic *exactly*, and further supportive interruption to complete an utterance as if the speaker and respondent were of one mind.

The first extract concerned the checking of ID cards in classrooms and at the gate:

H:	Yes, I've been there a couple of 'Excuse me, could I see your ID' and there were children from whatever school and they said 'I'm sorry, you're not allowed here.' But this year I haven't really been seeing any security at all aroun.	
N:	I just noticed that sometimes in the night, um, the back entrance...	4
H:	Mmhm –	
N:	Sometimes they might stop the cars going through.	6
H:	Mmhm.	
N:	But I mean that's not really often.	
L:	And if you just stick your head out and say you're going to one of the Halls	
N:	Mmhm.	
L:	They let you in.	
N:	Yeh. And that's the safest way.	12
L:	I mean nobody's going to be stupid enough to say I'm going to the campus to study, allright? You just say X Hall and they let you in because who are they to say that (.)	
H:	that you're not going	15
L:	that you're not going to Y Hall. Because you have no document to say well (Laughs) I goin to whatever Hall.	
N:	And that's when they do ask you!	
L:	Exactly!	19

It must already be clear that the conversational dynamic was quite different here from the previous interactions with minimal response (examples in lines 5, 7 and 9) and supportive completion following from speaker pause (line 15). Only three questions occurred in the entire extract, and they followed directly from one another. All three were semi-rhetorical and served to highlight the dilemma being dealt with. Two from Naomi (line 21) were followed by one from Liz (line 22) which in itself served as minimal response–support.

N:	I think you jus have to change the system or something bursts. (.) But they have done that in the past, haven't they? Changed it several times?	21

239

Due Respect

L: To what?

N: *That's it. It just doesn't work. Every time they change it*
      (Group laughter)
      I don't know what you're going to do. Changes.   24

The former dynamic immediately reasserted itself and was sustained to the end of the interaction.

L: *But they, you see, I think they've done it on a very superficial level because people are complaining, not about the lack of security, but about how the security treated you.*   26

H: *Well, they have made changes, you know, because Milner Hall has changed. Now you can't walk in and out as you like.*

Others: *Yeh?*

H: *OK. So in that way they're almost like X Hall where you have to say who you're going to etc. and they call the person =*

L: *Enter =*

H: *as you pleased.*   33

- All in all it is to be noted that there was an equal sharing of the floor among speakers and collaborative support throughout.

- Adversariality did not enter this interaction as it had the others and questioning was minimal. It would be dangerous out of this single conversation to make generalizations on the basis of gender, and we should note that the topic is one in which the girls are motivated to unity against an external threat. However, it is useful to note the differences from the other interactions and to note that questioning plays a minimal role in an interaction with this level of collaborative support.

Discussion

1. Consonant with the findings of Maltz and Borker (1982) in the context of their propounding the cultural difference approach to gender-based differences in conversational style, we found an adversariality to charac-

terize all three of the interactions involving males and males and females, and to be absent from the interaction among females only. The adversariality entailed a jostling for dominance within the group which was supported by the question type used. We should note, however, that in the first of the mixed-sex interactions, this adversariality passed from males to females, but in the second it was directed from male and female towards an elsewhere assertive male. Further, the mixed-sex topics lent themselves to side-taking in a way that the all-female topic did not. The extent of humorous adversariality in Conversations 1 and 3, its more serious nature in Conversation 2 and its total absence in Conversation 4, are interesting as potential support for different conversational styles according to gender balance in group settings in the Caribbean context, which demands further investigation. In this context, too, the humorous bantering which characterizes Trinidadian "picong" warrants further study in itself, and conversations like those discussed here need comparison with comparable data sets from other English-speaking cultures, for it seems that a peculiarly Caribbean dynamic is operable in such contexts.

2. Gender relations play a significant part in the overall interactional dynamic as is illustrated, for example, by speaker Alan's retreat from adversariality in Conversation 2, as well as Chris's heavy-handed manner in the same, but personality and speaker knowledgeability on topic also accounted partially for the shifting nature of the power dynamic.

Gender-oriented conversational studies have not focused specifically on mixed-sex conversational behaviour in the teens and twenties when assertiveness in some males may be mitigated by a concern/goal to make a positive impression on particular females in the group setting. This concern/goal may well account for the shift in Speaker A's behaviour in Conversation 2, where he modified his adversariality and cast C in the antagonistic role. Since C took up this role so readily, he may have been more preoccupied with his relative status vis-à-vis the females involved in this particular interaction.

If Conversation 2 had a primarily gender-oriented differential, Conversation 3 was mitigated strongly by personality factors and indi-

Due Respect

vidual sets towards the given topic, with knowledgeability and conviction conferring concomitant authority and respect. The study as a whole gives support to Meyerhoff's (1996: 216–17) model by showing that any given interactional network crucially determines an individual's conversational behaviour by calling upon a unique set of individual and social identities each time it is set up. Relative dominance, as determined by the interplay of personalities and gender dynamics, and individual sets towards the topic, was constantly changing throughout the conversation series. Personality and gender were the critical factors and role relations, topic and goals the stylistic determinants, in the particular interactional networks under discussion, but in another data set other variables, such as ethnicity (social) or setting (stylistic) might be the determining ones.

3. Questions played a significant role in controlling the discourse and working out the role relationships within the context. At this point it seems important to distinguish small-group interactions (in this case there were three parties to the first conversation and four to the other two) from conversational dyads, since the more parties there are to an interaction the more jostling for position within the group is likely to occur. It is worth noting that in the fourth conversation, in which no questioning occurred, there was no jostling for position among the speakers, but a sharing of the floor and collaborative support, maintained by minimal response and supportive completion. Gender and personality balance, as well as attitude towards topic and role relations, were key factors determining the extent of collaboration versus competition.

If we consider the whole question of face, first raised by Brown and Levinson (1978) and subsequently elaborated by Deuchar (1988), we can see that adversariality, sustained largely through challenging questioning techniques, threatened the negative face of respondents by imposing on them, while preserving that of the questioner, who was relieved of responding to challenges him- or herself. Power was seized in the very act of assuming the questioner role. Ultimately it must be clear that aggressive questioning tactics may themselves be perceived as defensive, guarding both the privacy and the ability to respond to the interrogator. This has not sufficiently been taken into account in considering differing male and female styles in formal and informal interactions. Antagonistic interrogating tactics may not always be a sign of empoweredness, but need to be considered as a potential cover for insecurity and uncertainty in themselves.

4. Questions served not only to sustain interactions which would not necessarily have sustained themselves (the students had been required to discuss a given topic for a given period of time), but defined and developed speaker identity throughout the interactions. Roles were not entirely consistent with the first three interactions or constant among them, but rather negotiated throughout each and may have been as important to the participants as the topic itself, which became a tool for working out the relationships within the group. Among the males, Alan sets out to enforce a leadership role which Brian and Chris acknowledged and supported through their responsiveness to him. At the same time, even as he supported his given role, Brian challenged this role in Conversation 1 through retaliatory questions, which attempted role reversal, and he succeeded in achieving the role reversal in Conversation 3, when Alan became vulnerable through topic uncertainty.

In Conversations 1 and 3, Brian looked for opportunities to take over the leading role in the interaction by adopting the strategies used by the conversation leader. This indicates that conversational strategies can be seized upon opportunistically as speakers recognize their potential usefulness to the playing out of a particular role. Their selection in such a case does not imply convergence to another speaker for purposes of identification with the individual but rather convergence to a speech ploy which generates a sought-after conversational role.

Finally, each question-type proved to have a pragmatic utility of its own:

- IS-questions got the interactions underway and sustained them, while at an interpersonal level they frequently challenged the respondent and simultaneously freed him or her from any statement of opinion or self-justification. In a conversation set which showed itself to be more competitive than collaborative and more hierarchical than egalitarian, they served as a basis for attack tantamount to a courtroom interrogation, save for the element of humour which was usually retained.

- Questions for clarification (talk questions) might sometimes be taken at face value but were also used to embarrass the respondent by asking him or her to clarify a definition or statement which clearly gave difficulty.
- Repetition of questions served as a defensive tactic giving time to the speaker to think through a response, as well as allowing him or her to attempt to reverse the conversational roles in some cases and to put the original questioner on the defensive.
- Rhetorical and semi-rhetorical questions (expressive questions) attracted attention to the speaker without adding anything significant to the content of the interaction.

All in all, a power dynamic was being worked out which went far beyond the surface meaning of the questions. Information exchange was supported but seemed less important than the working out of the relative positions of the parties to each interaction. It is clear that, even within a friendly undergraduate chat session, both meaning and relationships are being negotiated, and questions of different types are used as prime negotiating tools.

We must bear in mind ultimately that the sample was small in size and the number of variables investigated sufficiently large to make these findings preliminary in nature. However, they do provide cues for further research into the working out of speaker identities through conversational interaction and the specific role which questions play in this regard. The nature and function of adversariality in single- and mixed-gender interaction is of particular concern for future investigation, as well as more investigative study into Trinidad "picong" in relation to other interactive formats.

Notes

1. It has only recently begun to be investigated with work by Shields-Brodber (1998), on the Jamaican female's role in call-in talk shows, and the work of Youssef and Silverman (1992) and Youssef (1993) on AIDS counselling interactions.

2. In a relatively small-scale study, my intention was not to attempt generalizations concerning gender identification in Trinidad but to observe trends within the conversational interactions and salient features within the discourse and to allow these to speak for themselves.
3. Numbering represents the lines of transcribed conversation.
4. A metaphor for going through the voting procedure.

References

Bergvall, V. et al., eds. 1978. *Rethinking Language and Gender Research*. London: Longman.

Brown, P., and S. Levinson. 1978. *Politeness: Some Universals in Language Usage*. Cambridge: Cambridge University Press.

Deuchar, M. 1988. A pragmatic account of women's use of standard speech. In *Women in Their Speech Communities*, edited by J. Coates and D. Cameron. London: Longman.

Edelsky, C. 1981. Who's got the floor? *Language and Society* 10. (Reprinted in D. Tannen, ed. 1993. *Gender and Conversational Interaction*. Oxford: Oxford University Press.

Fishman, P. 1978. Interaction: The work women do. *Social Problems* 25.

Freed, A. 1996. Language and gender research in an experimental setting. In *Rethinking Language and Gender Research*, edited by V. Bergvall. London: Longman.

Freed, A., and A. Greenwood. 1996. Women, men and type of talk: What makes the difference? *Language and Society* 25, no. 1.

Hogg, M., and D. Abrams. 1988. *Social Identification: A Social Psychology of Intergroup Relations and Group Processes*. London: Routledge.

Holmes, J. 1995. *Women, Men and Politeness*. London: Longman.

James, D. 1996. Women, men and prestige forms: A critical review. In *Rethinking Language and Gender Research*, edited by V. Bergvall et al. London: Longman.

Lakoff. R. 1975. *Language and Women's Place*. New York: Harper and Row.

Le Page, R., and A. Tabouret-Keller. 1985. *Acts of Identity*. Cambridge: Cambridge University Press.

Maltz, D., and R.A. Borker. 1982. A cultural approach to miscommunication. In *Language and Social Identity*, edited by J. Gumperz. Cambridge: Cambridge University Press.

Meyerhoff, M. 1996. Dealing with gender identity as a sociolinguistic variable. In *Rethinking Language and Gender Research*, edited by V. Bergvall et al. London: Longman.

O'Barr, W., and B.K. Atkins. 1980. Women's language or powerless language. In

Women and Language in Literature and Society, edited by S. McConnell-Ginet et al. New York: Praeger.

Perakyla, A., and D. Silverman. 1991. Reinterpreting speech exchange systems: Communication formats in Aids counselling. *Sociology* 25.

Shields-Brodber, K. 1998. Hens can crow too. In *Studies in Caribbean Language II*, edited by P. Christie et al. St Augustine, Trinidad: School of Education, University of the West Indies.

Tannen, D. 1990. *You Just Don't Understand: Women and Men in Conversation*. New York: William Morrow.

Ten Have, P. 1991. A reconsideration of the asymmetry of doctor–patient interaction. In *Talk and Social Structure*, edited by D. Boden and P.H. Zimmerman. Oxford: Polity Press/Basil Blackwell.

Trabelsi, C. 1991. De quelques aspects du langage des femmes de Tunis. *International Journal of the Sociology of Language* 87.

Uchida, A. 1992. When 'difference' is dominance: A critique of the antipower-based cultural approach to sex differences. *Language in Society* 21, no. 4.

West, C. 1984. *Routine Complications: Troubles with Talk between Doctors and Patients*. Indiana: Indiana University Press.

Youssef, V. 1993. Marking solidarity across the Trinidad speech community: The use of An Ting in medical counselling to break down power differentials. *Discourse and Society* 4, no. 3.

Youssef, V., and D. Silverman. 1992. Normative expectations for medical talk. *Language and Communication* 12, no. 2.

Glossary

Acrolect The level of speech in a Creole continuum which is considered closest to the standard language.

Affix Usually a prefix (*re-* in *rebuild*) or a suffix (*-er* in *dancer*).

Afrogenesis Used to refer to the African origin of Creoles.

Aktionsart The inherent aspectual characteristics of a predicate as contrasted with the grammatical expression of aspect.

Anglophone An English-speaking person or territory.

Apodosis The consequence clause of a conditional sentence, for example, *you will be punished* in *if you disobey, you will be punished*.

Aspect A grammatical category concerned with the duration or type of action performed or the existence of a state. Habitual aspect expresses repetition of an action, Perfective or Completive aspect a completed action or an existing state, Imperfective Aspect an incomplete action, and Progressive/ Durative aspect an ongoing action.

Bajan Barbadian speech.

Basilect The level of speech in a Creole continuum considered furthest removed from the standard language.

Bilingualism The case in which speakers speak more than one language.

Cassidy–Le Page A writing system, first used for writing Jamaican Creole, in which each symbol represents one particular sound. (An illustration is given in Appendix 1.)

Codemixing The use of two languages by bilinguals in the course of a single utterance.

Codeswitching The moving from one language to another according to circumstances, characteristic of bilinguals.

Codification The drawing up of guidelines governing the use of a language, including the setting up of a writing system where necessary.

Glossary

Cognition verbs Verbs which refer to some intellectual activity, such as *think, know.*

Competence In the sense used by Chomsky, the unconscious knowledge which every speaker has of his or her language. In language pedagogy, however, the term is often used synonymously with *proficiency*, a speaker's ability to use a language.

Complementation The addition of a phrase or clause to "complete" the meaning of a noun, verb or adjective, for example, *the game* in *played the game*, or *that they were leaving* in *The men said that they were leaving*.

Complementizer A word or phrase used to introduce a complement clause, for example, *that* in *The men said that they were leaving*.

Completive See **Aspect**.

Consecutive clause A clause expressing result, for example, *that I slept* in *I was so tired that I slept*.

Continuum A way of representing Creole situations typified by a range of intermediate language varieties stretching between the standard language and the variety furthest removed from it.

Copula A verb which links the subject and the predicate of a sentence, but has little or no meaning of its own. *Be, seem* and *become* function as copulas.

Counterfactuality A situation which does not conform to reality.

Declarative Utterances that are statements, not questions or commands.

Decreolization The process by which a Creole becomes more like its coexisting standard language.

Diachronic Concerned with a language's historical development (see **Synchronic**).

Dialect Any variety of language used regularly by a group of speakers. The term, however, is often used to refer to a variety which diverges from a more socially accepted one.

Discourse analysis Analysis of samples of language based on units longer than a sentence, including oral narratives, conversations, written texts.

Djuka (Ndjuka) One of the Creole languages spoken by "Bush Negroes" in Suriname.

Dread Talk The dialect of the Rastafari, a Jamaican subgroup.

Final clause A clause expressing purpose, for example, *. . . so that we might know the truth*.

Garifuna An Arawakan language spoken by the Garifuna ("Black Caribs") of Belize and some surrounding coastal areas.

Glossary

Grammar The rule system of a language or a description of it.

Grammaticalization The process by which a structure becomes part of the grammar of a given language.

Habitual See **Aspect**.

Hypercorrection The overgeneralization by a speaker of a sound or grammatical form, sometimes in an effort to avoid stigmatized nonstandard usage.

Imperfective See **Aspect**.

Implicational scale A hypothetical scale on which it is assumed that the presence of one linguistic feature in someone's speech predicts the presence of another, for example, that the Jamaican speaker who uses *nyam* 'eat' will also use *pikni* 'child'.

Inflection The process by which the form of a word is changed by the addition of an affix. (See **Affix**.)

Interlanguage The temporary system(s) that second-language learners use during the process of learning a new language.

Intonation The pitch contour or "tune" of a stretch of speech.

Kekchi A Mayan variety spoken in Belize.

Krio A Creole spoken in Sierra Leone, West Africa.

Kriol/Kryol A Creole spoken in Guinea-Bissau, West Africa.

Language bioprogramme hypothesis The theory that, in Creole genesis, children invented the new language by relying on their innate knowledge of Universal Grammar. (See **Universal Grammar**.)

Lexicography The writing of dictionaries.

Lexicon The set of words in a language.

Lexifier The language from which a Creole derived most of its words, English, for example, in the case of Bajan, Jamaican, and so on.

Lingua franca A language used as a medium of communication between people who don't speak a common language.

Linguistics The objective study of language as a human phenomenon. It includes, among other things, analysis of its structure (structural linguistics), of the relationship between language and social factors (sociolinguistics), of language history (diachronic or historical linguistics).

Marked verb A verb which is modified for tense, aspect, or mood, either by an affix or by another word.

Mesolect The level of speech in a Creole continuum which is considered to lie between the acrolect and the basilect.

Glssary

Modality The expression of mood. (See **Mood**.)

Modal (verb) An auxiliary verb that expresses mood; *must*, *can*, *will*, and *ought* are all modal verbs.

Monogenetic theory A view that all the Creoles which arose out of African slavery had a single genesis.

Mood A grammatical category which expresses possibility, obligation, or certainty.

Morphology The aspect of language or language study which is concerned with word formation.

Noun complement A clause which adds something to a noun, for example, *that he had arrived* in *the news that he had arrived.*

Obstruent A sound in the pronunciation of which the flow of air is constricted. The majority of consonants are obstruents. (See **Sonorant**.)

Overgeneralization The extension of a feature or a rule to areas of a language to which it does not apply, for example, the addition of *-s* for the plural of *foot* or to a present tense English verb which has a plural noun as its subject.

Papiamentu/Papiamento A Creole spoken in Aruba, Curaçao and Bonaire in the Netherlands Antilles.

Perception verbs Verbs such as *see* and *hear* which refer to the senses.

Phonology The aspect of language study concerned with linguistic sound systems or such systems themselves.

Polylectal grammar A single model of grammar which aims to account for several lects or varieties of language.

Polygenetic theory A view that Creoles spoken by West African slaves had different origins.

Pragmatics The aspect of language or language study which focuses on the principles governing the communicative use of language.

Predicate One of the two basic parts of a sentence, the other being the subject.

Predicate cleft construction A structure such Jamaican *a sik dem sik* 'sick, they are' in which the predicate is considered "split".

Predication The way(s) in which predicates are expressed in a language.

Progressive See **Aspect**.

Prosody A term used in phonology to refer to elements of sound that accompany the speech stream, for example, stress, pitch, and intonation. (See **Suprasegmental**.)

Protasis The *if*-clause of a conditional sentence.

Glossary

Prototype The best example of a thing, concept, and so on.

Reduplication The repetition of a form in a single word, as in *fool-fool* 'foolish'.

Saramaccan A Creole spoken by "Bush Negroes" in Suriname.

Serial verb construction A structure consisting of a string of two or sometimes three verbs, as in Jamaican and other Caribbean Creoles *bring the book come give me*.

Sonorant A sound in the pronunciation of which the air flow is unconstricted. All vowels are sonorants, as are the liquids [l] and [r] and nasal consonants [m] [n] [ŋ]. Sonorants contrast with obstruents. (See **Obstruent**.)

Speech act verbs Verbs such as *say, tell, promise*. In using one of these the speaker is simultaneously performing the action to which it refers.

Sranan The main Creole spoken in Suriname.

Stative verbs Verbs which refer to a state as opposed to an action, for example, *seem, have* (meaning 'own').

Stereotype A model based on a general impression rather than on close observation of the facts.

Substrate language/substratum The native language of the original pidgin/Creole speakers, seen as underlying the Creole. (See **Superstrate**.)

Subtractive bilingualism The kind of bilingualism which eventually leads to the loss of one of a bilingual's languages.

Superstrate language Usually the European language to which a Creole is "related". (See **Substrate language**.)

Suprasegmental An element of the speech stream, for example, stress, pitch and intonation, which, in transcription, is sometimes represented by a notation placed above the symbols that represent consonants and vowels.

Synchronic Concerned with the study of a language at a given point in time. (See **Diachronic**.)

Syntax The aspect of language or language study which is concerned with the grammatical rules that govern word order and the ways in which words can be combined.

Tag question A question attached to the end of a sentence, for example, *don't you?* in *You like mangoes, don't you?*

Target language (TL) The language being learned or attempted in production by a nonnative speaker.

Tense/Mood/Aspect (TMA) The marking of predicates with respect to tense (present, past), mood (obligation, possibility), or aspect (duration, completion).

Glossary

Tone Change of pitch that brings about a change of meaning. Tones are described as High, Low, Rising, or Falling, for example.

Tone language A language in which differences in word meaning or grammar are systematically indicated by differences in pitch (tone).

Universal Grammar (UG) The features shared by languages in general which, according to Chomsky, form part of the innate knowledge of children acquiring a first language.

Vernacular (language) The native language of a speech community, often used to contrast with the institutionalized standard language.

Vocative A term used in addressing or calling someone/something.

WH-movement A transformation in which a word or phrase, most usually an interrogative (*who, what, how*) is considered to have been moved to the beginning of a clause or sentence. For example, it is posited in the derivation of *Whom did you see?*

Appendix 1

Cassidy–Le Page Writing System: An Illustration

Symbols	Jamaican examples
/ii/	/piis/ 'piece', 'peace'
/ie/	/fies/ 'face'
/o/	/wod/ 'word', /mos/ 'must'
/ai/	/bait/ 'bite', /fait/ 'fight'
/aa/	/paat/ 'part', 'path'
/uu/	/fuul/ 'fool', 'foolish'
/uo/	/guot/ 'goat', /buol/ 'bold', 'bowl'
/j/	/jam/ 'jam', /brij/ 'bridge'
/k/	/kom/ 'come', /kiip/ 'keep'
/z/	/luuz/ 'lose', /zip/ 'zip'
/ng/	/tong/ 'tongue', 'town'
/ks/	/veks/ 'vexed', 'angry'

Appendix 2

Caribbean Students who Gained Higher Degrees in Linguistics at the University of York, 1967–1988

Year	Name	Degree	Title of Thesis
1967	Maureen Warner(-Lewis)	MPhil	Language in Trinidad with special reference to English
1969	Pauline Christie	PhD	A sociolinguistic study of some Dominican Creole speakers
1972	Donald Winford	PhD	A sociolinguistic description of two communities in Trinidad
1973	Colville Young	PhD	Belize Creole: A study of creolized English spoken in the city of Belize, in its cultural and social setting
1975	Walter Edwards	PhD	Sociolinguistic behaviour in rural and urban communities in Guyana
1978	Hubert Devonish	PhD	Selection and codification of a widely understood and publicly useable language variety in Guyana to be used as a vehicle of national development
1980	Savitri Rambissoon (Sperl)	MPhil	From Indians to Trinidadians
1982	Kean Gibson	PhD	Tense and aspect in Guyanese Creole: A syntactic, semantic and pragmatic analysis
1988	Alison Irvine	MPhil	The linguistic markers of social differentiation in two Jamaican communities

Contributors

Pauline Christie, retired Senior Lecturer, Department of Language, Linguistics and Philosophy, University of the West Indies, Mona, Jamaica.

Kathryn Shields-Brodber, Lecturer, Department of Language, Linguistics and Philosophy, University of the West Indies, Mona, Jamaica.

Beverley Bryan, Lecturer, Department of Educational Studies, University of the West Indies, Mona, Jamaica.

Lawrence D. Carrington, Pro Vice Chancellor, Professor of Creole Linguistics, Director, School of Continuing Studies, University of the West Indies, Mona (formerly of the Department of Education, University of the West Indies, St Augustine, Trinidad).

Dennis R. Craig, Director, Education and Development Services Inc., Diamond, EBD, Guyana. (Former Professor of Language Education, University of the West Indies, Mona, Jamaica and former Vice Chancellor, University of Guyana.)

Hubert Devonish, Professor of Linguistics, Department of Language, Linguistics and Philosophy, University of the West Indies, Mona, Jamaica.

Dhanis Jaganauth, temporary Lecturer, Department of Language, Linguistics and Philosophy, University of the West Indies, Mona, Jamaica.

Silvia Kouwenberg, Senior Lecturer, Department of Language, Linguistics and Philosophy, University of the West Indies, Mona, Jamaica.

Darlene La Charité, former part-time Lecturer, Department of Language, Linguistics and Philosophy, University of the West Indies, Mona (currently Professor, Université Laval, Québec, Canada).

Velma Pollard, retired Senior Lecturer, Department of Educational Studies, University of the West Indies, Mona, Jamaica.

Contributors

Hazel Simmons-McDonald, Senior Lecturer, Department of Language, Linguistics and Literature, University of the West Indies, Cave Hill, Barbados.

Monica Taylor, Lecturer, Department of Language, Linguistics and Philosophy, University of the West Indies, Mona, Jamaica.

Donald Winford, Associate Professor, Department of Linguistics, Ohio State University, United States. (Former Senior Lecturer, Department of Language and Linguistics, University of the West Indies, St Augustine, Trinidad.)

Valerie Youssef, Senior Lecturer, Department of Liberal Arts, University of the West Indies, St Augustine, Trinidad.

www.ingramcontent.com/pod-product-compliance
Lightning Source LLC
Chambersburg PA
CBHW031310150426
43191CB00005B/157